Why You Need This New Edition
Simonds & Cooper (Ninth Edition)

There are many changes to this ninth edition of *Communication for the Classroom Teacher*. In this edition, we have tried to maintain a multidisciplinary approach and to focus on an audience of "teachers of all disciplines." In doing so, we have changed some communication-specific vocabulary (specifically as it relates to theory) to reach a wider audience. We have also attempted to make the ninth edition more "student friendly," while promoting an interactive classroom.

You'll find that this edition provides:

1. **Reading Objectives** and **Discussion Prompts** located at the end of each chapter objective to help teachers and students engage in a more interactive classroom. These tools provide opportunities to prepare for participation in an instructional discussion.

2. **Bolded key terms** throughout each chapter with a **summary of key terms** at the close of each chapter will help students better prepare for exams.

3. A new section on **Out of Class Communication** in Chapter 2.

4. A new section on the **Importance of Listening** in Chapter 3.

5. A new title (Language) and reorganization of Chapter 4 with an expansion of the coverage on verbal communication, which includes **Teacher Clarity, Teacher Appropriateness, and Verbal Delivery**.

6. A reorganization of Chapter 5 to include **Lesson Planning** based on state or national standards and more practical suggestions on how to plan and prepare a lecture.

7. Significant reorganization and streamlining of the information in Chapter 9 with a new section on **Handling Crisis Situations**.

PEARSON

COMMUNICATION FOR THE CLASSROOM TEACHER

Ninth Edition

COMMUNICATION FOR THE CLASSROOM TEACHER

Cheri J. Simonds
Illinois State University

Pamela J. Cooper
University of South Carolina, Beaufort

Allyn & Bacon

Boston   Columbus   Indianapolis   New York   San Francisco   Upper Saddle River
Amsterdam   Cape Town   Dubai   London   Madrid   Milan   Munich   Paris   Montreal   Toronto
Delhi   Mexico City   São Paulo   Sydney   Hong Kong   Seoul   Singapore   Taipei   Tokyo

Editor-in-Chief, Communication: Karon Bowers
Senior Acquisitions Editor: Jeanne Zalesky
Editorial Assistant: Stephanie Chaisson
Senior Managing Editor: Linda Mihatov Behrens
Associate Managing Editor: Bayani Mendoza de Leon
Manufacturing Buyer: Mary Ann Gloriande
Marketing Manager: Blair Tuckman
Art Director/Cover Designer: Nancy Wells
Editorial Production and Composition Service: Chitra Ganesan, PreMediaGlobal
Cover Image: Ryan McVay/Getty Images/Digital Vision

Library of Congress Cataloging-in-Publication Data

Simonds, Cheri.
    Communication for the classroom teacher / Cheri J. Simonds, Pamela J. Cooper. — 9th ed.
        p. cm.
    Prev. ed. cataloged as: Communication for the classroom teacher / Pamela J. Cooper, Cheri J. Simonds.
    Prev. ed. cataloged under Simonds, Cooper, Pamela J.
    Includes bibliographical references and index.
    ISBN-13: 978-0-205-74777-1 (alk. paper)
    ISBN-10: 0-205-74777-9 (alk. paper)
    1. Teacher-student relationships.   2. Interaction analysis in education.   3. Oral communication.
4. Communication in education.   I. Cooper, Pamela J.   II. Cooper, Pamela J. Communication for
the classroom teacher.   III. Title.
    LB1033.S63 2011
    371.102'3—dc22

                                                                                2010012088

Allyn & Bacon
is an imprint of

www.pearsonhighered.com

ISBN-10:   0-205-74777-9
ISBN-13: 978-0-205-74777-1

Contents

Unit Two: **Instructional Strategies**

Chapter 5   **Sharing Information   80**

Unit Three: Communication Impact

Preface

I have decided that real learning involves a change of attitude and behavior no less than does real teaching. I have come to believe that teaching is more of a calling forth of wholeness to be a better person than just a jamming in of information, that it must deal with the entire person, not just the mind. Teaching should make students and teachers aware of their sacredness, give them high expectations of themselves, and change their lives.

—Schmier, 1995, p. 21

Teachers and students become aware of the sacredness of which Louis Schmier writes through communication with one another. This text is about communication—the very essence of teaching and learning. It provides educators (from pre-service or in-service teachers to corporate trainers) the means to analyze, develop, and facilitate their own and their students' communication behaviors. It is designed to be both theoretical and pragmatic, providing educators the rationale for using certain communication strategies and the practical means to employ those strategies in the classroom. The text's discussions are supported by numerous and varied activities.

NEW TO THIS EDITION

There are many changes to this ninth edition of *Communication for the Classroom Teacher*. Although we have updated material key to current classroom practices, we made a conscious decision to preserve the historical value of the textbook by maintaining information from renowned educators. In this edition, we present a multidisciplinary approach and focus on an audience of teachers of all disciplines. In doing so, we have changed some communication-specific vocabulary (specifically as it relates to theory) to reach a wider audience. We have reorganized (particularly Chapters 4 and 5) and streamlined (significantly Chapters 9 and 10) some of the content and provided more practical examples including lesson planning for future teachers. We also attempted to make the ninth edition more student friendly while at the same time promoting an interactive classroom. We have included a set of reading objectives and discussion prompts at the end of each major section, which will help students to prepare to participate in classroom discussions. We have also bolded key terms and included a list of key terms at the end of each chapter to help students better prepare for exams. Finally, we moved selected activities and further readings to a more in-depth instructor's manual.

As you read this text, please be aware of the following styles and treatments. First, we have chosen to avoid the somewhat awkward "he/she" construction. Instead, we alternate "he" and "she" throughout the text. Second, while the intended audience for this text is educators from all disciplines and educational contexts, we sometimes refer to the pre-service or in-service teacher for purposes of clarity. Third, even though this is a coauthored text, in some instances, we have chosen to write the text in the first person singular when personal stories and examples are used. Finally, this text, like teaching, is highly personal. Much of what we have written comes from our own experiences in the classroom, both as students and as teachers. What you will read are guidelines, ideas we have found to work.

ACKNOWLEDGMENTS

Many people have contributed to this ninth edition of *Communication for the Classroom Teacher*. Our students continue to influence our ideas about teaching and learning, and hence, the text itself. They have challenged, criticized, and sometimes praised us. We are grateful for their insights and their enthusiasm for the teaching-learning process.

Our colleagues Kathleen Galvin, Gus Friedrich, and Steve Hunt have influenced our ideas about classroom communication. They have stimulated our thinking, challenged our conclusions, and helped us to find our own sacredness. We are also grateful to the staff at Allyn and Bacon, in particular to Jeanne Zalesky, Megan Lentz, and Stephanie Chaisson. They "took us on" and supported our endeavors. In addition, we would like to thank our assistant, Lindsay Soliman, who helped in the task of preparing these revisions and instructor's manual. Your assistance and support have not gone unnoticed. We would also like to thank the reviewers of this edition: Michelle Alise Brown-Grant, Felician College; Nathan Carter, California State University, San Bernardino; George M. Lawson, Jr., University of Nebraska at Kearney; Keith Nainby, California State University, Stanislaus; and Patricia Tarry-Stevens, Central New Mexico Community College.

Finally, our families deserve a very special thanks—our husbands, Rick and Brent, for teaching us that love gives strength, beauty, and meaning to life; our children, Jenifer, Bryan, Jamie, Dylan, and Addison, for teaching us a whole new meaning of the word *teacher*; and our grandchildren, Emma, Jack, and Kate, who remind us that teaching is indeed sacred and gives us another chance.

Cheri J. Simonds
Pamela J. Cooper

CHAPTER

1

Foundations of Classroom Communication

OBJECTIVES

After reading this chapter, you should be able to:

- Situate the field of instructional communication within communication education.
- Understand how instructional communication theory relates to research and practice.
- Provide an overview of the units and themes of this text.
- Define classroom communication.
- Define teacher communication competence.
- Differentiate between supportive and defensive classroom climates.
- Discuss the importance of understanding student diversity in the classroom.

Without communication, teaching and learning would be impossible. You communicate with your students, parents, administrators, and fellow teachers. Sometimes your interactions with these various groups will be under less than ideal circumstances. For example, a parent may need to be consulted concerning a student's behavior or academic difficulty. An administrator may discuss a student's dissatisfaction with your class. A fellow teacher may complain to you about the lack of fairness of the educational system, about a student he dislikes, or about his workload. On other occasions your interactions will be very enjoyable. Regardless of the circumstances surrounding your interactions, the more competent a communicator you are, the more effective you can be.

This book addresses the communication competence of educators in all disciplines. But, before we talk about the theory and research that frames this area of study, let's put it within the context of the larger field of communication education.

COMMUNICATION EDUCATION

Researchers in the field of communication education are interested in what happens in the classroom and how we develop the ability to communicate competently. This field of study is composed of three domains: communication pedagogy, developmental communication, and instructional communication.

Communication Pedagogy

Pedagogy is the art of teaching. Thus, researchers who study **communication pedagogy** are interested in determining appropriate ways of teaching communication competencies. For example, the most effective methods of teaching public speaking, interpersonal communication, or small group communication might be studied by these individuals. Communication pedagogy researchers also might look at issues such as what are the most useful methods for providing effective feedback on students' speeches or what techniques a teacher might use to help a student who has high communication apprehension (CA). In fact, communication apprehension has been the most widely researched topic in the communication discipline.

Questions a communication pedagogy scholar might ask include: What particular assignments or activities enhance student learning of communication? What content should be covered in a basic communication course? How does communication apprehension affect a student's ability to prepare for a public speech? What is the most effective way to provide feedback to students after they present speeches? The answers to these types of questions allow teachers of communication to be more effective and to have a greater impact in the communication classroom. For example, if you get the opportunity to teach a communication class, you will rely on this kind of research to decide which textbook to use, which assignments to give, and which assessments are appropriate given the age group and learning styles of your students.

Developmental Communication

Developmental scholars are interested in determining how individuals acquire, or develop, communication skills. For example, a **developmental communication** scholar might investigate how infants develop language skills or how college students enhance their interpersonal communication skills as they work toward earning a communication degree. Developmental scholars have argued that the most effective way to understand communication is to examine how it develops over time. These researchers use longitudinal research techniques and developmental theories. For instance, rather than studying the phenomenon of communication apprehension in a college public speaking classroom, developmental researchers would be more interested in tracking CA levels in such a way that they could explain how such anxiety changes over time. Typically, research would be conducted that follows student anxiety levels from grade school to college.

Nussbaum and Prusank (1989) suggest that communication education researchers should concern themselves with how students develop communication competencies, how teachers and students develop and maintain interpersonal relationships, and how teachers socialize into their roles and develop a teaching style. Questions a developmental scholar might ask include: What cultural or environmental factors affect how children develop a learning style? How do a teacher's attempts to build relationships with students through self-disclosure change from grade school to high school? How do a teacher's verbal and nonverbal communication styles change with each year of experience? In other words, developmental scholars focus on the long-term impact of communication issues in educational settings. For example, let's say that you have been teaching a fifth grade language arts class but have recently been asked to teach kindergarten. What will you need to know about the language skills of your new students? Research in developmental communication might give you the answers you need.

Instructional Communication

While communication pedagogy scholars study how to teach communication, **instructional communication** scholars study how to use communication to teach. In other words, instructional communication scholars are concerned with the communication skills that all teachers need, regardless of the subject they teach, to function competently in the classroom. This research area emphasizes the central role of communication in the learning process. All teachers need to have a certain level of communication competence to be effective in the classroom. As Hurt, Scott, and McCroskey (1978) aptly state, "The difference between knowing and teaching is communication" (p. 8). That is, a teacher might be an expert in her field, but if she cannot communicate that information in a way that students understand, learning is not achieved. The research of instructional communication scholars is intended for a much broader audience than the other two types of communication education research. It is designed to inform teachers of all disciplines how to prepare and present clear and effective lectures, how to lead classroom discussions, and how to use communication to establish positive relationships with students. While much of the research in communication pedagogy (e.g., effective group communication, communication apprehension) and developmental communication (e.g., interpersonal relationship development) inform other aspects of instructional communication, this text focuses on instructional communication. As such, our audience comprises current and future teachers, as well as trainers or educators in other contexts.

The research of instructional scholars is message centered: It focuses on the impact of different types of verbal and nonverbal messages on the classroom. Some topics that have been studied in this domain include teacher clarity, teacher immediacy (behaviors that indicate approachability, availability, and warmth), teacher credibility (competence and character), student questioning techniques, and student challenge behavior (strategies students use to question classroom rules and norms). Questions an instructional scholar might ask include: How does a teacher's clarity relate to student perceptions of a teacher's credibility? How do teacher immediacy behaviors affect student learning? How do teachers facilitate effective class discussions? Does a teacher's use of classroom activities expand students' critical-thinking skills? Instructional communication research, then, can be characterized by considering the central role of communication in all learning experiences. As a classroom teacher, think about how you will use communication in a given day. You use communication to interact with students, other teachers, administrators, and parents. In the classroom, you present material to students in a variety of ways. All of these are communication acts and can be informed by the research of instructional communication scholars.

Reading Objectives and Discussion Prompts

1.1 Domains of Communication Education

What do you know?
What are the three domains of communication education?

What do you think?
Why is it important to understand the distinction between the three domains of communication education? As a researcher, what questions would you be interested in asking?

THE RELATIONSHIP BETWEEN THEORY, RESEARCH, AND PRACTICE

Three methodological traditions have been used to guide instructional research—the empirical, interpretive, and critical perspectives. The **empirical tradition**, or scientific perspective, aims to provide systematic explanation for behavior that can be directly observed (Berger, 1977), and attempts to explain and predict future behaviors. For instance, instructional scholars from this tradition are interested in determining why some interactions between teachers and student are successful, but others are not. Many scholars have studied the link between teacher immediacy (behaviors that signal approach, availability, and warmth) and student learning (cognitive, affective, and behavioral) from this approach (Gorham, 1988; Gorham & Zakahi, 1990; McCroskey & Richmond, 1992). For example, if a teacher uses verbal and nonverbal behaviors that signal to students that they are friendly and easy to talk to, then students will have greater liking for the course and be more motivated to learn.

If the goal of the empirical approach is to explain and predict, then the goal of the **interpretive tradition** is to understand. For instructional communication scholars this goal translates into an understanding of the meaning of classroom processes. In this tradition, meaning, or reality, is negotiated through the interactions of teachers and students (Greene, 1983). Research in the area of teachers' and students' socialization provides an example of the interpretive tradition. For instance, Staton and Hunt (1992) describe a model of teacher socialization that includes biography, agents, changes, and context. Prospective teachers come into training with their own ideas and attitudes about what it means to be a teacher (biography). Through communication with others (agents) and by experiencing the dilemmas (changes) associated with being a new teacher, they work their way through the socialization process (context).

Teachers must acquire the skills and knowledge necessary to teach and to become a part of the culture of teachers (Staton & Darling, 1986). They must not only learn the content they want to teach but also the skills of being a teacher. This book addresses the communication skills that all teachers need to effectively socialize into their roles as teachers.

As teachers you will not only be concerned with teaching your own classes but with "fitting" in with colleagues, supervisors, support staff, students, and so on. You may feel unprepared to deal with the complexities you encounter in your roles as a teacher, your place in school, and especially your relationship with students.

Communication is the key to effective socialization. However, your students will be the primary agents of socialization in the classroom. The role of your students will be developed through interactions with you and the other students (Staton, 1990). The resulting relationships will help define the culture of the classroom.

Scholars from both the empirical and interpretive perspectives would agree that research should be value free. This is not the case for scholars with a **critical tradition**. Critical scholars reject the idea of value-free research, taking into account the historical, ideological context of the classroom and the influence it has on both teacher and students. According to Friedrich (1987), critical scholars "are interested in making us aware of and helping us challenge the values that are inherent in the status quo of the educational enterprise" (p. 9). Work in areas such as gender issues in the classroom (Sandler, 1991) and teacher empowerment (Sprague, 1992) would be examples of the critical tradition. What characterizes critical scholarship is moral reflection: questions about what should be and a focus on ethical standards, ideology, and social change (Bochner, 1985). Critical scholars would certainly agree that the classroom is a place of social influence (which we'll discuss more in Chapter 9). But they would question how that influence is used, or abused, in the classroom. They would acknowledge that teachers have influence over students and that educators wield a form of social influence toward a desired end. Critical scholars would challenge instructors to examine how this might affect the less empowered, such as minority students, in the classroom. For example, in your classroom, you notice that male students are commenting more than female or minority students. You might critically reflect on why this might be happening. Is there something happening in the classroom or in the way you are asking the questions that might empower this group over others? Answers to these questions might allow you to change the status quo and social climate of the classroom.

Based on the preceding descriptions, it is evident that the assumptions that guide the research process will vary extensively depending on a scholar's theoretical orientation. The argument posed in this chapter suggests that while scholars may gravitate toward a specific approach for research, each has value for enhancing the understanding of teaching and learning. And each will be highlighted at various points throughout this text. The theoretical traditions of instructional communication have the potential to assist teachers as they carry out the day-to-day tasks of their profession. What is important is that, as teachers, you understand how these theoretical traditions inform the research that is presented in this text. In addition, you should consider how theory and research guide daily decisions about how you run a classroom. In other words, how do theory and research help you as an educator answer questions about your own **teaching philosophy**? For example, what is the nature of teaching and learning? What are the roles of the teacher and student in the classroom? What are the implications for the way you conduct class? To illustrate, one of your authors, Dr. Simonds, shares her teaching philosophy, which is based on both theory and research:

> I believe that communication plays a central role in the process of teaching and learning. I believe that teachers should communicate their expectations clearly and follow through with them consistently. I feel that teacher

clarity affects the relational climate of the classroom and that teachers and students share in the responsibility of clarifying classroom content and processes (e.g., If teachers are unclear, students will use some type of clarification strategy: asking, observing, or testing the expectation in the form of a challenge).

I view the classroom as a secondary socialization process and a unique culture where the teacher is the only native. That is, the teacher is the only one who knows, in advance, what the expectations of the classroom are. Students must identify the environmental demands and speculate about the strategies necessary to meet these demands successfully. Because students have a vested interest in the outcome of their own instruction, they attempt to share ownership of the culture. They will seek to reduce uncertainty about classroom expectations by using one of three clarification strategies: asking, observing, or challenging. In short, challenge behavior is a mediational strategy that students may use to share ownership of the classroom culture and may be manifested by behaviors that are contrary to teacher expectations.

I view students as active agents in establishing, maintaining, and changing the conventions of the classroom culture. This may sound counterintuitive to the teacher being the only native. However, I also feel that teachers should be student-centered in creating rules, standards, and expectations. That is, teachers should consider the rights and learning styles of the students and the climate/culture of the classroom. It is in this way that students do have an indirect influence on teacher decisions.

These beliefs about teachers, students, and the classroom truly reflect my teaching philosophy and have implications for the way I conduct class. Because I consider the classroom to be a secondary socialization process and a unique culture, I pay special attention to the communication of classroom expectations on the first day of class. I also try to get students involved in a class assignment where they can introduce and get to know each other within the first week of class. Because I believe that students have a vested interest in the outcome of the class, I provide them the opportunity to critically reflect on course grades and challenge them constructively. Because I believe that students take an active role in the classroom and help to negotiate the climate of the classroom culture, I try to get the students involved in the learning process. One way that I attempt to do this involves having students evaluate their active preparation for and participation in class. I also give students opportunities to lead classroom discussions and process classroom activities with regard to course content. Additionally, students are provided many opportunities to apply course material to real-life experiences. Because I think that effective teaching requires that we (teachers) strike a balance between the way we teach and the way students learn, I feel strongly that we should incorporate a variety of instructional strategies to meet the diverse needs of our students. All this—to create a positive classroom environment which is conducive to learning. (Adapted from Simonds, 2001)

Reading Objectives and Discussion Prompts

1.2 Theory, Research, and Practice

What do you know?
What are the three methodological (or research) traditions used to guide instructional communication research?

What do you think?
What do you think is the nature of teaching and learning? What do you think are the roles of the teacher and students? How might each of these traditions inform your teaching philosophy? How will you implement these beliefs in your classroom?

UNITS OF THE TEXT

This text is divided into three units: communication competence, instructional strategies, and communication impact. The first unit provides a foundation of how communication works to affect the positive or negative encounters we have with students, parents, administrators, and colleagues. In other words, this unit (beginning with this chapter) focuses on the **communication competencies** (including interpersonal communication, listening, verbal and nonverbal communication) that all teachers need to function successfully in their role as teachers as well as their communication in the classroom. We will address how understanding the communication process helps us to develop more positive relationships with our students, how we can improve our listening skills and enhance the relational climate of the classroom, and how our verbal and nonverbal messages affect our ability to communicate effectively with our students, their parents, and our administrators and colleagues.

The second unit focuses on particular communication skills that all teachers need to incorporate a variety of instructional strategies in the classroom. There are many **instructional strategies** that teachers can choose—lecture, discussion, activities, and so forth. During any one day, a teacher may use several of these strategies. None has been found to be superior than any other, but some are better suited to your needs or your student's needs at various times. We'll discuss the advantages and disadvantages of each strategy within the various chapters; however, there are certain considerations that teachers should follow in deciding which strategy is appropriate given your particular needs, including the teacher, the objective, students, and environment. For example, you should consider your own personality and expertise as the teacher. You should also consider the objective of the lesson. If the objective is information acquisition, perhaps lecture is best. However, if you want to develop the critical-thinking skills of your students, then discussion might be more appropriate. You should also consider your students—their age, intelligence, motivational level, previous knowledge of the subject matter—before choosing a strategy. Finally, consider your environment—the time of day, classroom setting, class size—when choosing a strategy. Discussion and activities work best in smaller class sizes, while lecture is appropriate for larger classes.

The third unit considers the **impact** of our communication in the classroom. Our communication choices influence our students and our students' communication choices influence us. What does this mean? It means that we need to be attuned to our ethical behavior, our strategies for classroom management, and our use of power in the classroom. We also need to be aware of factors that affect how classroom interaction is perceived, such as racism, sexism, ethnocentrism, ableism, and classism.

There are several themes that run throughout all units of this text. First, we want to discuss the role of communication in the classroom. What is classroom communication and how do we become **competent communicators**? Next, we discuss the role of communication in creating a **positive classroom climate** throughout the text. Finally, we consider how **student diversity** may affect communication in the classroom. Please understand that diversity takes many forms. You may have students from different cultures, varying family backgrounds, different gender or sexual orientations, and with varying learning styles or special needs. Though we discuss issues of diversity throughout the text, we introduce why such considerations are important in this chapter. As you read and discuss the text, we ask that you consider how each concept might be considered from an alternative perspective.

Reading Objectives and Discussion Prompts

1.3 Units of the Text

What do you know?
What are the units and themes of the text?

What do you think?
Think about your subject matter (what you will be teaching) and your audience (who you will be teaching). How might each of these units inform you as a teacher? Why do you think the authors chose these themes to run throughout the text?

CLASSROOM COMMUNICATION

Communication scholars have long pondered the question: What is communication? The term *communication* is abstract, and like all words, has several meanings. For purposes of our discussion, **classroom communication** consists of the verbal and nonverbal transactions between teachers and students and between or among students.

In order for us to communicate, several **elements** are necessary. These include people (speaker and listener), the message, channel, interference, feedback, and context. First, communication involves interaction between **people**. It is important to understand that the speaker and listener, or interactants, involved in the communication event each bring to the encounter a number of things. The speaker and listener each have personal experiences, goals, values, attitudes, knowledge, gender, culture, and beliefs that affect everything they say and interpret in the event. This is known as a **frame of reference**. Because the people involved in the communication event have different frames of reference, they may interpret messages very differently.

Communication also involves verbal and nonverbal messages (which we discuss in detail in Chapter 4). **Verbal messages** include the words you use in the encounter. **Nonverbal messages** are how you say your words. In other terms, verbal messages are what you say, whereas nonverbal messages are how you say it. Your goal is to construct a message, verbally and nonverbally, in such a way that your students understand your intended meaning. Given what we know about differing frames of reference, this can sometimes be challenging.

We also need **channels** (face-to-face, e-mail, text messaging, telephone, etc.) through which messages can be sent and received. It is important to consider the implications of the channel you choose to communicate certain messages. For example, if you want to tell a parent that his child is struggling with a certain subject, what is the most appropriate channel for doing so? What implications will your choice have on the likelihood of getting cooperation from the parent in assisting the student?

Communication is not always easy, however, and it is sometimes affected by interference. **Interference** is anything that gets in the way of shared meaning between the teacher and the students. Interference may be physical (someone tapping a pencil on a desk, students talking, noises from outside the classroom) or psychological (daydreaming, personal problems or ailments, attitudes or conflict). These are all distractions that can cause inaccuracy in communication—preventing the message sent from being the message received. In the English classroom, for example, a student's dislike for the subject could function as noise by prohibiting the student from accurately receiving messages concerning, say, Shakespeare. Regardless of what messages the teacher sends about Shakespeare and his relevance today, the student will find it difficult to receive any message that would enhance his liking for Shakespeare.

Feedback is very important to the communication process and involves both the teacher and the students simultaneously. As you teach a lesson, the listener is responding either verbally or nonverbally. As you send a message you look to see whether your students understand you. Your students may ask questions for clarification, nod their heads in agreement, or express confusion in their faces or eyes. This feedback tells you, the teacher, what to say next.

Finally, communication happens in **context**. The time of day, location, or social situation all provide context to the communication encounter. As teachers, we all know how the time of day affects our students' ability to concentrate on our message. Though time and place are important factors to consider, perhaps even more important is the social context of the communication event. What implications do the current economical, political, and social climates have on your lessons? Everything you say and do happens in a climate that either makes your message appropriate or inappropriate, effective or ineffective, at any given time or place. In the educational context, this environment is termed *classroom climate*. Much of what is discussed in this text concerns how to build a supportive classroom climate through communication. A supportive classroom climate is important because it promotes fuller development of a student's positive self-image and enhances self-concept. We discuss ways to build a supportive classroom climate in more depth later in this chapter as well as throughout the text. For now, keep in mind that a supportive classroom climate is one characterized by openness rather than defensiveness, confidence rather than fear, acceptance rather than rejection, trust rather than suspicion, belonging rather than alienation, order rather than chaos, and high rather than low expectations.

We know that communication involves all of these elements, but it is also important to understand that communication is a **transactional process**. That is, communication is the simultaneous sending and receiving of messages that occur in context. Feedback is constantly being shared verbally and nonverbally between both people

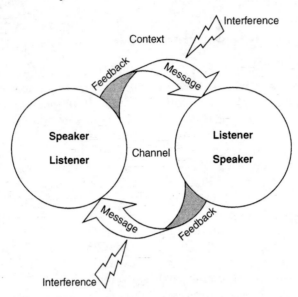

FIGURE 1.1 A Transactional Model of Communication.

From Public speaking: Prepare, present, participate *by Cheri J. Simonds, Stephen K. Hunt, & Brent K. Simonds. Copyright Allyn & Bacon, 2010.*

involved in the encounter. There is no one speaker or listener, but transactions that take place between people. The transactional nature of communication takes into account the context of the situation and the relationship between individuals (see Figure 1.1). As you consider how all of these elements of communication work together, you are beginning to develop your own ideas of how you can use communication in your classroom. This, in turn, will improve your classroom communication competence.

Reading Objectives and Discussion Prompts

1.4 Classroom Communication

What do you know?
Define classroom communication. What are the elements of communication?

What do you think?
How do you think all of these elements fit together? Describe a verbal and a nonverbal transaction between a teacher and a student that would commonly take place in the classroom.

CLASSROOM COMMUNICATION COMPETENCE

What is **communication competence**? To be effective communicators, we must be flexible and possess a variety of communication acts. Different communication behaviors may be required depending on the situation, the people involved, the topic being discussed, and the task at hand. In terms of classroom communication, the National Communication Association has outlined the communication competencies teachers need to be effective (Cooper, 1988a). These are listed in Table 1.1. In addition, we know that effective teachers

- Make clear their instructional goals.
- Know their content and the strategies for teaching it.
- Communicate to their students what is expected of them and why.
- Know their students, adapt instruction to students' needs, and anticipate misconceptions in students' existing knowledge.
- Address higher-level as well as lower-level cognitive objectives.
- Monitor students' understanding by offering regular, appropriate feedback.
- Reflect on their practice.

Much of the research reviewed in this text suggests that teaching effectiveness is intrinsically related to the way one communicates. The basis of communication effectiveness is the appropriateness of the communication act. The competent communicator carefully examines the components of the communication situation—the participants, the setting, the topic, and the task. Based on an analysis of these components, the competent communicator chooses the appropriate communication act.

Imagine for a moment that you and another teacher, Ms. Smith, are alone in the faculty lounge after school. Ms. Smith is complaining loudly to you about a student who is disruptive in class—refuses to work, arrives late to class every day, whispers constantly to other students, and "talks back" when Ms. Smith tells him to "behave." You have the student in a class and have had no difficulties with him. You know that Ms. Smith has the reputation among students of being "incompetent" and is perceived by the faculty as unable to "keep order" in her classroom. Ms. Smith, after complaining at length, turns to you and asks, "What should I do?" Several communication choices are open to you. Some of them include persuading Ms. Smith to quit teaching, informing her of how students and faculty perceive her, accepting her feelings of anger and telling her you understand, and theorizing with her about what she might do to solve the problem. Based on your analysis of the communication situation, you choose one of the possible choices—the one you think most appropriate.

After choosing from the variety of possible communicative acts, you'll implement the one you've chosen. Finally, you'll evaluate the effectiveness of the choice you implemented. Was it appropriate to the communication situation? Was it satisfactory to you? To the other person? The judgments you make concerning the effectiveness of your communication choice will depend on feedback from others as well as information from your personal experiences.

Poor parent-teacher, administrator-teacher, and teacher-teacher communications can seriously interfere with your relationship with your students. If you respond inappropriately to a parent, for example, you may foster defensiveness or hostility that the parent, intentionally or not, may communicate to the student. This, in turn, affects how the student behaves in your classroom. Thus, communication competence will enhance your interaction with others in the educational environment.

TABLE 1.1   Communication Competencies for Teachers

I. **Informative Messages.** Teachers should demonstrate competence in sending and receiving messages that *give or obtain information.*
   A. To *send* these messages effectively:
      1. Structure information by using devices such as preview questions and comments, transitions, internal summaries, and concluding summaries.
      2. Amplify information graphically through the use of verbal and audiovisual supporting materials.
      3. Ask incisive questions to assess how well students understand the information given in lectures.
      4. Present information in an animated and interesting way.
   B. To *receive* these messages effectively:
      1. Identify the main point of students' informative messages.
      2. Discern structural patterns and problems in the information they present.
      3. Evaluate the adequacy of one's verbal and audiovisual supporting material in terms of the students' responses.
      4. Formulate questions that probe for the informative content.
      5. Differentiate between informative messages that students deliver in an interesting manner and those that are dull—but still say something.

II. **Affective Messages.** Teachers should demonstrate competence in sending and receiving messages that *express or respond to feelings.*
   A. To *send* these messages effectively:
      1. Reveal positive and negative feelings about self to students.
      2. Express positive and negative feelings about students to students.
      3. Offer opinions about classroom content, events, and real-world occurrences.
      4. Demonstrate openness, warmth, and positive regard for students.
   B. To *receive* these messages effectively:
      1. Recognize verbal and nonverbal cues that reveal students' feelings.
      2. Invite students to express their feelings.
      3. Be nonjudgmental in responding to their feelings.
      4. Ask open-ended questions in response to their expressions of feelings.
      5. If necessary, offer advice tactfully.

III. **Imaginative Messages.** Teachers should demonstrate competence in sending and receiving messages that *speculate, theorize, or fantasize.*
   A. To *send* these messages effectively:
      1. Use vivid descriptive language.
      2. Use expressive vocal and physical behavior when creating or recreating examples, stories, or narratives.
   B. To *receive* these messages effectively:
      1. Respond to students' use of imagination with appreciation.
      2. Be nondirective when encouraging their creativity.

IV. **Ritualistic Messages.** Teachers should demonstrate competence in sending and receiving messages that *maintain social relationships and facilitate interaction.*
   A. To *send* these messages effectively:
      1. Demonstrate appropriate behavior in performing everyday speech acts such as greeting, taking turns in conversation, and leave-taking.
      2. Model appropriate social amenities in ordinary classroom interaction.

3. Demonstrate speaking and listening competence when participating in or role-playing interviews, conversations, problem-solving and legislative groups, and public ceremonies.

B. To *receive* these messages effectively:
   1. Comment favorably when students perform everyday speech acts appropriately.
   2. Acknowledge appropriate performance of social amenities; diplomatically correct inappropriate behavior.
   3. Recognize competence and incompetence when students participate in interviews, conversations, problem-solving and legislative groups, and public ceremonies.

V. Persuasive Messages. Teachers should demonstrate competence in sending and receiving messages that *seek to convince.*

A. To *send* these messages effectively:
   1. Differentiate between fact and opinion.
   2. Be aware of audience factors that may encourage or constrain acceptance of ideas, such as peer pressure, fatigue, bias, and so on.
   3. Offer sound reasons and evidence in support of ideas.
   4. Recognize underlying assumptions in one's own arguments.

B. To *receive* these messages effectively:
   1. Admit one's own bias in responding to ideas.
   2. Question the adequacy of reason and evidence given.
   3. Evaluate audience evidence and reasons presented.
   4. Recognize underlying assumptions in the arguments of others.

From *Communication Competencies for Teachers,* by Pamela Cooper. Copyright © 1988 by National Communication Association. Reprinted by permission of the publisher.

Reading Objectives and Discussion Prompts

1.5 Communication Competence

What do you know?
Define classroom communication competence.

What do you think?
What do you think competent teachers do? How will you specifically try to incorporate these behaviors into your classroom?

CLASSROOM COMMUNICATION CLIMATE

As we suggested earlier in this chapter, a **supportive classroom climate** fosters fuller development of a student's positive self-image and enhances self-concept. In addition, when students are free of disruptive anxiety, fear, anger, or depression, they are more likely to make desirable cognitive and affective gains. More than any other person, the teacher sets the classroom climate. Productive student behavior is related to the following teacher characteristics: understanding/friendly teacher behavior, stimulating/imaginative teacher behavior, student-centered educational philosophy, favorable attitudes toward students, and democratic classroom procedures (Cooper & Galvin, 1983).

In his book *The Geranium on the Window Sill Just Died but Teacher You Went Right On,* Cullum (1971) writes of what students experience in a nonsupportive classroom climate:

> *It's September again*
> *—the time of jumping when you call,*
> *doing cartwheels for you,*
> *nodding yes.*
> *It's September again*
> *—standing on my head for you,*
> *leaping high*
> *hoping to please.*
> *It's September again*
> *—taking your tests,*
> *finding my lost pencil,*
> *losing ground.*
> *It's September again*
> *—hiding behind my reading book,*
> *breathing quietly,*
> *afraid!*

So what specifically and behaviorally can you do as a teacher to create a supportive classroom climate and, therefore, positive attitudes in your students? You want to focus on the positive, not the negative. Mayer (1968) defines these concepts for us; an aversive or negative consequence is "any event that causes physical or mental discomfort. It is an event that causes a person to think less highly of himself, that leads to a loss of self-respect or dignity, or that results in a strong anticipation of any of these. In general, any condition or consequence may be considered aversive if it causes a person to feel smaller or makes his world dimmer" (p. 47). Pain, anxiety, fear, frustration, embarrassment, boredom, and physical discomfort are all aversive stimuli and encourage a defensive classroom climate.

A positive consequence or condition is "any pleasant event that exists during the time the student is in the presence of the subject matter, or that follows his approach to the subject matter. In the way that an aversive condition or consequence causes the student's world to become dimmer or causes him to think less highly of himself, a positive condition or consequence causes the student to think a little more highly of himself, causes his world to become a little brighter" (Mayer, 1968, p. 58). Personal feedback, the use of praise, and the lack of blame increase student participation and performance. These practices communicate respect for students, or indicate to students that they are valued. It's important to remember that simply providing feedback or praise is not sufficient in itself. The feedback must be effective. Suggestions for effective feedback are presented in Box 1.1.

Classroom climate has two dimensions: supportiveness and defensiveness (Gibb, 1961). A supportive climate has few distortions, effective listening behaviors, and clear message transmission (Darling & Civikly, 1987). A supportive climate reduces defensiveness and allows students to focus on the content and structure of the message (Gibb, 1961). In contrast, a defensive climate interferes with the communication process and creates an atmosphere in which the sharing of ideas is stifled (Gibb, 1961, pp. 142–148). Table 1.2 lists Gibb's definitions of each of the components of both climates.

BOX 1.1

Effective Feedback

1. *Make your messages clearly your "own" by using the first person singular pronouns* I *and* my.
2. *Make your messages complete and specific.* Include clear statements of all necessary information the student needs in order to comprehend the message.
3. *Make your verbal and nonverbal messages congruent.* Communication problems arise when a person's verbal and nonverbal messages are contradictory.
4. *Be redundant.* Repeating your messages more than once and using more than one channel of communication (such as pictures and written messages as well as verbal and nonverbal cues) will help the student understand your messages.
5. *Ask for feedback concerning the way your messages are being received.*
6. *Make sure your feedback is helpful and nonthreatening:*
   a. *Focus your feedback on the person's behavior, not on her personality.*
   b. *Focus your feedback on descriptions rather than on judgments.* Refer to what occurred, not to your judgments of right or wrong, good or bad, or nice or naughty.
   c. *Focus your feedback on a specific situation rather than on abstract behavior.* What a person does is always related to a specific time and place. Feedback that ties behavior to a specific situation and is given immediately after the behavior has occurred increases self-awareness. The more immediate the feedback, the more helpful it is. Instead of saying, "Three weeks ago you didn't hand in your homework," say "You didn't hand in your homework today. Is something wrong?"
   d. *Focus your feedback on sharing your perceptions and feelings rather than on giving advice.*
   e. *Do not force feedback on people.* Feedback is given to help people become more self-aware and to improve their effectiveness in relating to other people.
   f. *Do not give people more feedback than they can understand at the time.* If you overload people with feedback, it reduces the chances that they will use it.
7. *Make the message appropriate to the receiver's frame of reference.* The same information will be explained differently to an expert in the field than to a novice, to a child than to an adult, or to a boss than to a coworker.
8. *Describe your feelings by name, action, or figure of speech.* When communicating your feelings, it is especially important to be descriptive. You may describe your feelings by name ("I feel sad"), by actions ("I feel like crying"), or by figures of speech ("I feel down in the dumps").
9. *Describe other people's behavior without evaluating or interpreting.* When reacting to the behavior of other people, be sure to describe their behavior ("You keep interrupting me") rather than evaluating it ("You're self-centered and won't listen to anyone else's ideas").

Adapted from Curwin & Mendler (1999).

Reading Objectives and Discussion Prompts

1.6 Classroom Climate

What do you know?
Describe a supportive and defensive classroom climate.

What do you think?
How will you communicate your classroom climate to your students? What do you think are the student's responsibilities in maintaining a positive classroom climate?

TABLE 1.2   Defensive versus Supportive Communication Climates

Defensive Climates	Supportive Climates
1. *Evaluation.* To pass judgment on another; to blame or praise; to make moral assessments of another; to question another's standards, values, and motives and the affect loadings of the person's communication.	1. *Description.* Nonjudgmental; to ask questions that are perceived as genuine requests for information; to present "feelings, events, perceptions, or processes that do not ask or imply that the receiver change behavior or attitude." If we use "you" language—"You are not doing your best"—we are evaluating. If we use "I" language—"When you don't do as well as I think you can, I get frustrated"—we are describing.
2. *Control.* To try to do something to another; to attempt to change an attitude or the behavior of another; to try to restrict another's field of activity; "implicit in all attempts to alter another person is the assumption of the change agent that the person to be altered is inadequate."	2. *Problem Orientation.* The antithesis of persuasion; to communicate "a desire to collaborate in defining a mutual problem and in seeking its solution" (thus, tending to create the same problem orientation in the other); to imply that he has no preconceived solution, attitude, or method to impose on the other; to allow "the receiver to set his own goals, make his own decisions, and evaluate his own progress—or to share with the sender in doing so." Control is an "I know what's best for you" attitude. Problem orientation is "We have a problem. What can we do to solve it?" attitude.
3. *Strategy.* To manipulate others; to use tricks to "involve" another, to make her think she was making her own decisions, and to make her feel that the speaker had genuine interest in her; to engage in a stratagem involving ambiguous and multiple motivation.	3. *Spontaneity.* To express guilelessness; natural simplicity; freedom from deception; having a "clear id"; having unhidden uncomplicated motives; straightforwardness and honesty. Whenever we try to trick or manipulate another person into doing what we want, we are using a strategy. Spontaneity is expressing ourselves honestly. How many of us wish for a simple, honest "I just didn't get the paper done" instead of the "My dog ate the paper" excuse!
4. *Neutrality.* To express lack of concern for the welfare of another; "the clinical, detached, person-is-an-object-of-study attitude."	4. *Empathy.* To express respect for the worth of the listener; to identify with his problems, share his feelings, and accept his emotional values. Students feel defensive when they perceive our neutrality—"She doesn't really care about me. I'm just another student to her." Being empathic—putting ourselves in another's shoes—can communicate to students that we care about them personally. Remember, being empathetic doesn't mean we agree with the student's feelings—only that we respect those feelings.

5. *Superiority.* To communicate the attitude that one is "superior in position, power, wealth, intellectual ability, physical characteristics, other ways" to another; to tend to arouse feelings of inadequacy in the other; to impress the other that the speaker "is not willing to enter a shared problem-solving relationship, that he probably does not desire feedback, that he does not require help, and that he will be likely to try to reduce the power, the status, or the worth of the receiver."

5. *Equality.* To be willing to enter into participative planning with mutual trust and respect; to attach little importance to differences in talent, ability, worth, appearance, status, and power.

   We have all had teachers who constantly remind us that they are the teacher—the superior intellectual being in the classroom. Remember how thrilled you were when the teacher made a mistake? A teacher who believes in equality communicates that everyone has value—regardless of their intellectual capabilities. In addition, such a teacher communicates that everyone makes mistakes and that everyone—teacher and students—can learn from one another.

6. *Certainty.* To appear dogmatic; "to seem to know the answers, to require no additional data"; and to regard self as teacher rather than as coworker; to manifest inferiority feelings by needing to be right, wanting to win an argument rather than solve a problem, seeing one's ideas as truths to be defended.

6. *Provisionalism.* To be willing to experiment with one's own behavior, attitudes, and ideas; to investigate issues rather than taking sides on them, to problem solve rather than debate, to communicate that the other person may have some control over the shared quest or the investigation of ideas. "If a person is genuinely searching for information and data, he does not resent help or company along the way."

   We have all known people who are always right—who believe they have a corner on ultimate truth. Generally, we expend a great deal of energy trying to prove these people wrong. In provisionalism, although the person may have a strong opinion, she is willing to acknowledge another's viewpoint.

Adapted from "Defensive Communication" by J. Gibb, *Journal of Communication, 11* (1961), pp. 142–148. Copyright © 1961 by Oxford University Press. Reprinted by permission.

TEACHING DIVERSE STUDENTS

Many of the communication principles discussed in this text come from research based on more traditional populations. Some of the information may be generalized across various groups, but other information may not. As you read and discuss this text, we want you to consider how each concept may be applied to different student groups based on gender, ethnicity, culture, and sexual orientation, as well as to students with varying backgrounds, learning styles, and needs. For example, how does nonverbal feedback work with students who have physical disabilities? How would someone from another culture perceive the curriculum provided in U.S. history? How do gay or lesbian students react when assumptions about male-female relationships abound in our textbooks? How might various teaching strategies affect students with differing learning styles? All of these are important questions to ask if we want to be competent and effective teachers striving to create a supportive classroom climate for all of our students, not just some of them.

These examples tell us that teaching in a diverse classroom is not an easy task. Teachers need special training (Simonds, Lippert, Hunt, Angell, & Moore, 2008; Salinas, 2002). In preparing to teach a diverse group, Chism, Cano, and Pruitt (1989) suggest the following six competencies:

- Understand nontraditional learning styles.
- Learn about the history and culture of nontraditional groups.
- Research the contributions of women and ethnic minorities.
- Uncover your own biases.
- Learn about bias in instructional materials.
- Learn about your school's resources for nontraditional students.

Teachers should also consider ways to teach from a more **global perspective**; that is, taking into account the diverse student population you may have in a classroom. We recommend that teachers avoid, or at least recognize our propensity for, stereotyping. In addition, teachers should consider the **inclusion-exclusion rule**. Can everyone in your classroom comfortably participate in your curriculum? Consider, for example, how American Indian children feel when we talk about "Columbus discovering America" when their ancestors were here before Columbus and didn't feel they needed to be discovered. How do Jewish children feel when we celebrate Christmas in our classrooms? We also recommend that teachers begin the process of perspective taking—putting yourself in the place of your students. Teaching from a global perspective doesn't privilege one group, it rather takes into consideration the values and beliefs about varying groups. This is where real learning about differences can take place.

All cultures share certain elements such as language, patterns of thought, values, and beliefs. The way we view these elements makes up of our frame of reference or **worldview**. There is an adage that says, when you learn about another culture, you learn about yourself. Think about this saying as you read about the communication variables that affect your interactions with students from differing backgrounds.

In the next few chapters, several communication variables are discussed. Paying particular attention to these variables can enhance your communication competence in the educational environment while at the same time help you to create a more positive climate for your students. We feel that if you take time in the beginning of your classes to consider these issues, you will see that the rest of your time is better spent on teaching.

Reading Objectives and Discussion Prompts

1.7 Teaching Diverse Students

What do you know?
What are the six suggestions for teaching in a diverse classroom?

What do you think?
What do you think makes students diverse? How might a student's worldview, or frame of reference, affect your communication with him/her?

In Sum

This chapter has provided a basic introduction to instructional communication theory and research and how they may be applied in the classroom. We have provided a theoretical foundation for communication education and discussed the relationship between theory, research, and practice. Several important topics that provide the foundation for our study of classroom communication were presented: classroom communication competence, classroom climate, and student diversity. These ideas are important. Yet, we would caution that teachers must consider all these ideas in relationship to their students. As Hugh Prather (1970, p. 20) reminds us:

> *Ideas are clean. They soar in the serene supernal. I can take them out and look at them, they fit in books, they lead me down that narrow way. And in the morning they are there. Ideas are straight—*
> *But the world is round, and a messy mortal is my friend.*
> *Come walk with me in the mud . . .*

Key Terms

Communication Pedagogy
Developmental
    Communication
Instructional
    Communication
Empirical Tradition
Interpretive Tradition
Critical Tradition
Teaching Philosophy
Communication
    Competencies

Instructional Strategies
Communication Impact
Classroom Communication
Elements of Communication
    (People, Verbal and
    Nonverbal Messages,
    Channels, Interference,
    Feedback, Context)
Frame of Reference
Transactional Process

Classroom Climate
    (Supportive and
    Defensive)
Student Diversity
Global Perspective
Inclusion-Exclusion Rule
Worldview

2 Interpersonal Communication

OBJECTIVES

After reading this chapter, you should be able to:

- Explain the importance of good interpersonal relationships in the classroom and describe the relationship stages.
- Understand the relationship between self-concept and communication.
- Define self-disclosure.
- Understand the role of immediacy in the classroom.
- Define communication style.
- Discuss the dimensions of teacher credibility.
- Describe the process of teacher expectancy and how they can be communicated.
- Describe student expectancies.
- Discuss seven guidelines for parent-teacher conferences.
- Provide guidelines for effective communication online.

Former NFL quarterback and congressman Jack Kemp is quoted as saying, "People don't care what you know until they know who you are" (Knoblock, 2003). Carl Rogers (1962) suggests that in our work with students it's the quality of our relationship with them, not the content we teach, that is the most significant element determining our effectiveness. When asked to rate behavior they consider important to effective teaching, teachers often cite interpersonal communication and relationship skills (c.f. Frymier & Houser, 2000; Morganett, 1995; West, 1994).

How do we build relationships in the classroom? We build these relationships through communication with our students—through interpersonal communication. It is through communication that we develop, maintain, and terminate relationships. A teacher must possess a well-developed repertoire of interpersonal communication skills in order to establish, maintain, and promote effective interpersonal relationships in the classroom.

RELATIONSHIP DEVELOPMENT

Communication has two major dimensions: content and relational. Teachers and students not only share content but also share a relationship. Graham, West, and Schaller (1992) base their relational teaching approach on the belief that "teaching involves a process of relational development and requires effective interpersonal communication skills to achieve satisfying outcomes" (p. 11). Frymier and Houser (2000) examined student perceptions of teacher behaviors to observe any similarities between the student-teacher relationship and other interpersonal relationships (e.g., friends).

Frymier and Houser found that students perceived communication skills, particularly the ability to convey information clearly, the ability to make people feel good about themselves, and conflict management skills as important to good teaching. The researchers also found that all communication skills studied were significant predictors of student learning and motivation. In other words, the teacher-student relationship is indeed an interpersonal one—with both content and relationship dimensions.

How are relationships formed between people? The basic stages of relationship development are initiating, experimenting, and intensifying. The termination stages are deterioration and dissolution. It is important to note that communication changes as people progress through the stages.

According to Knapp and Vangelisti (2008) our communication becomes more broad, unique, efficient, flexible, smooth, personal, spontaneous, and overt as we progress through the stages of relationship development. Knapp and Vangelisti also speculate that as relationships deteriorate, communication becomes more narrow, stylized, difficult, rigid, awkward, public, and hesitant, and overt judgments are suspended.

Relationship Stages

INITIATING.   This first stage is one of first encounters. On the first day of class we begin **initiating** our relationships with students. Much goes into this first stage. Our prior knowledge of the students and theirs of us, our mutual expectations, and our initial impressions all affect the initiation stage. Much has been written in teacher education concerning the importance of the first day of class. First impressions have a great impact on how the student-teacher relationship progresses. First impressions are difficult to change. The first impression we have of a class or a student determines our expectations of how effective or pleasant future interactions will be.

Getting off on the wrong foot—either as a teacher or a student—can have very detrimental effects (Friedrich & Cooper, 1999; Goza, 1993).

EXPERIMENTING.   In this stage, students and teachers test one another and try to discover the unknown. Students **experiment** with behaviors—"How much can I get away with?" and "How can I please this teacher?" Teachers seek to identify the teaching methods and classroom management techniques that work best. Each person is trying to answer questions such as "Who are you?" "What do we have in common?" and "What do you expect from me?"

Much of the communication in this stage is stereotypical. Teachers aren't perceived by students as unique individuals, but only in their role as teachers. In like fashion, students are viewed in their role and not as individuals with unique ways of behaving or learning.

INTENSIFYING.   In the **intensifying** stage, teachers and students communicate on a more interpersonal level. That is, communication is not role-to-role but person-to-person. A larger variety of topics may be discussed in greater depth than in the experimenting stage. Behavior is more easily predictable and explainable because teachers know students better and vice versa. For example, at this stage of the student-teacher relationship, a teacher will be able to predict how a particular student will react to humor or criticism and to adapt communication accordingly.

DETERIORATION AND DISSOLUTION.   We often consider **termination** of relationships as negative. However, in the student-teacher relationship, the termination stages of deterioration and dissolution are a natural phenomenon. Classes end and students leave. Patrick Walsh (1986), in his book *Tales Out of School*, describes the feelings many teachers experience as the school year ends:

> Nowadays I make my June farewells to students by writing them notes on the blackboard. A couple of years ago I was checking the roll for the last time when I suddenly got choked up. I made a quick exit, returned, but had to leave again. The next year, confident I'd be able to control my emotions, I started to tell a fourth-period how much I'd enjoyed teaching them. I got about five words out and had to stop.
>
> Another time I was collecting the last set of tests when it hit me that this would be the last time these kids would come together as "my" students. I could feel the tears starting, so I turned and pretended to look for papers on my desk. Finally, I grabbed some chalk and scribbled a note on the blackboard: "You've been one of the most talented, wild, fun classes I've ever taught. Thanks for a great year." As I finished writing, I thought of a line from T. S. Eliot: "It is impossible to say just what I mean." (p. 211)

Reading Objectives and Discussion Prompts

2.1 Relationship Stages

What do you know?
Describe the relationship stages between teachers and students.

What do you think?
How are teacher-student relationships similar to other interpersonal relationships? How are they different?

COMMUNICATION VARIABLES IN INTERPERSONAL RELATIONSHIPS

Several communication variables contribute to building a positive relationship between student and teacher. The following variables are discussed in this chapter— self-concept, teacher expectancy, self-disclosure, immediacy, communication style, and teacher credibility.

Self-Concept

Basic to all interpersonal communication is the question, "Who am I?" Finding the answer to this question is prerequisite to being able to communicate effectively with others. Only when we know who we are can we proceed to communicate effectively with others. Your **self-concept** is your total image of yourself. It is made up of four parts:

- How you perceive yourself intellectually, socially, and physically.
- How you would like to be.
- How you believe others perceive you.
- How others actually perceive you.

Although we'll use the term *self-concept* throughout this chapter, it's important to remember that this term is somewhat misleading. Many self-concepts make up our general self-concept. For example, a student may have a concept of self as an athlete and a concept of self as a math student. For each of these concepts, the student has ideas about the four parts previously listed. You not only describe yourself but also appraise or evaluate yourself. This appraisal reflects your **self-esteem**. In other words, I have a concept of myself as a teacher: I am dedicated and hardworking. If I value those qualities, I will have high self-esteem. If I do not value my concept as a teacher, I will have low self-esteem. When people have high self-esteem, they feel likable, productive, and capable.

COMMUNICATION AND SELF-CONCEPT. A reciprocal relationship exists between communication and self-concept: Communication affects our self-concept, and our self-concept affects how and what we communicate. A model by Kinch (1963) demonstrates this reciprocal relationship (Figure 2.1).

We can begin looking at this model at any of the four circles. Beginning with (P), our perceptions of how others see us influence our self-concept (S). Our self-concept influences our behavior (B). Our behavior (B) in turn influences the actions of others toward us (A). These actions influence our perceptions of how others see us, and we are back to the starting point again. As a teacher you can affect the self-concepts of students by the nature of the communication you direct toward them. Several researchers have found support for this idea. For example, Cooper, Stewart, and Gudykunst (1982) conducted studies that demonstrate that students with high and low self-concepts as public speakers perceive messages differently and that these perceptions are related to changes in their self-concept, their motivation to achieve, and their rating of both the instructor and their relationship with the instructor. Thus, how we perceive the communication we receive from others influences our self-concept and our subsequent communication.

One of the major ways self-concept affects communication in the classroom is through the **self-fulfilling prophecy,** which suggests that we behave in ways people expect us to. Self-concept affects communication because we communicate and behave in

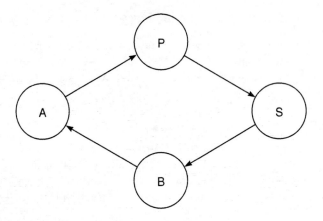

P = Perception of others' responses
S = Self-concept
B = Behavior
A = Actual responses of others

FIGURE 2.1 Kinch's Model of the Relationship between Self-Concept and Communication.

From "A Formalized Theory of Self-Concept" by J. W. Kinch, *American Journal of Sociology*, 68:4 (January 1963), pp. 481–486. Copyright © 1963 by The University of Chicago Press. Reprinted by permission of the publisher.

accordance with our self-concept. Our self-concept is formed, to a large extent, by our perception of the communication we receive from others. Consider the student who believes he is "dumb" in math. His attitude might be, "I don't do well, so why try?" As a result, he doesn't do math homework, doesn't study for exams, and doesn't pay attention in class. Because of these behaviors, he subsequently fails math. He has fulfilled his own prophecy, "I don't do well in math."

SELF-CONCEPT AND ACADEMIC PERFORMANCE.   A logical question at this point is, "What effect does self-concept have on academic performance?" Bassett and Smythe (1979) outlined the characteristics of a student who demonstrates high academic achievement and the characteristics of a student who demonstrates low academic achievement (see Table 2.1). These authors indicated that many of the variables affecting academic achievement are related to student self-concept. If this is the case, it becomes crucial to consider the impact that teachers can have on student self-concepts.

In general, teachers who appear to enjoy teaching and facilitate good student-student interaction, shared decision making, and positive student-teacher interactions foster more positive self-concepts in students. For example, your concept of self can greatly affect your teaching effectiveness. One way that this can happen is through a concept known as **teacher efficacy**—a teacher's belief that she can influence how well students learn (Berman et al., 1977, Guskey & Passaro, 1994; Knobloch, 2003). Teachers who have a high sense of efficacy were more satisfied with teaching, experienced less stress (Burley, Hall,

TABLE 2.1   Characteristics of Students Demonstrating High and Low Academic Achievement

Students Demonstrating High Academic Achievement	Students Demonstrating Low Academic Achievement
1. Have high regard for themselves	**1.** Have unfavorable attitudes toward school and teachers
2. Are optimistic about their potential for success in the future	**2.** Do not assume responsibility for learning
3. Possess confidence in their competence as persons and students	**3.** Have low motivation
4. Believe they are hard workers	**4.** Have low morale and are dissatisfied with their school experience
5. Believe other students like them	**5.** Participate in class infrequently
	6. Act in ways that create discipline problems
	7. Have high dropout rates
	8. Have difficulty adjusting personally and socially

Villeme, & Brockmeier, 1991), and exhibited greater enthusiasm for teaching and levels of planning and organization (Allinder, 1994). High teacher efficacy has also been shown to be related to student achievement and motivation (Midgley, Feldlaufer, & Eccles, 1989), increased self-esteem (Borton, 1991), improved self-direction (Rose & Medway, 1981), and more positive attitudes toward school (Miskel, McDonald, & Bloom, 1983). It appears that teacher efficacy is somewhat contagious and cyclical. It works like this: a teacher who has confidence in his ability will have more positive interactions with students, who will, in turn, do better in school. It should be noted that the reverse is also true. A low sense of efficacy can create a self-defeating and demoralizing cycle of failure (Bandura, 1997). In this way, a teacher's concept of self has a great impact on student success.

Not only does positive student behavior affect our self-concepts as teachers, but negative student behavior can also influence the way we feel about ourselves as teachers. One of your authors, Dr. Cooper, shares the following:

> Recently I began teaching a class in communication and socialization. I had never taught the class before and was somewhat nervous. One student began to argue with me about the requirements for the course and became quite hostile. Perhaps because she was not completely confident about this new course, she left class questioning my ability to teach this course effectively. As teachers we all have days when we don't get positive reactions from students. Often when we receive negative reactions, we feel inadequate. At this point, it is necessary to honestly reevaluate our teaching techniques and skills. However, it's just as important to keep things in perspective and not overreact to unpleasant situations. As I reflected on the student's hostile behavior and reevaluated what I wanted to accomplish in the course on communication and socialization, I decided I had been

correct in my choice of requirements for the course. One student's negative behavior had thrown me temporarily, but a reevaluation of myself and the situation convinced me I was still adequate as a teacher.

Reading Objectives and Discussion Prompts

2.2 Self-Concept

What do you know?
Define self-concept. What is the relationship between self-concept and communication?

What do you think?
Describe your teacher self-concept. Do you think this will change with experience? How do you think your self-concept as a teacher will affect the way you communicate with your students? How will it affect the way they communicate with you?

Understanding the role that self-concept plays in our communication with others also allows us to understand how teacher expectancies may play a role in how students view themselves.

Expectancy

TEACHER EXPECTANCIES.   With the publication of Rosenthal and Jacobson's *Pygmalion in the Classroom* in 1968, a controversy began about the effect of **teachers' expectations** on students. Basically, the expectancy process works as follows:

- Teachers expect certain behaviors from certain students.
- These expectations influence the teacher's behavior toward these students.
- The teacher's behavior indicates to the students what the teacher expects of them. These expectations affect the students' self-concept, motivation to achieve, and achievement.
- If the teacher's behavior is consistent over time and the students do not resist it, high-expectation students will achieve well and low-expectation students will not.

Although much disagreement has been generated about the teacher expectancy issue, the evidence does suggest that teacher expectations can be self-fulfilling.

One of the clearest models of teacher expectancy is proposed by Braun (1976). The model suggests that, based on the teacher's perceptions of student ability and background (input), expectations are formed (see Figure 2.2). These expectations are then communicated to students in various ways (output). Students read and internalize the teacher's output and form a self-expectation. The student's output, based on the self-expectation, produces new input (represented by the dotted line in the model), and the cycle continues.

Should a teacher strive to have only positive expectations? Appropriate expectations, not necessarily high expectations, are what you as a teacher should strive for, according to Good and Brophy (2007):

Expectations should be appropriate rather than necessarily high, and they must be followed up with appropriate behavior. This means planned learning experiences that take students at the level they are now and move them along

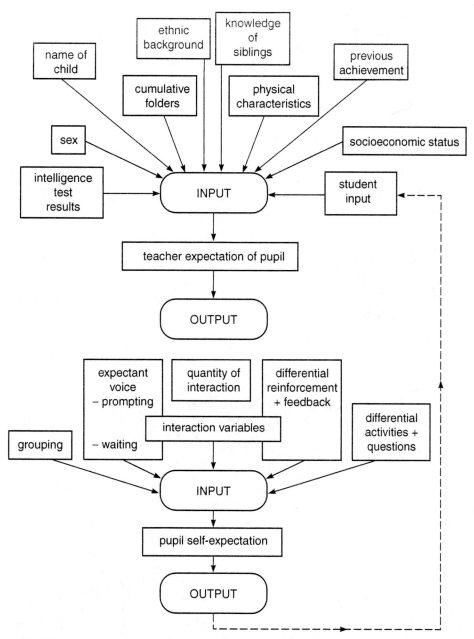

FIGURE 2.2   A Model of the Expectation Process.

From "Teacher Expectation: Sociopsychological Dynamics" by C. Braun, in *Review of Educational Research*, *46* (1976), p. 206.

at a pace they can handle. The pace that will allow continued success and improvement is the correct pace and will vary with different students. Teachers should not feel guilty or feel that they are stigmatizing slower learners by moving them along at a slower pace. As long as students are working up to their potential and progressing at a steady rate, the teacher has reason to be satisfied. There will be cause for criticism only if the slower children are moved along at a slower pace than they can handle because the teacher's expectations for them are too low, are never tested out or re-evaluated, and consequently, are unalterable. (p. 42)

Certain teacher expectations are recommended for an effective learning experience. Without them, teachers would not be very effective. Box 2.1 provides a useful list of

---

BOX 2.1
Teacher Expectations

1. *The teacher should enjoy teaching.*
2. *Teachers should understand that their main responsibility is to teach.* Your job involves many roles besides that of instructing students. Although these other roles are necessary aspects of your job, they are subordinate to and in support of the major role of teaching—instruction.
3. *Teachers should understand that the crucial aspects of teaching are task presentation, diagnosis, remediation, and enrichment.* Failure to be clear about crucial aspects of teaching characterizes teachers who favor high achievers over low achievers or who pay more attention to answers than to the thinking processes a student goes through in reaching an answer.
4. *Teachers need to assess student understanding regularly.* There may be disparity between what teachers think they have communicated and what students actually heard. Teachers should monitor the work of their students regularly and talk to them about their understanding of classroom instruction.
5. *Teachers should expect all students to meet at least the minimum specified objectives.* Although all students cannot be reasonably expected to do equally well, reasonable minimal objectives can be established for each of your classes.
6. *Teachers should expect students to enjoy learning.* When you do have the appropriate attitude toward your subject, you present it in ways that make your students see it as enjoyable.
7. *The teacher should expect to deal with individuals, not groups or stereotypes.* As a rule, you should think, talk, and act in terms of individual students. In the final analysis, you are teaching Johnny and Susie, not Group A or "slow learners." The way you talk about your students is an indication of how you think about them and how you'll relate to them.
8. *The teacher should assume good intentions and a positive self-concept.* Teachers must communicate to their students the expectation that the students want to be—and are trying to be—fair, cooperative, reasonable, and responsible. This includes even those students who consistently present the same behavior problems. Your basic faith in a student's ability to change is a necessary (but often not sufficient) condition for such change. If students see that you do not have this faith in them, they will probably lose whatever motivation they have to keep trying.
9. *The teacher should expect to be obeyed.* Obedience is usually obtained rather easily if you establish fair and appropriate rules, are consistent in what you say, say only what you really mean, and follow up with appropriate action whenever this is necessary.

things that you as a teacher should expect of yourself and your students. As you reflect on this list (both now and when you begin teaching), consider how these expectations will influence the way you approach teaching and your students. Consider how your approach will affect your continued desire to teach and your student's motivation to learn.

STUDENT EXPECTANCIES.   Remember that expectancies exist on the part of students as well as teachers. Lim (1996) asked fifty of his students their expectations for an outstanding professor. Their expectations are provided in Box 2.2. The profiles in Box 2.2 provide a set of guidelines that can prompt careful self-evaluation and motivate instructors toward "A" professor behaviors (pp. 3–4).

Students avoid some teachers and flock to others based on their expectations of what a particular teacher's class will be like. The expectancies a student has for a teacher will affect communication in the classroom. Students will communicate more with teachers they expect to be positive in responding. Student expectancies can affect student perceptions of a teacher's messages. If students expect to receive negative feedback, chances are they'll perceive messages from the teacher as negative. If they expect to receive positive messages, they'll perceive the teacher's communication as positive. For example, if a student raises his hand and is not called on, he may perceive the message negatively—"Ms. Miller never calls on me"—if he expects a negative message. If a positive expectation is present, the student could interpret the message, "Ms. Miller wanted to give someone else a chance to talk."

Finally, student expectations can affect learning. Consider how learning might be affected by such expectations as, "You never have to do anything. Just go to class and you'll get an A," or "Mr. Brommel really knows his stuff. You'll learn a lot."

Reading Objectives and Discussion Prompts

2.3 Teacher Expectancies

What do you know?
Describe the teacher expectancy process.

What do you think?
How will you communicate your teacher expectations in the classroom? What should your students expect from you?

Self-Disclosure

Self-disclosure—voluntarily giving others information about ourselves that they are unlikely to know or discover from other sources—is important in the development of relationships. If we're going to communicate effectively with our students, we need to know how they view themselves (their self-concepts). The only way to really know how students view themselves is through their self-disclosures. Likewise, if our students are going to communicate effectively with us, they need to know how we view ourselves. The underlying assumption of interpersonal communication is that the more we know about another, the more effective our communication will be with that person. Although the focus in this chapter is on verbal self-disclosure, you should remember

BOX 2.2

Student Expectations

The "A" Professor—An Outstanding Professor

Preparation: "A" professors are able to prepare well-organized syllabi and follow them. They always bring a complete set of notes to class and are prepared to lecture the materials thoroughly and efficiently.

Enthusiasm: "A" professors are enthusiastic about teaching. They make students feel welcome when seeking help, be it personal or academic. They have a genuine desire and interest in the subject they are teaching.

Clarity: "A" professors answer their students' questions clearly, accurately, and specifically. They make homework assignments clear and to the point.

Research: "A" professors are always up-to-date with new information. They are able to introduce the latest research into classrooms and always keep an eye on the latest technology and prepare their students for the future.

Assignments: "A" professors give out assignments regularly to reinforce class materials. Their assignments are challenging and pertain to class discussions. They always make sure that the students have the tools and knowledge to finish the assignments on time. They grade the assignments promptly and make adequate comments on homework and tests.

Humor: "A" professors have a sense of humor that makes the class more fun to attend. They bring to the class a level of dynamics that helps to maintain the interest of students when the materials become dry.

Fairness: "A" professors treat students fairly. They grade students according to the students' performance and efforts. They are not biased, but assign grades impartially.

The "C" Professor—An Average or Typical Professor

Preparation: "C" professors do not prepare their lectures well. They do not have syllabi that students can follow. They often misplace their notes or forget to bring them to class. They frequently find themselves trying to figure out where they were previously. They do not have a clear plan about what to cover.

Enthusiasm: "C" professors usually do not show a strong commitment toward the class. They will be half-hearted when it comes to teaching, and they usually are not focused on the task at hand.

Clarity: "C" professors present their lectures in such a way that the students feel lost. They are vague about the requirements for assignments.

Research: "C" professors are not up-to-date in their field of study. They do not have full command of the subject and often try to conceal it.

Assignments: "C" professors give minimal assignments, and they do not grade the assignments for weeks after. They pile up assignments and assign all of them at once without proper warning. They give assignments that are unreasonable, expecting students to know more than they do. They also give poor guidance on assignments.

Humor: "C" professors present the materials in a monotone voice and manner that could make an interesting subject boring. They appear aloof and intimidating.

Fairness: "C" professors do not necessarily treat students fairly. They favor students whom they know prior to class and project a sense of inequality in the classroom.

that we disclose information about ourselves nonverbally as well as verbally. The clothes you wear, the way you walk, and your smile all communicate things about you—your likes and dislikes, your emotional states, and so forth. We discuss nonverbal communication in Chapter 4.

The more information you have about how students view themselves, the better able you'll be to see the world through their eyes and thus better understand their responses to you, to other students, and to the instructional process.

A major characteristic of effective self-disclosure is **appropriateness**. To be effective communicators, we need to consider the timing of our disclosure, the other person's capacity to respond, the short-term effects, the motives for disclosure, how much detail is called for, whether the disclosure is relevant to the current situation, and the feelings of the other person as well as our own.

Another characteristic of self-disclosure is that it occurs **incrementally**. It's unlikely a student will come into your office following the first day of class and tell you anything very personal. In order to self-disclose, we have to trust the other person, and it takes time to build trust in a relationship. We must believe that the other person will not reject us, but will accept us for who we are. In addition, we must trust that they will respect the confidentiality of the information. As soon as someone violates our trust, self-disclosure stops or decreases significantly.

Self-disclosure is **reciprocal**. We disclose to the people who disclose themselves to us. It's primarily up to the teacher to begin this reciprocal process. If we are willing to share ourselves with our students, they'll be more willing to share themselves with us. The effect of this reciprocity is that we can develop a more positive classroom atmosphere and enhance effective communication.

Numerous factors influence self-disclosure. Self-disclosure occurs more readily under some circumstances than others. Children disclose more than adolescents or adults. Elementary school teachers receive some rather interesting (and unsolicited) information concerning a student's home life, likes and dislikes, fears, and so on. However, children learn to temper their disclosures so that by the time students reach adolescence, they are fairly secretive.

Females disclose more than males. Men have traditionally been seen as the stronger of the sexes physically as well as emotionally. Many men don't cry or reveal their feelings because this would seem to show weakness. As traditional sex roles are reevaluated, this tendency may well begin to disappear.

Finally, race, culture, and nationality affect self-disclosure. European American students have been found to disclose more information than African American students. Students from the United States disclose more than similar students in Puerto Rico, Great Britain, West Germany, or the Far East.

What does all this information on self-disclosure have to do with classroom communication? Self-disclosing messages can be used to clarify course content and have been linked to affective learning, teacher effectiveness (Holladay, 1984; Downs, Javidi, & Nussbaum, 1988), student cognitive learning (Wambach & Brothen, 1997), more communication inside and outside the classroom (Knapp, Martin, & Myers, 2003), and increased student interest (Cayanus & Martin, 2004). Research has clearly demonstrated that the attitudes you have toward students affect the quality and quantity of communication you have with your students. In addition, students' behavior toward you can affect how you feel about yourself as a teacher. This feeling can, in turn, influence your teaching, which can influence student learning.

Reading Objectives and Discussion Prompts

2.4 Self-Disclosure

What do you know?
What are the characteristics of effective self-disclosure? What factors influence self-disclosure?

What do you think?
What do you think is appropriate self-disclosure in the classroom? How much will you disclose to your students? How much will you allow them to disclose to you?

Immediacy

Immediacy is verbal and nonverbal communication behaviors that enhance physical and psychological closeness (Mehrabian, 1969). Immediacy includes such behaviors as praising, use of humor, addressing another by name, using personal examples, using the words *our* and *we*, smiling, eye contact, and changes in vocal and facial expression.

Immediate teachers are viewed as approachable, friendly, open, and responsive to student needs (see, for example, Andersen, 1979; McCroskey, Richmond, Plax, & Kearney, 1985; and Richmond, Gorham, & McCroskey, 1986). In addition, immediate teachers are perceived as warm and relaxed. Nonimmediate teachers are perceived as cold, distant, and unfriendly (see, for example, Kearney, Plax, Smith, & Sorensen, 1988).

A great deal of research has investigated the immediacy variable. In general, findings indicate that teacher immediacy (vocal expressiveness, smiling, gestures, eye contact, movement around the classroom, and a relaxed body position) is associated with cognitive learning (Gorham, 1988; Richmond, McCroskey, & Payne, 2007; Chesebro & McCroskey, 2001; McCroskey, Valencic, & Richmond, 2004), affective learning (Andersen, 1979; Gorham, 1988; Kearney, Plax, Richmond, & McCroskey, 1985), recall of information (Kelley & Gorham, 1988), classroom management (Kearney, Plax, Richmond, & McCroskey, 1984; Kearney et al., 1988; Richmond, 1990), humor (Gorham & Christophel, 1990; Wanzer & McCroskey, 1999; Wrench & Richmond, 2004), motivation (Christophel, 1990; Christophel & Gorham, 1995; Frymier, 1994a; Gorham & Christophel, 1992; Richmond, 1990), willingness to communicate in and out of the classroom (Menzel & Carrell, 1999; Mottet, Martin, & Myers, 2004), and positive evaluation of the teacher by students (Thweatt & McCroskey, 1996).

Why does teacher immediacy have such a positive impact? As Frymier and Shulman (1995) suggest

> Initially, an immediate teacher gains students' attention. Immediate teachers move about the classroom, make eye contact, use vocal variety, and address students by name, all of which are attention getting. Use of immediacy behaviors may also help to build confidence in students. An immediate

teacher seems to produce liking and positive feelings among students, which creates an environment where success may seem more likely. Students with such a teacher are also likely to be more satisfied with the learning experience than are students with a low immediacy teacher (Frymier, 1994b). . . . Immediacy behaviors are likely to increase motivation because of their positive impact on (a) attention, (b) confidence, and (c) satisfaction. (p. 41)

Some research has focused on the student behaviors that influence teachers. Students' verbal and nonverbal communication has been found to influence how teachers perceive students (Mottet, 2000; Mottet & Richmond, 2002). In terms of immediacy, students who are perceived to be less nonverbally responsive and immediate have been shown to be at a disadvantage in the classroom (Barringer & McCroskey, 2000; Mottet, 2000). For example, Mottet (2000) found that teachers' perceptions of student nonverbal responsiveness were positively related to teachers' impressions of student competence. In a similar vein, Barringer and McCroskey (2000) found that as teachers perceived students to be more nonverbally immediate, teachers' perceptions of student credibility, interpersonal attraction, and liking increased significantly.

One word of caution is necessary. Several researchers suggest that immediacy is influenced by culture (McCroskey, Fayer, Richmond, Sulliven, & Barraclough, 1996; McCroskey, Sallinen, Fayer, Richmond, & Barraclough, 1996; Neuliep, 1995)—a topic we will discuss more fully in Chapter 10. For example, Fayer, Gorham, and McCroskey (1993) examined teacher immediacy in the United States and in Puerto Rico. They found immediacy to be positively related to affective and cognitive learning in both cultures, but more so for U.S. students than for Puerto Rican students.

Collier and Powell (1990) found significant differences in the ways European Americans, Hispanic Americans, African Americans, and Asian Americans evaluated teacher immediacy. Although all four groups perceived a positive relationship between immediacy and teacher effectiveness, immediacy cues functioned differently across groups. For European Americans, the degree to which the teachers oriented their body positions toward the students contributed significantly to teacher effectiveness. For Hispanic Americans, smiling, vocal expressiveness, and body position were most important. Teacher relaxedness and smiling were perceived by African Americans to be important contributors to teacher effectiveness. Finally, for Asian Americans, vocal expressiveness, smiling, and teacher relaxedness contributed significantly to their perception of teacher effectiveness.

Based on data drawn from the cultures of Australia, Finland, Puerto Rico, and the United States, McCroskey, Richmond, Sulliven, Fayer, and Barraclough (1995) found that nonverbal teacher immediacy behaviors related, in all four cultures, to positive teacher evaluation and willingness to take another course with the teacher. Immediacy behaviors that contributed to higher teacher evaluations were vocal variety, relaxed body position, eye contact with students, and smiling at students. Moving around and gesturing were also viewed positively by students (less so by Australian students) but were less important in students' evaluations of teachers. McCroskey and colleagues (1996) found that increased teacher immediacy was associated with increased affective learning across the cultures of the United States, Puerto Rico, Australia, and Finland.

Recently, a group of researchers developed a training program on communicating social support to diverse learners. Immediacy was an important part of that training (Simonds, Lippert, Hunt, Angell, & Moore, 2008). The researchers argued that immediacy behaviors would help K–12 teachers communicate more effectively with diverse student populations. These studies suggest that teachers need to be concerned with being both verbally and nonverbally immediate to their students. Perhaps what these multicultural studies suggest is that a large repertoire of immediacy behaviors is necessary for a teacher to be perceived as immediate by all students.

Reading Objectives and Discussion Prompts

2.5 Teacher Immediacy

What do you know?
Define immediacy. How does immediacy affect student perceptions of the teacher? How does immediacy affect learning?

What do you think?
What teacher immediacy behaviors will you feel comfortable demonstrating in the classroom? Do you think a teacher can be too immediate?

Communication Style

Communication style can affect interpersonal communication in the classroom. It is "the way an individual verbally and paraverbally interacts to signal how literal meaning should be taken, interpreted, filtered, or understood" (Norton, 1978). Communication style describes whether a person is precise, contentious, relaxed, dominant, dramatic, open, attentive, animated, and friendly, and the voice and impression he leaves. These characteristics influence communicator image. In his research, Norton (1977) found strong evidence that students' perceptions of effective teaching are related to a teacher's communication style. The effective teacher was rated as attentive, relaxed, not dominant, friendly, and precise; further, this study found that effective teachers created positive, lasting impressions on their students. Myers, Mottet, and Martin (2000) found that when students perceived their teachers as friendly, they were more motivated to communicate with them.

Potter and Emanuel (1990), in their research with students in grades 8 through 12, found that adolescents identify the instructor communication styles of friendly, attentive, and relaxed as the most desirable and the styles of dominant and contentious as the least desirable. Potter and Emanuel refer to these three styles as Human, Actor, and Authority. The Human teacher is one who carefully listens to student needs, talks to them on a friendly and informal basis, and is open to changing the course to meet student needs. The Actor teacher is a good storyteller who moves around a lot with gestures and facial expressions. The Authority teacher is well organized, has a command of all details, and puts students on the spot with probing questions and difficult arguments.

To give you a better understanding of each communication style, the items related to each variable are presented in Table 2.2. Norton (1983) examined the question of which of these variables strongly profile the ineffective teacher. He found that the ineffective teacher is not very animated or lively, does not show enough attentiveness or

TABLE 2.2 Communicator Style Variables

Communicator Style Variable	Questionnaire Item
Attentive	This person can always repeat back to someone else exactly what was said.
	This person deliberately reacts in such a way that people know that he or she is listening to them.
	This person really likes to listen very carefully to people.
	This person is an extremely attentive communicator.
Impression making	What this person says usually leaves an impression on people.
	This person leaves people with an impression that they definitely tend to remember.
	The way this person says something usually leaves an impression on people.
	This person leaves a definite impression on people.
Relaxed	This person has no nervous mannerisms in his speech.
	This person is a very relaxed communicator.
	The rhythm or flow of this person's speech is not affected by nervousness.
	Under pressure this person comes across as a relaxed speaker.
Not dominant	In most social situations this person (does not) generally speak very frequently.
	This person is (not) dominant in social situations.
	This person (does not) try to take charge of things when she is with other people.
	In most social situations this person (does not) tend to come on strongly.
Friendly	This person readily expresses admiration for others.
	To be friendly, this person habitually acknowledges others' contributions verbally.
	This person is always an extremely friendly communicator.
	Whenever this person communicates, he tends to be very encouraging to people.
Precise	This person is a very precise communicator.
	In an argument this person insists on very precise definitions.
	This person likes to be strictly accurate when he or she communicates.
	Very often this person insists that other people document or present some kind of proof for what they are arguing.

From *Communicator Style: Theory, Applications, and Measures* by R. W. Norton, p. 41. Copyright © 1983 by Sage Publications, Inc. Reprinted by permission of Sage Publications, Inc.

friendliness, does not have a very precise style, is not very relaxed, and does not use a dramatic style.

In addition, Norton examined the dramatic style more closely and found that the teacher with a highly dramatic style always scored high on three variables: (1) uses energy, (2) catches attention, and (3) manipulates moods. Norton makes the following recommendations to help ineffective teachers do a better job of teaching:

Use more energy when teaching.   The primary problem at this point is defining what constitutes energy. It probably entails being more dynamic, active, open, mentally alert, enthusiastic, and forceful. The dynamic speaker employs vocal variety (emphasis, intonation, rate) and nonverbal variety (gestures) to increase expressiveness.

Anticipate how to catch attention.   The classes of communicative behaviors to do this include use of humor, curiosity, suspense, emotion, analogy, metaphors, surprise, and narratives.

Learn how to make a class laugh.   This is not to say that the teacher needs to become a clown. The more important dynamic entails audience analysis. Learning how to make someone laugh requires understanding shared premises. Even if laughter is never evoked, thinking about the problem is useful. A teacher might use humor to reduce tension, facilitate self-disclosure, relieve embarrassment, disarm others, save face, entertain, alleviate boredom, or communicate goodwill. The assumption is that humor enhances student-teacher relationships and thus enhances learning.

Gorham (1988) found that the amount of humor teachers are perceived to use is positively related to the students' perceptions of how much they learn and how positive they feel about the course content, instructor, and the behaviors recommended in the course. Examining students' perceptions of teachers' humor, Gorham and Christophel (1990) found that male and female students perceive humor differently, and the effect of humor on learning differs by student gender. Females seem to prefer the use of stories or anecdotes, particularly personal stories related to the topic. Male students seem to prefer tendentious comments, reporting these as things their teachers did to "show he had a sense of humor." Darling and Civikly (1987) and Stuart and Rosenfeld (1994) found that humor was positively related to classroom climate.

Observational and experimental research indicates humor is capable of improving student perception of teachers, facilitating student-teacher rapport, reducing negative affective states, and enhancing perceptions of competence, appeal, delivery, perceived intelligence, character, and friendliness. High school teachers use humor less frequently than college teachers. High school teachers use humor as a way of putting students at ease, as an attention getter, as a way of showing they are human, and to make learning fun. In other words, humor is used as a way to make the classroom environment more conducive to learning (Neuliep, 1991). In a recent study Wrench and Richmond (2004) found that student perceptions of teacher humor were also associated with more affective and cognitive learning, more motivation, and more teacher credibility.

One note of caution is necessary. Downs and colleagues (1988) found that award-winning college teachers used less humor than did a comparison group of non-award-winning teachers. The researchers suggest that "too much humor or self-disclosure is inappropriate and moderate amounts are usually preferred" (p. 139). It should also be noted that the majority of communication style research has been conducted in the United States. Thus, little is known about teacher communication style from an intercultural perspective. For example, strategies usually proposed in the United States to enhance teacher effectiveness may be anxiety-provoking and misunderstood by Asian American students. In addition, Eastern Europeans experience difficulties in classrooms when teachers are perceived as being too informal and friendly (Borisoff, 1990).

Reading Objectives and Discussion Prompts

2.6 Communication Style

What do you know?
Define communicator style. What are the characteristics of communicator style?

What do you think?
How would you describe your communicator style? Which of these characteristics do you think are most appropriate for the classroom?

Credibility

A **teacher's credibility** has three dimensions: competence, character, and caring. Competence is perceived knowledge and expertise in an area; character refers to perceived trustworthiness, goodness as a person, ability to be sympathetic, and willingness to act in the best interest of others; and caring refers to the degree the teacher is concerned about students' welfare. Teachers who are competent are perceived as intelligent, trained, expert, informed; teachers who have character are perceived as honest, trustworthy, honorable, moral, ethical, and genuine; and teachers who are caring are perceived as concerned, sensitive, not self-centered, and understanding as well as having students' interests at heart (McCroskey & Teven, 1999).

Research evidence suggests that increasing a teacher's credibility has a positive impact on learning outcomes for students (Beatty & Zahn, 1990; Butner, 2004; Tantleff-Dunn, Dunn, & Gokee, 2002; Teven & McCroskey, 1997; Wheeless, 1974, 1975), and negative teacher behaviors such as verbal aggressiveness have a negative effect (Myers, 2001; Schrodt, 2003). When students perceive their teachers as credible, they report greater amounts of self-motivation, affective learning, and cognitive learning (Frymier & Thompson, 1992; Johnson & Miller, 2002; Russ, Simonds, & Hunt, 2002; Teven, 2001). Credibility has also been associated with increased out-of-class communication between teachers and students (Dobransky & Frymier, 2004; Myers, 2004).

What affects the perception of credibility? Research indicates that the communication variables previously discussed—namely communicator style and immediacy—can affect students' perceptions of teacher credibility. For example, Rubin and Feezel (1986) found that teacher credibility and teacher effectiveness were best predicted by the communication style variables of making an impression and being relaxed. Beatty and Behnke (1980) found that a teacher's consistent verbal and nonverbal messages lead to perceptions of greater character, whereas positive vocal cues predict perceptions of competence.

Thweatt and McCroskey (1998) found that students perceive instructors with high immediacy to have more credibility. They also note that students perceive nonimmediacy as a form of teacher misbehavior and suggest that teachers engage in immediate behaviors to protect their credibility. Teven and Hanson (2004) found that when teacher caring was low, regardless of whether immediacy was high or low, students rated the credibility of their instructors as low.

Myers and Bryant (2002) were interested in students' perceptions of how teachers conveyed credibility. Their research demonstrates that teacher credibility is conveyed in numerous ways. Competence was conveyed in three ways:

- *Content expertise*—providing examples, having a command of the material, having experience with the material, answering and encouraging student questions, demonstrating knowledge beyond the textbook, providing real-world examples, and using PowerPoint
- *Affect for students*—expressing feelings for a student's problems, being reasonable and respectable toward students, and being available outside of class for personal one-on-one discussions
- *Verbal fluency*—using a strong voice, showing confidence through tone of voice and looking at students' faces, avoiding "uh" and "ah" and pauses

Instructor character was conveyed in three ways:

- *Immediacy*—expressiveness, being friendly and asking how students are doing, and using humor, nonverbal cues, and enthusiasm
- *Promotion of understanding*—being knowledgeable about the material, providing examples, expressing expectations
- *Trustworthiness*—keeping promises made to students, behaving appropriately, being respectful to students

Instructor caring was conveyed in three ways:

- *Responsiveness*—answering and encouraging questions, being willing to help, being immediate, having patience with students, providing encouragement, and using humor
- *Accommodation*—not penalizing work (e.g., giving a day for makeup exams with no excuse necessary), providing study guides, adjusting the exams (e.g., changing date of exam so as to avoid students having several tests on one day), providing extra credit opportunities.
- *Accessibility*—holding office hours, sending and responding to e-mail messages, providing multiple ways to be contacted (e.g., home telephone number, e-mail address, and office hours)

Some researchers have explored the relationship between several of the communication variables discussed in this chapter. For example, Comadena, Hunt, and Simonds (2007) studied the effects of teacher immediacy, teacher caring, and teacher clarity (to be discussed in Chapter 5) on student motivation and learning. They found that these behaviors play complementary roles in enhancing learning.

Reading Objectives and Discussion Prompts

2.7 Teacher Credibility

What do you know?
Define teacher credibility. Describe the dimensions of teacher credibility.

What do you think?
What specific things can you do to influence your students' perceptions of your credibility?

OUT OF CLASS COMMUNICATION

Several of the communication concepts we have discussed thus far in this text will transcend the classroom. As teachers, you will communicate with parents, administrators, colleagues, and students outside the classroom. For example, you can use what you know about the communication process (e.g., frame of reference and feedback) to inform your discussions with parents (what is their background, what are their concerns, and how can you address them?). You can use your immediacy and credibility behaviors to help you communicate more sensitively and confidently with administrators. Much of this communication may take place online. In the next couple of sections, we will discuss a couple of these out of class communication encounters.

Parent-Teacher Conferences

Interaction between the school and the home seems to be increasing, so that the home environment affects the classroom. For this reason, and because parent-teacher conferences are one of the most important interpersonal communication events, we discuss these briefly. Because parents and teachers each hold the other primarily responsible for school-related problems, parent-teacher conferences deserve special attention. Your goal during a parent-teacher conference is to discuss a student's progress. In order to meet that goal, you and the parents must communicate effectively. Several guidelines should prove helpful:

- *Know the child's home background.* Does she live in a single-parent home or with a parent or stepparent? Such information will often influence how you structure the conference.
- *Create a positive atmosphere.* Make sure your meeting room is clean and attractive. Choose furniture that is all the same height. If you sit in a higher chair and remain seated behind your desk, parents may feel intimidated.
- *Make the right comments.* Don't outline all of a student's shortcomings. Choose those essential to the student's improvement. State your "problem" in positive terms: "Jane did not finish her assignment because she was reading the school newspaper" rather than "Jane is lazy."
- *Offer practical, realistic suggestions.* Ask parents for their suggestions and solutions for solving a problem. Your attitude ought to be: "How can we best work together to help Jane?"

- *Listen to parents.*   Don't get defensive. If a conflict arises, remember the behaviors discussed earlier about managing conflict and apply them to this situation.
- *Conclude the conference by asking parents questions that will tell you whether your message was clearly understood.*   Make sure you understood them correctly also.
- *Don't leave a parent hanging.*   Request a follow-up conference if necessary or report back to parents on their child's progress.

Parent-teacher conferences can be enjoyable and helpful. Much of what occurs during the conference will be your responsibility. By following these guidelines, most of your conferences should prove to be quite productive.

Box 2.3 provides a letter from a parent to a teacher discussing how she views the parent-teacher conference. In this letter, a concerned parent provides useful suggestions about how to communicate during the "dreaded" parent-teacher conference. Notice how many of these suggestions support the guidelines previously suggested. Also keep in mind that many parents will feel just as anxious as you will about this encounter (as the letter in Box 2.3 intimates). In the future, you may want to refer to this letter just prior to your first parent-teacher conference.

Communicating Online

Earlier in this chapter, we discussed the relationship between immediacy and learning as well as student perceptions of teacher credibility. Recall that immediacy includes verbal and nonverbal behaviors that signal approachability, availability, and warmth. This notion of immediacy has been expanded recently to include mediated forms of communication. O'Sullivan, Hunt, and Lippert (2004) discuss ways that teachers can communicate mediated immediacy, which they describe as a "language of affiliation" (p. 471), by demonstrating behaviors that signal approachability (e.g., self-disclosure, accessibility, informality, and familiarity) and regard (personal, engaged, helpful, and polite). Researchers have investigated the relationship between immediacy and student willingness to communicate with instructors outside of the classroom setting (Fusani, 1994; Jaasma & Koper, 1999). With the prevalence of personal home computers and increasing computer literacy, one form of extra-class communication can take place online. In fact, many schools provide family access to student daily progress through various online means. Waldeck, Kearney, and Plax (2001) found that when teachers demonstrate immediacy behaviors, students are more willing to communicate with them online. When doing so, students interacted with their teachers (1) to clarify course material and procedures, (2) for personal/social reasons, and (3) because it was convenient. There are many advantages to communicating with administrators, colleagues, students, and parents using e-mail (Dorman, 1998). First, online communication is convenient and efficient because you can send and receive messages on your own time and to many people at once. Second, online communication provides opportunities for increased contact between students and parents when school is not in session. Third, online communication can provide a central source of information from which you can announce assignments or special events, respond to frequently asked questions, and provide feedback to individuals or groups. Fourth, online communication can facilitate communication with parents and is a cost-effective way to ensure parents obtain information

BOX 2.3

Letter from a Concerned Parent

Dear Mrs. McCrea,

About that conference next week. . . . It's a week until our conference about David, and I already have a knot in my stomach. Even having sat behind the desk as a teacher doesn't make it any easier when it's my child. I still have a knot.

I guess I'm like most people in that I don't deal very well with the unknown. I start weaving dreadful fantasies, anticipating the worst. Oh, I know David is a terrific kid. The question is, do you? I also know I shouldn't get anxious; when I'm anxious, I don't listen very well, and that's not a great way to go into a conference that's supposed to be for my benefit, is it? So I've been trying to think of ways to make our getting together a little easier for me, and maybe for you, too. Here are a few suggestions:

Information in advance about what we'll be talking about would definitely help loosen that knot in my stomach. You might send a general note to all the parents outlining the topics you usually cover—and maybe even ask us what we'd like to hear about on a tear-off at the bottom (that way you won't have to wait and wonder what I'm going to spring on you!). If you have a sense of what's on the agenda, I can pull my thoughts together and formulate reasonable-sounding questions (my words just get jumbled up if I don't have a chance to plan a bit). I could also talk with David's father about his ideas, and bring them along, since he can't always get away for daytime meetings.

It would help if you went over, at the outset of the meeting, what you plan to cover during the meeting—as well as what you don't plan to discuss. That way I'll know what to expect and can dispel those dreadful fantasies right from the start. At the same time, it would be useful if you told me how you want to structure the meeting. Should I interrupt with questions or wait until you ask for them? Will there be things for me to look at or read? How much time will we have? Much as I hate to admit it, we parents are a bit like students when it comes to parent-teacher conferences. The more that's laid out for us at the beginning of the lesson, the more we're apt to learn.

What I really want to know about David is how he's doing—both in relation to his own ability (and certainly I want to know if he's slacking off), and in comparison with other children. I know comparisons aren't supposed to be important, but I do wonder where he stands. Eventually he'll be getting some kind of comparative grades; I don't want to be taken by surprise. Hearing for years that "he's working up to his ability" in spelling won't prepare me for his official low grade in the subject. I want to know as much as you can tell me about my child's schoolwork.

If you do have bad news for me, tell me at the start, so I don't have to spend my time waiting for the other shoe to drop. Let me know exactly what you see to be the problem. Show me the papers, tell me the episodes, put everything out for me to look at, I'll probably be upset, but I'll react more calmly if I get clear, specific information. I'd like to know how serious you think the problem is, too. Is it a big issue that you think will have long-term effects, or do you see it as a minor annoyance that will go away by itself? Is it a part of a larger concern, or is it an isolated event? Help me to keep my perspective by telling me just how worried I should be.

Please tell me, too, what you plan to do about any problem David is having—and how I can help. The worst feeling for me is helplessness. If you can give me some guidance about what David needs (a special tutor, less help with homework, whatever), I'll have something to do besides worry.

Which brings me to another point. Even though I think I know what "fine motor skills" and "set theory" mean, some real-world examples will help me to be sure we agree on their meaning and purpose. I like seeing David's work. I'm also interested in what you see in his writing and art. Don't worry about boring me with lots of examples; where my child's progress is concerned, I'd rather see his work than listen to lots of fancy talk about it.

(Continued)

Finally, please plan to reserve some time to listen to me. I want to be able to tell you how I think David's doing, to ask you some questions, to respond to what you've told me. I know that I do go on at times, so I won't mind if you remind me that we have only a few minutes left and ask if I have any last things to say. If I feel there's a lot more to talk about, I hope we can schedule another conference.

If all this makes you think I'm an overly concerned parent, well, maybe I am. I admit I'm something of a zealot where David's skills, competence, and progress are concerned. I want what's best for him, of course. I've put him under your care and tutelage for six hours a day. Now I expect to know what's been going on during that time, how he's doing, and what I can do to help. I think we can be a terrific team—if I can just untie that knot in my stomach.

(Gerritz, 1983, p. 46)

that may get lost between school, a student's backpack, and home. Thompson (2008) found that parents appreciated being able to talk with teachers about their student's academic, behavioral, and social struggles via e-mail. Parents reported this outlet as being less time-consuming and more immediate than a parent-teacher conference, which can be intimidating for both the parents and the teacher.

When using online communication, however, there are several issues to consider. If requiring the use of online communication as an opportunity for extended learning, you will need to be sure that all students have both access and the skills necessary to use this medium. It should be noted that teachers should communicate their expectations about online interactions at the beginning of the class. For example, be clear to students and parents about when to expect a response and what information should be exchanged. Keep in mind that online communication leaves a permanent record of your interactions and that information that should be confidential should be protected. In addition, online communication does not contain a nonverbal component and some messages could be misinterpreted. Finally, online communication has a unique set of rules or norms (DeFleur, Kearney, & Plax, 2004), commonly referred to as "netiquette." These rules recommend that users keep messages brief; avoid using all uppercase letters; use correct spelling and grammar; use "emoticons" to convey emotion, for example, "LOL" for "I'm laughing out loud" and ":-)" for "I'm smiling"; and avoid hostility or "flaming."

Another consideration for online communication is social networking. While many discussions have taken place about the pitfalls of teachers communicating with students or parents via social networking sites, some research suggests that, if used properly, this form of communication can be beneficial. Mazer, Murphy, and Simonds (2007, 2009) studied student perceptions of teachers who used Facebook. Participants who accessed the Facebook website of a teacher high in self-disclosure anticipated higher levels of motivation and affective learning and a more positive classroom climate. They also rated this teacher as higher in credibility. However, in their responses to open-ended items, participants emphasized possible negative associations between teacher use of Facebook and teacher credibility. Because Facebook is a very public space, teachers should be careful to present a professional image at all times. It should be noted that the participants in these studies were college students and that these implications may not apply to other age groups.

Reading Objectives and Discussion Prompts

2.8 Out of Class Communication

What do you know?
What are some guidelines for parent-teacher conferences? What are some guidelines for online communication?

What do you think?
How will your understanding of the following concepts help you communicate better with parents, administrators, colleagues, and students outside the classroom?

Communication Process
Supportive Climate
Diversity
Self-Concept
Self-Disclosure
Immediacy
Communication Style
Credibility
Expectancies

In Sum

Teaching is not simply talking, just as learning is not simply listening. Rather, teaching and learning involve a communication relationship. Research suggests that good teachers differ from poor teachers in that good teachers:

- Have generally more positive views of others—students, colleagues, and administrators
- Are less prone to view others critically or to accuse people of having ulterior motives; rather, they see them as potentially friendly and worthy in their own right.

- Have a more favorable view of democratic classroom procedures.
- Have the ability and capacity to see things from another's point of view
- Don't see students as persons "you do things to" but rather as individuals capable of doing for themselves once they feel trusted, respected, and valued

Good teachers are able to communicate what they know in a way that makes sense to their students. They are good also because they view teaching as primarily a human process involving interpersonal communication in human relationships.

Key Terms

Relationship Stages
  (initiating, experimenting,
  intensifying, terminating)
Self-Concept
Self-Esteem
Self-Fulfilling Prophecy

Teacher Efficacy
Teachers' Expectations
Student Expectations
Self-disclosure
  (appropriateness,
  incremental, reciprocal)

Immediacy
Communication Style
Teacher's Credibility

CHAPTER

3　Listening

OBJECTIVES

After reading this chapter, you should be able to:

- Understand the importance of listening.
- Describe the process of listening.
- List, define, and provide examples of the types of listening.
- Discuss the barriers to effective listening.
- Improve your own listening skills.
- Discuss active listening.

> *After too many days of*
> *"learning"*
> *I stopped long enough*
> *to simply LISTEN,*
> *It was then that I found that*
> *LEARNING is*
> *that soft*
> *quiet thump*
> *beneath the*
> *fall*
> *of*
> *the*
> *leaf*
> (Welch, 1991, p. 7)

Listening is a key component of the teaching-learning process. Most of us need to improve our listening skills. In this chapter we discuss not only the importance of listening but also the types of listening, barriers to effective listening, and methods of improving our listening.

THE IMPORTANCE OF LISTENING

Why is effective listening important? First of all, we spend a great deal of time listening. Research demonstrates that 70 percent of our waking time is spent participating in some form of communication. Of that time, 9 percent is spent writing, 16 percent reading, 30 percent talking, and 42 to 57 percent listening.

Interestingly, although listening is the type of communication we engage in the most and learn first, it requires a skill we are taught the least. The following chart shows the order in which we learn the four types of communication, the degree to which we use them, and the extent to which we are taught how to perform them (Steil, 1980):

	Listening	*Speaking*	*Reading*	*Writing*
Learned	1st	2nd	3rd	4th
Used	45%	30%	16%	9%
Taught	Least	Next least	Next most	Most

In the classroom, listening is the main channel of instruction. Estimates of the amount of time students are expected to listen range from 53 to 90 percent of their communication time (Galvin, 1988). When such a large portion of time is spent listening, ineffective listening can be quite costly to students. Most of us are inefficient listeners, retaining only about 20 percent of what we hear.

Finally, listening is important because it is a survival skill. For example, in the business community, listening is cited as one of the top skills necessary for effective performance (Wolvin & Coakley, 1991). We acquire knowledge, develop language, increase our communication ability (the good listener is also a good communicator), and increase our understanding of ourselves and others through listening. Listening, then, is an important skill to develop and improve because we cannot be effective in our relationships or our professions without it.

Listening is also an extremely important way to communicate respect. One of your authors, Dr. Simonds, shares the following:

> In the first year of my teaching career, I had a parent visit me after class who was apparently quite upset. She stormed into my classroom in a very heated manner, and with a raised voice, to discuss her daughter's sudden sense of apathy toward the drama program I was directing and school in general. My first thought was to defend myself immediately, but I held back that instinct when I remembered my own rules of listening: look people directly in the eye when they are talking, smile and nod, and avoid interrupting. In other words, I demonstrated active listening skills to allow the parent to express her concern. I noticed that as I engaged in these behaviors, the parent softened

in her approach and by the time she was done communicating with me, she thanked me for listening and admitted that her daughter's apathy probably had little or nothing to do with my teaching.

Reading Objectives and Discussion Prompts

3.1 Importance of Listening

What do you know?
Why is listening important?

What do you think?
As a teacher, when do you think listening will be most important?

WHAT IS LISTENING?

If communication is the difference between knowing and teaching (Hurt, Scott, & McCroskey, 1978), then listening is the difference between hearing and learning. The following scenario exemplifies this notion:

STUDENT: What do you mean the unit test is today? I thought you said it was Friday! We always have unit tests on Fridays!

TEACHER: As we discussed last week, the test is today because we have an assembly scheduled during this period on Friday. I know you heard me explain that!

The teacher involved in this conversation is operating under the misconception that hearing and listening are the same activity. However, listening is much more than simply hearing.

Listening is a much more complicated process than simply hearing. Judi Brownell describes listening according to what she calls the **HURIER model,** which represents six interrelated activities associated with listening—hearing, understanding, remembering, interpreting, evaluating, and responding (2009).

Since **hearing** involves the physiological process of accurately receiving sounds, we must focus our attention and concentrate to begin the process of listening. For example, close your eyes and attend to the sounds around you, what do you hear . . . the rustling of pages in a book, the tapping of pencils, the whirring of a computer? You may be able to hear things you might not have heard otherwise. This is because you stopped to call attention to the sounds you were hearing.

We may hear sounds, but may not always comprehend them. Listening for **understanding** improves with practice. It involves a thought process within us and requires reflection. We begin to think of the sounds around us and what they mean. For example, you hear a student in the classroom cough and you kindly ask if they need a drink of water.

According to Brownell, "remembering is essential if you intend to apply what you have heard in future situations." How often have you been introduced to someone and forgotten his or her name only moments later? Perhaps this is because you are not attending to the name, rather forming in your mind first impressions of the person. **Remembering** requires a conscious effort on the part of the listener. For example, if you repeat each student's name just after being introduced, you are more likely to remember their names and be able to call on them in future classes.

Interpreting messages involves the ability to see a situation from another person's perspective. Would someone else interpret the message differently than you (perhaps someone from another culture)? For example, when an American Indian child hears in her history classes that *"In 1492, Columbus sailed the ocean blue,"* thus discovering the new world, she might be a little confused and think *"Wait a minute . . . our ancestors were here before Columbus and didn't need to be discovered!"* In addition, interpreting requires that you pay attention to the meaning and the context of the message. For example, would a student's message change if the situation were different? For example, a student tells you she needs to leave the class to make a phone call. What will you say? What if you happen to know that this student's mother had a very important doctor's appointment earlier in day? Or, perhaps the message remains the same, but the context causes you to interpret the meaning of the message differently.

We **evaluate** messages through our past experiences, attitudes, and values. Based on these predispositions, we evaluate the messages we receive. Are they consistent with your beliefs? If not, how are they different, and will you accept or reject the messages? In our example above, the American Indian child is confused when the teacher talks about Columbus discovering America because it is not consistent with what she knows about her own heritage. Thus, while most European American children may take this part of their history lesson for granted, it causes the American Indian child to wonder.

Once we have listened to a message, we must decide how we will **respond**. What will we do with the information? Will we use it to form new information? Or, will we reject it because it is not consistent with what we already know? Given our previous discussion, what do you think the American Indian child will do with the notion of Columbus discovering America?

Reading Objectives and Discussion Prompts

3.2 The Listening Process

What do you know?
Describe the listening process.

What do you think?
Can you think of an example of when each of these activities will take place in the classroom?

TYPES OF LISTENING

There are basically four types of listening: informative, appreciative, empathic, and critical. However, these categories are not mutually exclusive. We may engage in all four in any given communicative situation.

Much of the listening we do is **informative**. Informative listening occurs when we are attempting to understand a message for a particular reason—to gain knowledge or complete a task. Informative listening requires that you retain the information for future use. Thus, as your students listen to you provide directions for a task or how to prepare for an exam, they are listening for specific information and details. On the other hand, as your students provide answers to your questions, you may be listening to see if they understand the concepts you have been teaching. Obviously, this type of listening is particularly important in the classroom. Errors in informative listening can be extremely detrimental to classroom learning. We will discuss strategies for clarifying informative content in Chapter 5 when we talk about teacher clarity behaviors.

We engage in **appreciative** listening when we listen for enjoyment. We may simply want to gain a sensory impression of the tone, mood, or style of another person. For example, we've all heard teachers or speakers we like to listen to because their voices are pleasant or because they are stylistically unique.

Another type of listening is **empathic**. In this type, we are listening for the feelings of another person. Often we are simply sounding boards; people say, "Thank you for listening. I guess I just needed someone to talk to." Thus, in empathic listening we may not be asked to provide any service other than simply listening. This should indicate how important listening is. And when we need someone to listen to us, we are grateful when that person gives us the full attention we seek.

As we become more familiar with students, we find ourselves increasingly engaging in empathic listening. A student came to one of the authors for some personal advice on a problem she was having at home. She talked and talked. Suddenly, she jumped up and said, "Thanks for all your help. I know now what I need to do!" She had thought through her problem and had come to a solution with no input except a willingness to let her verbalize her thoughts and feelings.

Empathy is not an easy concept to define (Weaver & Kintley, 1995). For our purposes, empathy is the capacity of a person to put himself into the shoes of another, to see things from another's viewpoint. The empathic listener strives to thoroughly and accurately understand the person communicating. This doesn't direct the conversation but encourages the other person to share her ideas and feelings. The empathic listener doesn't impose her own opinions and values. When you listen empathically, you don't evaluate. Instead you promote honest, engaged communication through total other-centered involvement in the encounter (Brownell, 2009). Empathy involves two steps: predicting accurately the motives and attitudes of others and communicating in ways that are rewarding to the other person who is the object of prediction.

The first step—predicting accurately—involves an awareness of what the other person is like and what can realistically be expected from him. However, just because we accept another person for "who he is" doesn't mean we agree with what he says or does. For example, you can accept students' feelings, ideas, and behaviors as legitimate and still not agree with them. However, students appreciate empathic understanding—the realization that they are understood, not evaluated or judged, but understood from their own point of view rather than the teacher's.

In terms of the second component of empathy—communicating empathy to students—several guidelines should be followed:

- *Be willing to become involved with the student.* When students who are graduating from high school or college are asked to identify the best teachers they had, they often identify teachers who were available or accessible to them. The willingness to become involved with another person can be more important at times than the quality of the interaction itself. Knowing that someone who is important to you cares enough about you to devote time to the relationship and to focus on matters of mutual interest can make quite a difference.

- *Communicate positive regard for the student.* Positive regard for another person is expressed not so much by the specific content of our remarks when we interact as it is by the general way we treat that person. If we are manipulative, if we attempt to control or to coerce the other person, or if we prevent the other person from saying or doing things that displease us, then we are not displaying positive regard. Positive regard for another person can be said to exist when we treat that person with a basic respect as a person of integrity, regardless of the specific things that person says or does.
- *Communicate a supportive climate.* A supportive climate is one in which the emphasis is on understanding rather than on judging the behavior of others.
- *Listen to the person's nonverbal as well as verbal communication.* Effective listening requires that we respond to the content of the message and the information about the message, as well.
- *Accurately reflect and clarify feelings.* There is a tendency to respond more to the content of what others say—the ideas, thoughts, opinions, and attitudes conveyed—than to the feelings that others are expressing. Feelings are harder to respond to because in our culture most of us get less experience responding to feelings than to ideas.
- *Be genuine and congruent.* We are not as likely to develop a good relationship with others if we communicate in a false and misleading way. Facades are difficult to maintain and ultimately not very attractive. A constructive relationship is one in which the participants respond to each other in an honest and genuine manner. Our communication is congruent when the things that we do and say accurately reflect our real thoughts and feelings.

Finally, as teachers you will engage in **critical listening** in the classroom. Critical listening involves making judgments about the messages we receive. Is the information provided useful, meaningful, clear, valid, or reliable? Is it consistent with what you already know? Have all perspectives been considered? As a teacher, you will engage in critical listening in order to provide feedback for your students.

The purpose of feedback is for you to provide the student with a plan for improvement. The student will want to know what to repeat (things he/she did well) or change (things he/she could improve) next time. So, what kinds of comments can you provide to help the student? In a series of studies (Stitt, Simonds, & Hunt, 2003; Reynolds, Hunt, Simonds, & Cutbirth, 2004; Simonds, Meyer, Hunt, & Simonds, 2009), scholars found that generally instructors used four types of comments when providing feedback on speeches: positive nondescriptive, positive descriptive, negative, and constructive. Each of these are explained below. While this research was based on speech evaluation, these types of feedback can be used in other contexts.

Positive nondescriptive comments say that the student did a good job but do not describe or detail how the task was accomplished. Examples:

Good eye contact
Nice references
Excellent support
Plus marks (+).

Positive descriptive comments are those that say that the student did a good job, and specifically describe or detail what was liked about how the student accomplished their task. Examples:

Good job of engaging your audience through the use of facial expression and direct eye contact.
Nice job of incorporating full source citations into the flow of your presentation.
Your visual aids are very professionally produced and incorporated smoothly into the presentation.

Thus, positive-descriptive comments provide a better plan for improvement than positive comments alone.

Negative comments criticize the performance without providing suggestions for improvement. Examples:

Poor eye contact
Weak sources
Writing need work
Minus marks (−).

Constructive comments acknowledge the need for improvement and provide specific direction or detail on how to improve. Examples:

You need more direct eye contact. Try using fewer note cards and gaze more directly with more of your audience.
Try to provide more complete information for each source. I would suggest putting complete information on your note cards.
Your visual aids need to be larger and bolder. Practice incorporating them into the flow of your speech.

Thus, constructive comments should be used if the student is expected to improve next time. In short, if your feedback is to be effective (i.e., help the student improve), you should concentrate your comments on the positive descriptive and constructive aspects of the student's content, structure, and delivery.

Reading Objectives and Discussion Prompts

3.3 Types of Listening

What do you know?
What are the four types of listening?

What do you think?
Can you think of an example of when you might engage in each of these types of listening in the classroom? How will you communicate empathy in the classroom? How will you provide feedback to your students?

BARRIERS TO EFFECTIVE LISTENING

It's no wonder most of us are poor listeners. The factors that keep us from listening as effectively and efficiently as we could are numerous. These factors fall within four major categories: factual distractions, semantic distractions, mental distractions, and physical distractions.

Factual Distractions

Factual distractions occur because we listen for facts rather than for the main ideas and feelings behind the message. As a result, we fail to integrate what we hear into a whole, or we lose sight of the "big picture." Students sometimes have a problem pulling together facts into a coherent whole, particularly in essay exams, because they listen for facts but fail to analyze the ways in which the facts fit together. In other words, they may be able to define terms but cannot elaborate on the implications of the concepts to their own experiences. The same problem often occurs when students take notes based on lectures only. Perhaps if students are provided the opportunity to share their experiences and discuss concepts as they transfer to other situations, they may be able to engage in higher levels of learning.

Semantic Distractions

Semantic distractions occur when the other person uses unfamiliar terminology or when we react emotionally to words or phrases. These semantic distractions result from the fact that meanings are in people, not words. For example, Dr. Simonds shares the following story:

> When my son was 3 years old, he attended church with his grandparents. In his Sunday school class, the teacher asked, "Does anyone here know how to be saved?" Dylan excitedly raised his hand and said, "I do, I do!" The teacher then asked Dylan to share with the rest of the class how to be "saved." Dylan said, "You call 911!" The meaning of the word *saved* was very different for the teacher and my son. Now, to the teacher, the word *saved* was based on her experiences with the church. To Dylan, his notion of the word was based on watching entirely too much television.

The following exchange illustrates the confusion that can result if someone is using a term in a manner unfamiliar to you:

> ***What Did You Knott Say?***
> Hello, who's speaking?
> *This is Watt.*
> I'm sorry. What's your name?
> *Yes, Watt's my name.*
> Is this a joke? What is your name?
> *John Watt.*
> John what?
> *Yes. Look, who's this? Are you Jones?*

No, I'm Knott.
Will you tell me who you are?
Will Knott.
Why not?
My name is Knott.
Not what?
(Littell & Littell, 1972, p. 19)

When we hear words that carry emotional overtones for us, our anger, frustration, or resentment can impair our ability to listen. For some students, the word *math* has a negative connotation. If students have not done well in math, they may continue to fail because they believe failure is inevitable and, therefore, they do not listen in class.

Mental Distractions

Mental distractions are caused by intrapersonal factors. One form of mental distraction occurs when we focus on ourselves. We may be formulating what we will say when it's our turn to speak; we may be engrossed in our own problems or needs; we may be concentrating on our own goals and plans; we may be simply daydreaming.

Mental distractions can also occur when we focus on the other person, allowing our preconceived attitudes about the other to prematurely determine the value of what the person is saying. For example, we often listen more closely and with more interest to those we perceive as attractive. If the person belongs to a group we value, we may listen more closely and more positively. Other nonverbal factors, such as vocal cues, can also affect our listening.

Most of us stereotype others at some time or another. Often we aren't as tolerant of those who fit a stereotype we don't value. For example, if we stereotype a student as a low-level student and don't find any value to students with low academic ability, we will be reluctant to listen to the student's ideas. To be effective listeners, we have to consciously "unteach" ourselves prejudices and stereotypes—or at least understand that they may be affecting the extent to which we are willing to listen to others.

Finally, focusing on the status of the other person can cause a mental distraction that keeps us from listening. Sometimes we fail to listen critically to those we view as of a higher status. The ideas of teachers may be accepted simply because they are "experts." Similarly, we rarely listen to those we perceive as having lower status: "Jane's really artistic, but she's so quiet and boring. Let's ask Maria, the head cheerleader, to help with decorations instead."

Physical Distractions

The final barrier to listening, **physical distractions**, can take many forms. The color of the room, the time of day, uncomfortable clothing, and noises can all be physical distractions that interfere with one's ability to listen. We've all been distracted before in classrooms when the room was too warm or cold or noises outside kept us from listening. As teachers, it is important to understand that physical distractions should be reduced as much as we are capable of reducing them. And when we cannot remove the distractions, we should understand when our students may not comprehend all of the material covered during the distraction. Perhaps a review of this material would be warranted at another time.

Reading Objectives and Discussion Prompts

3.4 Barriers to Effective Listening

What do you know?
What are the barriers to effective listening?

What do you think?
Which barriers do you have the most difficulty with? Which barriers do you think your students will have difficulty with? What can you as a teacher do to overcome these barriers?

IMPROVING LISTENING SKILLS

Several behaviors can help you improve your listening skills. Some are fairly easy to master. Others will take a great deal of effort on your part.

- *Remove, if possible, the physical barriers to listening.*   You might simply move to another room, or move the furniture in the room, turn the thermostat up or down, or close the door to your classroom. Manipulate your environment to fit your needs.
- *Focus on the speaker's main idea.*   You can always request specific facts and figures later. Your initial purpose as a listener should be to answer this question: "What is this person's main idea?"
- *Listen for the intent, as well as the content, of the message.*   Ask yourself, "Why is this person saying this?"
- *Give the other person a full hearing.*   Don't begin your evaluation until you've listened to the entire message. When a student tells you that his homework is not finished, allow the student to complete his explanation before you respond. Too often as listeners we spend our listening time creating our messages rather than concentrating on the content and intent of the other's message.
- *Remember the adage that meanings are in people, not in words.*   Ask for clarification when necessary. Try to overcome your emotional reactions to words. Focus on what you can agree with in the other's message, and use this as common ground as you move into more controversial issues.
- *Concentrate on the other person as a communicator and as a human being.*   All of us have our own ideas, and we have deep feelings about those ideas. Listen with all your senses, not only with your ears. The well-known admonition to "stop, look, and listen" is an excellent one to follow when listening. Focus on questions such as, "What does she mean verbally?" "Nonverbally?" "What's the feeling behind the message?" and "Is this message consistent with those she has expressed in previous conversations?"

Reading Objectives and Discussion Prompts

3.5 Improving Your Listening

What do you know?
How can you improve your listening skills?

What do you think?
How will you apply these to your class?

ACTIVE LISTENING

The process of listening isn't complete until you have made some **active response**—verbal or nonverbal—to the other person. Your response can have an important impact on the communication climate.

The concept of active listening has been around for a number of years. The main idea of active listening is that the listener must get involved in the communication transaction. In other words, listening is not passive; rather, it is as active and behavioral as speaking. And, of course, the primary indicator of active listening is active responding. Several methods of active response are important.

Paraphrasing

Paraphrasing is a restatement of both the content and the feelings of another person's message. It is not, however, simply parroting another's words. Often, understanding a speaker's feelings is even more important to understanding her message than simply comprehending the actual words spoken. Thus, paraphrasing restates both the content and the feelings components of the message.

Suppose a student says to you, "I don't see how I can possibly finish this report by tomorrow. I have two major tests tomorrow. Boy, I've really gotten myself into a bind." Your paraphrase might be something such as, "It sounds like things are really hectic for you, and you feel frustrated."

If paraphrasing sounds trite, uncomfortable, or clumsy to you, keep in mind two important ideas: (1) Anytime you learn a new skill, it initially feels funny. Remember how clumsy you felt when you were first learning to ride a bike? Remember also, that with practice, riding a bike became easier and very natural. The same is true of paraphrasing. The more you practice and use the skill, the easier it will become. (2) Paraphrasing is not always appropriate or necessary. If someone says to you, "Wow, what fantastic weather!" there's no need for paraphrasing. Paraphrasing should be used to help you avoid confusion and misunderstanding. Overuse of the paraphrasing technique is just as detrimental to effective communication as its underuse.

Perception Checking

A second technique of active responding is **perception checking**. Perception checking is similar to paraphrasing—both seek to clarify the speaker's meaning. But a perception check, unlike paraphrasing, is not limited to the last utterance of the speaker. Perception checking refers to behavior over an extended period of time.

A perception check consists of stating three ideas: (1) sensory data that describes what you have heard and seen to lead to your conclusion; (2) the conclusion you've drawn; and (3) a question that asks the other person whether your conclusion is accurate.

Suppose you are a science teacher and one of your students has, for the past week, been late for class every day, been extremely disruptive, and failed to hand in homework. You have decided to call the student into your office to talk. How might you use perception checking?

You might say, "Martin, I am aware that you've been late every day this week, you have ridiculed other students when they answer questions, and your work has not been up to par. I suspect all this might mean you are having a problem—either with this class or at home. Is there any truth to that?"

The basic purpose of perception checking is to clarify our perceptions of another's thoughts, feelings, or intentions. Because it's impossible to communicate with others without making some inferences, it's important that we check on those inferences in order to make our communication as effective as possible.

Ask Questions

One of the communication strategies we all use less than we should is asking questions. Whenever we are not sure we have understood another person's content or relationship messages, we need to ask questions. Another result of asking questions is that it indicates to your conversational partner your interest in their ideas, experiences, contributions, and so forth. By asking questions, you communicate that you are willing to listen and interested in what someone else has to say. Let's face it. People like to talk about themselves and, when we ask questions, we are giving them license to do so. Hopefully, your partner will reciprocate and you will get your turn as well. A word of caution here: avoid questions that pry into irrelevant areas or issue a challenge to the other person in any way.

Say More

Closely related to asking questions is a technique discussed by Stewart and Thomas (1990) called "Say more," encouraging your conversation partner to keep talking. When ideas seem unclear or you're not sure you really understand what your partner means, ask that person to "Say more" or "Keep talking." For example, as a teacher, you may want to get your students involved in classroom discussions (which we'll discuss more in Chapter 6). You ask a question that calls for students to share an experience. A student responds to your question, but you think there is more he can say. You ask a probing question to get the student to elaborate on the contribution. In doing so, you validate the student's response and communicate your interest by wanting to know more.

Beware of Cultural Differences

Remember that cultural background can affect listening behavior. Nishida (1985) suggests that the most effective intercultural listeners have a high tolerance for ambiguity. In other words, they can see many points of view and they remain open-minded when confronted with information that contradicts their previously held beliefs.

In an article entitled, "Listening in the Global Marketplace," Jean Harris (2002) provides several strategies for listening interculturally. They include: (1) Listen for your own cultural/individual values; (2) when you are being introduced to someone from another culture, listen for their cultural/individual values; (3) expand your knowledge of the cultural norms of other peoples; and (4) listen with your eyes open and an open mind. These strategies allow one to become a global listener.

In addition, the competent intercultural listener recognizes differences in nonverbal systems and does not make assumptions about what various nonverbal behaviors mean. For example, in the United States, we often signal that we are listening to someone when we maintain eye contact, smile and nod, and physically lean toward the person who is speaking. The competent intercultural communicator understands that not all cultures interpret attentiveness in the same way. In some Asian, Latin American, and African cultures, for instance, direct eye contact is considered rude, threatening, and disrespectful, especially when communicating with a person of higher status, such as a teacher (Samovar & Porter, 2009). As teachers of the dominant Western culture, we appreciate when students look at us during the communication process so that we can gauge their level of understanding and comprehension through feedback. In fact, we might even become suspicious that students are not listening when we cannot see this behavior. But we should not assume that a student is not listening simply because she is not looking at us. Rather, the student may be showing a sign of respect and fully comprehending our message.

As educators, it is important that we communicate to our students a willingness to listen actively to their ideas. Hopefully, these strategies will help you to not only improve your own listening, but improve students' perceptions of you as an effective listener.

Reading Objectives and Discussion Prompts

3.6 Active Listening

What do you know?
What are some strategies for active listening?

What do you think?
Can you think of an example where some of these strategies might help you communicate with your students?

In Sum

Listening is an active process. It requires practice and concentration. Because it is a process in which you spend a great deal of time, it's important to do it well. As one author suggests, "A failure to listen probably creates more interpersonal problems than any other aspect of human behavior" (Barker, 1971). As a teacher, try to adhere to the following Code for Listening in order to avoid interpersonal problems and foster a supportive communication climate in your classroom.

Code for Listening
As a teacher I shall

- Be a good listener myself.
- Use a classroom voice that is relaxed, unhurried, and nonthreatening.

- Use sincere, varied, expressive facial expressions that promote accurate listening.
- Get everyone's attention before speaking.
- Teach students that directions and instructions will be given only once.
- Not repeat a student's contributions, answers, or remarks but encourage students to listen to each other.
- Ask questions that require more than "yes," "no," or other short answers.
- Take time to listen to my pupils before and after school as well as in school.
- Create an emotional and physical atmosphere conducive to good listening.
- Establish with my students the purpose for which they should listen to each activity.
- Be well prepared for the material to be taught or the activity to be directed.
- Vary my classroom program to include a variety of listening experiences, such as sound films, discussions, individual and group reports, dramatic activities, and demonstrations.
- Teach my students the value and importance of good listening.
- Build a program in which listening skills are consistently taught and practiced: for example, interpreting unknown words through context, noting details, finding main and subordinate ideas, evaluating expressed points of view in relation to facts or propaganda, and making valid inferences.
- Teach my students to form desirable listening habits: for example, disregarding distractions and mannerisms of speakers, exercising mental curiosity about what is heard, and being courteous to speakers by looking for something interesting about speaker and subject.

Key Terms

Listening
HURIER Model (Hearing,
   Understanding,
   Remembering,
   Interpreting, Evaluating,
   Responding)
Informative Listening
Appreciative Listening

Empathic Listening
Critical Listening
Positive Nondescriptive
   Comments
Positive Descriptive
   Comments
Negative Comments
Constructive Comments

Factual Distractions
Semantic Distractions
Mental Distractions
Physical Distractions
Active Response
Paraphrasing
Perception Checking

CHAPTER

4

Language

OBJECTIVES

After reading this chapter, you should be able to:

- Understand the importance and characteristics of language.
- Explain how to use effective verbal communication in the classroom.
- Explain how to use effective nonverbal communication in the classroom.
- Describe the functions and categories of nonverbal communication.
- Understand the relationship between nonverbal communication and culture.
- Describe ways to improve nonverbal communication.

In the first chapter we defined classroom communication as the verbal and nonverbal transaction between teachers and students and between or among students. In this chapter we examine more specifically the verbal and nonverbal aspects of communication. However, we first discuss the importance and characteristics of language.

THE IMPORTANCE AND CHARACTERISTICS OF LANGUAGE

Before you can consider how language affects classroom communication, it is important that you understand why language is so important. There are a few characteristics of language that will help us understand the implications of language in the classroom.

First, language is **symbolic** (Meade, 1934). That is, words stand for or symbolize things. They are not the actual things they represent. Thus, words can have several meanings. For example, consider the word *fish*. What immediately comes to mind?

Do you envision a large shark in the ocean or a tiny goldfish in a bowl? Or, do you see someone wading in a river casting a line? In this example, the word can function as a noun or a verb and represents multiple things given your interpretation.

Second, language is **arbitrary** (Meade, 1934). Words have no meaning in and of themselves. They get their meaning from the people who use them. There is nothing inherent in a *fish* that necessitates calling it a fish. We could call it anything really. For example, the French word for fish is *poisson*.

Figure 4.1 helps us to understand the symbolic and arbitrary nature of words by demonstrating the words have a **triangle of meaning.** The *symbol* is the word (lower left-hand corner). The top of the triangle is the *thought*—the meaning you give the word. The lower right-hand corner is the *referent*—or the actual thing itself.

So, if you hear the word *fish*, and you are planning a trip to Hawaii, you might think of a shark; whereas, if your goldfish just died, you might be lamenting your pet. From this triangle of meaning, we get the principle that *meanings are in people; not in words* (Berlo, 1960). We talked about this briefly in Chapter 3 as a semantic distraction. Recall the following example from one of your authors:

> *When my son was three, he attended an Easter worship service at his grandparent's church. The Sunday school teacher asked the class, "Does anyone here know how to be saved?" Dylan raised his hand eagerly and said, "I do, I do!" The teacher asked Dylan to share with the rest of the class how to be saved. And he said, "You call 911!"*

Now, in this example, the teacher and the student had two very different interpretations of the word *saved*. The teacher was thinking about a religious interpretation based on her experience and Dylan was thinking about a "search and rescue" interpretation based on watching entirely too much TV.

By considering these characteristics of language, we can understand why messages are often misunderstood or misinterpreted. As a teacher, recognizing that meanings are in people allows you to more carefully choose your words based on what you know about your students' experiences.

But why should you care? Language is important because, as many scholars agree, **language creates a social reality** (Young, 1931). What does this mean?

To illustrate, let's talk about the implications that word choice may have on reality. Years ago, people who protected our community were often referred to as *policemen* or *firemen*. During this time, a large percentage of that workforce was men. After all, why

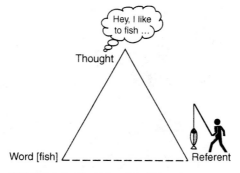

FIGURE 4.1 The Triangle of Meaning.

would a young girl grow up thinking she could be a policeman or a fireman? Now, we more accurately refer to the job they perform rather than the people they are and use words like *police officer* and *firefighter* As a result, our protective services include more women in that workforce than when the job was described in male terms. Language creates a social reality because it tells us *what* and *whom* to value in society.

Language used in the classroom context can affect learning. In general, positive language is more effective in terms of learning and creating a supportive classroom climate than is negative language. Good and Brophy (2007, pp. 234–235) provide excellent examples of the use of positive versus negative language (Table 4.1).

Research on teacher effectiveness (both from the students' and the teacher's perspectives) seems to suggest that communication variables such as humor, warmth, openness, enthusiasm, and attentiveness are extremely important in classroom interaction and in building a supportive classroom climate. For example, a group of researchers from both the communication and education disciplines (Angell et al., 2004) note that immediacy behaviors (discussed earlier in Chapter 2) have been shown to facilitate the

TABLE 4.1   Positive versus Negative Language

Positive Language	Negative Language
Close the door quietly.	Don't slam the door.
Try to work these out on your own without help.	Don't cheat by copying your neighbor.
Quiet down—you're getting too loud.	Don't make so much noise.
Sharpen your pencil like this (demonstrate).	That's not how you use a pencil sharpener.
Carry your chair like this (demonstrate).	Don't make so much noise with your chair.
Sit up straight.	Don't slouch in your chair.
Raise your hand if you think you know the answer.	Don't yell out the answer.
When you finish, put the scissors in the box and bits of paper in the wastebasket.	Don't leave a mess.
These crayons are for you to share—use one color at a time, then put it back so others can use it too.	Stop fighting over those crayons.
Use your own ideas. When you do borrow ideas from another author, be sure to acknowledge them. Even here, try to put them in your own words.	Don't plagiarize.
Speak naturally, as you would when talking to a friend.	Don't just read your report to us.
Note the caution statements in the instructions. Be sure you check the things mentioned there before proceeding to the next step.	Take time when doing this experiment, or you'll mess it up.
Be ready to explain your answer—why you think it is correct.	Don't just guess.

From *Looking in Classrooms*, 10th ed., by Thomas L. Good and Jere E. Brophy. Copyright © 2007 by Pearson Education. Reprinted by permission of Allyn and Bacon.

development of an open and supportive classroom climate and that, if employed effectively, communicate to all learners that they are respected.

Language involves our words (verbal messages) and behaviors (nonverbal messages). In the next sections of this chapter, we will discuss how teachers can use verbal and nonverbal communication in the classroom.

Reading Objectives and Discussion Prompts

4.1 Importance and Characteristics of Language

What do you know?

What are the characteristics of language?

What do you think?

How will understanding these characteristics help you communicate better with your students?

VERBAL COMMUNICATION

Verbal communication takes into account the effect that words have on your students and will affect your ability to teach competently. Thus, effective teachers will work to assure that their communication is clear, appropriate, and interesting.

TEACHER CLARITY.   To be clear, you need to use words that are specific and familiar to your students. There are several things you can do to promote **teacher clarity**. Remember the adage that the difference between knowing and teaching is communication (Hurt, Scott, & McCroskey, 1978)? Teacher clarity is the key to this distinction. That is, a teacher may be an expert in the field, but if she cannot communicate that knowledge in a clear and effective way, learning is not achieved. Clarity, then, is the teacher's ability to present knowledge in a way that students understand. Cawyer (1994) explains that, "when viewed in relationship to 'teacher knowledge,' clarity may be seen as a connecting element between content and pedagogy since it represents an instructor's capacity to transfer the cognitive dimension of teaching into visible instructional behaviors" (p. 30). Teachers should, therefore, have an appreciation for the principles of teacher clarity before attempting to construct a message for their students.

According to Civikly (1992a, p. 139), "The struggle encountered with the teacher clarity construct begins at the definitional level; specifically, what is teacher clarity and how do I know it when I see and hear it?" Several researchers have responded to the problems of definition and abstractness by developing low inference descriptors of teacher clarity. The behaviors that describe teacher clarity are provided in Box 4.1. You can use this list of behaviors to monitor your own clarity as you begin your teaching endeavors.

Many scholars have studied the construct of teacher clarity. Teacher clarity has been linked to student achievement, satisfaction, and student's perception of teacher caring (Frey, Leonard, & Beatty, 1975; Hines, Cruickshank, & Kennedy, 1985; Comedena, Hunt, & Simonds, 2007). French-Lazovik (1974) found that students judge a teacher's effectiveness, in large part, on clarity behaviors. And according to Gloeckner (1983),

BOX 4.1

Teacher Clarity Behaviors

1. Orient and prepare students for what is to be taught.
2. Communicate content so that students understand.
3. Provide illustrations and examples.
4. Demonstrate.
5. Use a variety of teaching materials.
6. Teach things in a related, step-by-step manner.
7. Repeat and stress directions and difficult points.
8. Adjust teaching to the learner and topic.
9. Cause students to organize learning in meaningful ways.
10. Provide practice.
11. Provide standards and rules for satisfactory performance.
12. Provide students with feedback or knowledge of how well they are doing.
13. Use concrete examples of concept.
14. Give multiple examples.
15. Point out practical applications.
16. Stress important points.
17. Repeat difficult ideas.

From Cruickshank (1985) and Murray (1985).

teacher clarity can be enhanced through training. Simonds (1997a) developed an instrument that measures not only content clarity but process clarity as well. Process clarity includes information that relates to various classroom expectations, such as standards for performance, feedback of how well students are doing, explanations of evaluation procedures, practical relevance, and tasks, among others (see Table 4.2).

Clarity can also improve relationships in the classroom. Civikly (1992a) extends the notion of clarity to include student clarification techniques. She argues that clarity highlights the central role of communication in the process of teaching and learning. Teacher clarity is a communication variable that may affect the relational climate of the classroom. Studies of the student's role in processing teacher information and of the teacher's clarification strategies indicate that students are part of the instructional clarity process (Darling, 1989; Kendrick, 1987; Kendrick & Darling, 1990; Simonds, 1997a; West & Pearson, 1994). For example, if a teacher is unclear about a classroom expectation, students will use some type of clarification tactic in order to reduce uncertainty. Students may ask questions, observe other students asking questions, or test the expectation in the form of a challenge. Simonds (1997a) examined the relationship between teacher clarity and student challenges. She found that the higher a teacher scored on teacher clarity, the fewer student challenges she faced with regard to evaluation procedures, practical relevance, procedural rules, and power plays. Teachers and students share in the responsibilities and the ability to clarify content. These studies demonstrate the principle that teacher clarity is the result of an interaction that takes place between teacher explanation and student clarification tactics. Because students are concerned about both content material and classroom processes, teachers must be able to identify the appropriate explanation to address student concerns.

TABLE 4.2 Teacher Clarity Report

My instructor	Very Often	Often	Sometimes	Almost Never	Never
is clear when presenting content.	____	____	____	____	____
uses examples when presenting content.	____	____	____	____	____
relates examples to the concept being discussed.	____	____	____	____	____
uses the board, transparencies, or other visual aids during class.	____	____	____	____	____
gives previews of material to be covered.	____	____	____	____	____
gives summaries when presenting content.	____	____	____	____	____
stresses important points.	____	____	____	____	____
stays on topic.	____	____	____	____	____
clearly explains the objectives for the content being presented.	____	____	____	____	____
defines major/new concepts.	____	____	____	____	____
communicates classroom processes and expectations clearly.	____	____	____	____	____
describes assignments and how they should be done.	____	____	____	____	____
asks if we know what to do and how to do it.	____	____	____	____	____
prepares us for the tasks we will be doing next.	____	____	____	____	____
points out practical applications for coursework.	____	____	____	____	____
prepares students for exams.	____	____	____	____	____
explains how we should prepare for an exam.	____	____	____	____	____
provides students with feedback of how well they are doing.	____	____	____	____	____
provides rules and standards for satisfactory performance.	____	____	____	____	____
communicates classroom policies and consequences for violation.	____	____	____	____	____

Note: The first ten items are content messages, whereas the last ten items are process items. From "Teacher Clarity Report," from Simonds, C. J. (Summer 1997). *Communication Research Reports* 14(3), 279–290.

TEACHER APPROPRIATENESS.   Teachers should be sure that the language used in the classroom is **appropriate** to the topic and the audience, or students. Recall that students may respond differently than anticipated to certain words or phrases.

An effective teacher will consider the implications word choices have on the way students understand a lesson. Teachers should strive to use language that is inclusive.

Inclusive language considers and respects all types of people regardless of gender, race, sexual orientation, and so forth. In other words, inclusive language avoids excluding anyone for any reason. Inclusive language avoids making assumptions about who can and cannot engage in certain activities. Inclusive language respects listeners and helps teachers accomplish their goals. For example, avoid using the generic "he" when referring to both sexes. Teachers may also want to avoid using gender terms to describe what people do. In other words, avoid making judgments about which gender should be in certain jobs or social roles.

VERBAL DELIVERY.   How can you use your voice to make yourself appear credible and your message sound conversational? The trick is variety! To be perceived as credible, you will want to have clear articulation and pronunciation. To sound conversational, you will want to vary your volume, rate, and pitch. All of these characteristics make up your **verbal delivery**.

Articulation is the clear formation of words. Your articulators are parts of your physical anatomy that allow you to form your words. To illustrate, try saying the following tongue twister: *A tutor who tooted the flute tried to tutor two students to toot. Said the two to the tutor, "Is it harder to toot or to tutor two students to toot?"* Now, what did you physically have to do to say this? Did you use your mouth, tongue, teeth, hard and soft pallet? These are your articulators and help you to form each sound in a word.

Sometimes people get lazy with their words and skip a few sounds. For example, has anyone ever asked you, "Yungry, lesqueet?" Did you understand what they were asking? Probably, but they were not clearly articulating. Lazy articulators say things like "gonna" instead of "going to" "din't" instead of "didn't," or "fishin" instead of "fishing." Lazy articulators lack a certain level of credibility in the eyes of their audience.

While many people can read or write a particular word, they may be less certain about how to pronounce it. **Pronunciation** is how a word is said and stressed. Which syllable is the strongest and which vowel sound is used? Is it a short *a* or a long *a*? Dictionaries provide information for how a word should be said. As you construct your lessons, be on the lookout for any words that you may not be sure how to pronounce. You will want to pay particular attention to how names of sources are pronounced, which can sometimes be tricky. For example, if you are talking about the German scholar, Max Weber, you will want to be sure to pronounce it as Max *Veber*, which is the correct pronunciation. Incorrect pronunciation will also affect teacher credibility if the students catch on.

The loudness or softness with which you speak should be varied to sound conversational. In natural conversation, no one really ever talks with the same amount of **volume** at all times. People tend to get louder when they want to stress a point or softer when they want to show effect. Try reading a passage from this chapter without varying your volume. It sounds monotonous, right?

Your volume should also be appropriate to the size of the room and audience. Do you know anyone who is a loud talker? This can be quite annoying and detract from a person's message. On the other hand, if students can't hear the message, nothing can be learned. You will want to project your voice so that students in the back of the room can hear you comfortably while not appearing to shout at the people in the front of the room.

You will also want to vary the speed with which you speak, or your **rate**. This might include some well-planned pauses for emphasis or effect. It is important to know that sometimes when you are nervous, you have a tendency to speak fast. You should look to your students for clues if this is happening. Remember, your students need time to grasp complex information and follow the organization of your lesson. On the other hand, speaking too slowly may bore students and ultimately decrease the amount of information they retain from your lesson. In fact, research has generally found that moderate speakers are perceived as more intelligent, competent, confident, credible, socially attractive, and effective than slow speakers (Simonds, Meyer, Quinlan, & Hunt, 2006).

One way to vary your rate is through the use of pauses. **Pauses** can be used to emphasize a point, collect your thoughts, or transition to a new point. The use of pauses can also demonstrate poise and confidence, which will enhance your credibility with your students.

Pitch is the highness or lowness of your voice. Have you ever known anyone with a particularly high voice? On the other hand, someone who attempts to speak in a low range can sound unnatural. When you vary your pitch, you are using **inflection** to help you communicate your ideas. When you do not, you become **monotone**. Perhaps you have known a teacher who speaks in the same pitch at all times and know exactly what we are talking about. A good example of a monotone voice comes from the ever popular movie, *Ferris Bueller's Day Off*, where the teacher calls roll, lectures, and then asks questions he never really intends for anyone to answer. And yet he continues with his monotone lecture after no one responds to: *anyone? . . . anyone? . . .*

The way that you vary the last four vocal qualities (volume, rate, pauses, and pitch) will enhance your overall **vocal variety**. Vocal variety allows you to become more conversational and expressive. Think about ways to vary your voice so that your students become more interested in what you have to say. Your voice can communicate your attitude. For example, if you say "Great job!" in an upbeat, somewhat loud, somewhat high pitch, you communicate your approval. If you say the same phrase in a lower, softer, sarcastic tone, you communicate your disapproval.

Your voice also communicates your feelings about yourself or others. Generally, the more positive your feelings, the faster the rate, louder the volume, and more varied the pitch will be.

Just as words don't have a single meaning, neither do nonverbal aspects of communication. The clothes you wear, the expressions on your face, the gestures you use may communicate different meanings than you intend.

Reading Objectives and Discussion Prompts

4.2 Verbal Communication

What do you know?
What are three considerations for effective teacher verbal communication?

What do you think?
What are some specific ways that you can use verbal communication to help your students learn? Take into account the subject matter and age group you will be teaching.

NONVERBAL COMMUNICATION

Nonverbal communication is important to the classroom teacher. A teacher's nonverbal behavior is an important factor in students' attitudes toward school. When teachers are trained in effective use of nonverbal communication in the classroom, student–teacher relationships improve. In addition, student cognitive learning and affective learning improve.

An important axiom of communication is that *one cannot not communicate.* When we are seen by another person, we communicate. As we will see, nonverbal gestures, facial expressions, touch, and so on can affect the content of your message. In addition, the relationship aspect of a message is communicated primarily through nonverbal means. Thus, students will discern how you view your relationship with them by analyzing your nonverbal communication.

Functions of Nonverbal Communication in the Classroom

Nonverbal communication serves many functions in the classroom. As in any context, a nonverbal message can repeat, substitute for, complement, contradict, or regulate the verbal message. However, in the classroom context, nonverbal communication also plays a significant role in several areas. These include self-presentation, identification of rules and expectations, feedback and reinforcement, liking and attitude, regulation of conversational flow, and classroom control. Let's briefly examine each of these.

SELF-PRESENTATION. If you were asked to describe teaching, you would have little difficulty describing what a teacher does and how a teacher acts. How we define the job of teaching influences how we present ourselves. For example, if you yourself as an authoritative information giver, your nonverbal cues will present this image. You will stand erect, speak in a commanding voice, and lecture from the front of the room. Students, too, present a particular image. They may nod their heads, take notes, and look very attentive. Your image of yourself will affect your nonverbal behaviors in the classroom.

IDENTIFICATION OF RULES AND EXPECTATIONS. Although most teachers will verbally state classroom rules to their students ("No late papers will be accepted. Class participation is expected. Misbehavior will not be tolerated."), most rules are communicated nonverbally. A gaze that connotes disapproval or the wagging finger tells you that your behavior is inappropriate, even though the teacher may never have verbally said so.

Similarly, expectations are communicated, in large part nonverbally. Rarely does a teacher say to you, "I expect you to do very well in this class." However, as we discussed in Chapter 2, teachers' expectations for student achievement are most often communicated by such nonverbal cues as eye contact, seating arrangement, body orientation, and facial expressions.

FEEDBACK AND REINFORCEMENT. Even when a teacher fails to tell us, "Good job," we know how we are doing by the teacher's facial expressions, gestures, and body movements. A smile, an affirmative head nod, or a pat on the shoulder can all communicate approval. Similarly, a frown, quizzical look, or shake of the head can tell us we are not "on the right track."

Reinforcement has a powerful effect on a student's perception of self, school, and instructor. Smiles, frowns, eye contact, touch—all give students a message about how worthwhile they are. This is an example of how nonverbal messages tell us the most about the relationship level of a message. Most of us can remember teachers we didn't like or teachers we felt didn't like us. Obviously the teacher did not say, "I don't like you," but nonverbally we got the message.

LIKING AND AFFECT.   As we discussed in Chapter 2, nonverbal immediacy is perceived positively by students and is related to numerous student outcomes. Nonverbal immediacy behaviors such as smiling, removing physical barriers, and eye contact go a long way to communicate to students your liking and affect not only for teaching, but for students as well. This, in turn, makes them feel that you are approachable, available, and warm. Recently, researchers have studied how immediacy cues make students feel accepted and supported (Hunt, Angell, Boyd, Lippert, & Moore, 2005).

REGULATION OF CONVERSATIONAL FLOW.   Because of their power position in the classroom, teachers determine who talks, how often, how long, and when. As Andersen (1986) suggests

> Nonverbally, instructors signal that it is a student's turn to talk by dropping their pitch, dropping gestures, relaxing and leaning back slightly, and ending a vocal phrase by looking directly at the student expected to respond. An instructor can shorten student responses and acquire the speaking floor more quickly by nodding his or her head rapidly, opening his or her mouth as if to talk, inhaling, gesturing, leaning forward, and verbalizing during the first pause that is accompanied by eye contact. (p. 46)

Teachers can also use nonverbal cues to signal that it is not time to talk. Sometimes a particular student will want to answer every question. Instead of ignoring the student, the teacher might make eye contact while in the middle of an utterance. Eye contact timed in this way recognizes the student, but does not invite her to participate verbally. After the teacher finishes talking, he can avoid eye contact with the overly verbal student and focus eye contact directly on another student.

CLASSROOM CONTROL.   Nonverbal communication can be used both to encourage desirable student behavior and control undesirable student behavior. Often nonverbal behavior is more effective than verbal behavior in controlling the classroom. None of us likes to be verbally reprimanded. Nonverbal behaviors create less of the "me against you" attitude that often occurs with verbal reprimands. Suppose three or four students are talking together while you are lecturing. Increasing your eye contact with these students or moving in their direction may be enough to stop their talking. Such nonverbal movements are far less likely to disrupt other students who have been listening than, "Juan, Mary, Kim, please be quiet."

Often teachers want to increase student participation in their classrooms. Teachers need to do more than say, "I'd like us all to participate in this discussion."

Their nonverbal behaviors such as eye contact, facial expressions, and gestures need to encourage participation. For example, smiling, gesturing, being vocally expressive, pausing to wait for student comments, and reducing spatial barriers can do much to encourage participation. One teacher I observed increased participation by doing three simple things: she had her students sit in a semicircle, she moved from behind her desk to sit in the semicircle with them, and she paused several seconds after asking a question so students could respond and participate.

Reading Objectives and Discussion Prompts

4.3 Functions of Nonverbal Communication

What do you know?
What are the functions of nonverbal communication?

What do you think?
What are some specific ways that you can use nonverbal communication in your classroom? How have you seen it used by your own teachers before?

CATEGORIES OF NONVERBAL COMMUNICATION

Nonverbal communication can be categorized in several ways. In the next section, we examine the following categories of nonverbal communication: proxemics, spatial arrangements, environmental factors, chronemics, physical attractiveness, artifacts, kinesics, and touch.

Proxemics

Proxemics is the study of how people use space. It includes territoriality and personal space. Territoriality is fixed space. You usually sit in the same place in the classroom, even if the seats aren't assigned. I have noticed this phenomenon in mass lectures of 300 students as well as in classrooms of 25 or 30 students. Personal space has been compared to a bubble surrounding us that we carry with us wherever we go and that expands or contracts depending on the situation.

If our personal space is invaded we usually become uncomfortable unless, of course, we know the person well and he or she is special to us. For most encounters in the classroom, more distance is needed for students and teachers to be comfortable. Consider how you feel when a teacher stands over you while you're working at your desk. As teachers, we need to be careful of invading the personal space of our students.

Spatial Arrangements

Think about the various classroom environments you have experienced and the effect these spatial arrangements had on the communication that occurred. **Spatial arrangements** (a form of territoriality) affect such communication factors as who talks to whom, when, where, for how long, and about what.

Instructor		
57%	61%	57%
37%	54%	37%
41%	51%	41%
31%	48%	31%

FIGURE 4.2   The Traditional Classroom Spatial Arrangement: Rows. Percentages Indicate Degree of Participation in Classroom.

You may choose any of several different spatial arrangements for your classroom. The most common is the traditional row arrangement. The effect this arrangement has on communication is pictured in Figure 4.2. Notice that the percentage of participation is greater for students in the front and center rows. In a straight row arrangement, students most willing to communicate will tend to sit front and center. Those less willing to communicate will tend to sit further from the teacher and on the sides.

Two other common classroom arrangements are the horseshoe and the modular. Probable participation level according to seat location in each of these arrangements is shown in Figures 4.3 and 4.4 (McCroskey & McVetta, 1978).

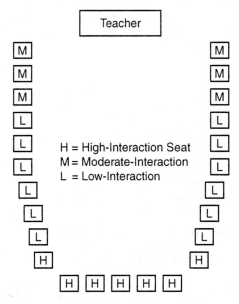

H = High-Interaction Seat
M = Moderate-Interaction
L = Low-Interaction

FIGURE 4.3   The Horseshoe Arrangement.

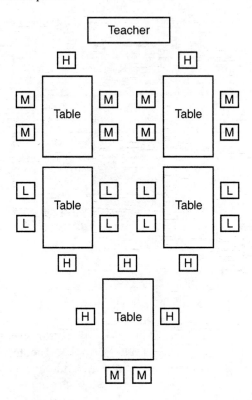

H = High-Interaction Seat, M = Moderate-Interaction, L = Low-Interaction

FIGURE 4.4 The Modular Arrangement.

From "Classroom Seating Arrangements: Instructional Communication Theory versus Student Preferences," by J. C. McCroskey and R. W. McVetta, *Communication Education, 27* (March 1978). Copyright © 1978. Reprinted by permission of Taylor & Francis Ltd. www.tandf.co.uk/journals.

Consider Figure 4.5. Psychologist Feitler (1971) and two fellow researchers showed this figure to 276 graduate and undergraduate students at Syracuse University's School of Education and asked them the following two questions:

- Which of the following classroom seating arrangements would you find the most and least comfortable if you were a student?
- Which would you find the most and least comfortable if you were the teacher?

Responses to the questions indicated that, whether the students thought of themselves as students or teachers, setting four was most comfortable. Settings three and seven were also chosen as comfortable. Least comfortable for both teacher and student were settings one and six. The researchers interpreted these results as indicating the need for teacher control. Perhaps, however, the results can be explained by remembering that students and teachers have little experience with seating arrangements other than those in which the teacher has control.

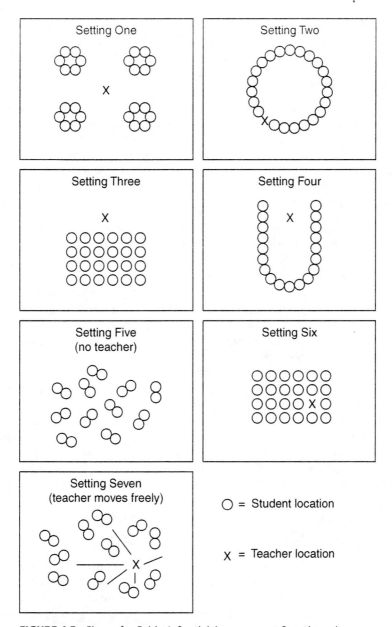

FIGURE 4.5 Figure for Feitler's Spatial Arrangement Questionnaire.

From "Tie Lane," by Kenneth Goodall, *Psychology Today, 5* (September 1971), p. 12. Copyright © 1971 by Sussex Publishers, Inc. Reprinted by permission from *Psychology Today Magazine.*

As a teacher, you need to be aware of how each of the three arrangements affects communication in the classroom. Your own experience as a student should tell you that the traditional row arrangement promotes teacher–student interaction. Very little communication occurs among students because the teacher dominates the classroom in this type of arrangement. The horseshoe arrangement increases student–student interaction.

The modular arrangement promotes the most student–student interaction. The arrangement you desire depends on many factors—the content you are teaching, the teaching style you use, the amount you want your students to communicate, and so forth.

Environmental Factors

Maslow and Mintz (1956) conducted a now-classic study in which they compared the interaction of people in an ugly versus a beautiful room. They found that:

> The ugly room was variously described as producing monotony, fatigue, headaches, discomfort, sleep, irritability and hostility. The beautiful room, however, produced feelings of pleasure, comfort, enjoyment, importance, energy, and desire to continue in the activity. (p. 256)

Several studies have confirmed this finding in the classroom. Sommer and Olsen (1980) remodeled a traditional classroom to create a "soft" classroom, one with cushioned benches, carpeting, and various decorative items. The percentage of students voluntarily participating was greater in the soft classroom (79 percent) than in the traditional classroom (51 percent). In addition, the mean number of comments per student doubled (2.5 per student in the traditional classroom compared to 5 per student in the soft classroom).

Teven and Comadena (1996) examined the effects of the aesthetic quality of faculty offices on students' perceptions of teacher credibility and communication style. Their research indicates that interactions outside of the classroom, especially those conducted in an instructor's office, may mediate students' perceptions of teacher credibility and communication style. Participants who visited an aesthetically pleasing office of an instructor prior to evaluating a videotape of that instructor's classroom behavior, compared to those who visited an office of low aesthetic quality or who had no office exposure at all, reported the instructor to be more friendly, more animated, more relaxed, more open, and more able to leave an impression on others. In addition, the aesthetically pleasing office produced higher ratings of trustworthiness and authoritativeness than the office of low aesthetic quality or the no office control condition (p. 105).

Todd-Mancillas (1982) reviewed research demonstrating that color, lighting, and temperature all affect the classroom climate. For example, warmer colors (yellows and pinks) are best for classrooms of younger children; cool colors (blues and blue-greens) are best for classrooms of older students.

Lighting can affect student–teacher communication. Poor lighting can lead to eye strain and fatigue, resulting in frustration and even hostility (Thompson, 1973). Another environmental factor affecting classroom communication is temperature. If a classroom is too hot, learning may be affected because students become irritable and anxious to leave. If a room is too cold, it's difficult to concentrate on learning. The classroom temperature for optimal student performance appears to be 66° to 72° Fahrenheit.

The implications for teachers are obvious. If you value some of the behaviors and attitudes that environmental factors have been found to influence, then you should consider your classroom environment. Changes in classroom environment may lead to changes in classroom climate. Eventually, these changes may lead to changes in achievement (Fouts & Myers, 1992). At any rate, it's important for students to feel comfortable in the learning environment, and you can have a significant impact on how the environment is arranged.

Chronemics

Chronemics is the study of people's use of time. Schools are organized temporally as well as spatially. Students often are admonished not to waste time, and classes are scheduled to meet at certain times and for specific lengths of time. The teacher's use of time in the classroom can greatly affect the communication that occurs. For example, the amount of time a teacher waits for a student to answer a question can affect interaction between teacher and student. Too often teachers fail to wait long enough for students to respond to questions—in fact, they seldom wait longer than 5 seconds. Silence certainly is not viewed as being golden in the classroom! Teachers seem to be afraid of silence and therefore answer their own questions or move rapidly from one student to another. This has a great impact on the communication interaction in the classroom. Few students will be willing to interact in such an environment—only those who are highly verbal will respond. In addition, when students know the teacher will answer her own questions if they simply wait long enough, the teacher will find herself doing just that!

Another area of chronemics involves the time spent on different subjects. The amount of time you spend on a given topic area communicates to students the importance of that area. How many times have you heard someone say, "I don't need to study that for the exam. The teacher spent hardly any time on it in class."

Time spent with individual students communicates our attitudes toward them. Teacher expectancy research indicates that high-expectancy students receive more teacher communication time than low-expectancy students. For example, teachers talk more to (praise more and have more academic interactions) and are more nonverbally active (head nods, smiles, supportive gestures) with high-expectation students.

Time can affect students in a number of other ways as well. Students may be either **monochronic** or **polychronic**; that is, they may work best when one activity, assignment, or project is scheduled at a time, or they may be able to engage in several activities at once. Students' biological clocks also affect their classroom performance. Morning-active students generally have higher academic achievement than those students who are most alert later in the day. Your awareness of the ways in which students are affected by time can enable you to meet their individual needs more effectively.

Finally, students use time to communicate. Putting away pencils and packing up books signals the instructor that the class period is nearly over. As we often tell our teachers in training: You don't need a clock in your classroom. Students will let you know what time it is!

Artifacts

One of your authors, Dr. Cooper, writes the following:

> I was recently reminded of the impact of artifacts in the classroom. I always wear an ankle chain. I entered a classroom on the first day of class wearing a business suit. One girl later told me she was "put off" by my clothing. It communicated a stiff, unyielding personality. But, she said, "I knew you would be human when I saw your ankle chain!"

An interesting study suggests the effects clothes can have in the classroom. High school boys who had much better achievement scores than some of their peers but wore "unacceptable" clothing (as deemed by their peers) had lower grade point averages than those boys who wore clothing deemed "acceptable" by their peers (Knapp & Hall, 2008). Anecdotal evidence suggests that students are ostracized if their clothing is tattered or out of fashion (Parsons, 1997).

In the classroom, researchers have examined student perceptions of "informally/casually dressed" and "formally dressed" teachers. Formally dressed teachers are perceived as more organized, more knowledgeable, and better prepared. Informally dressed teachers are perceived as more friendly, more sympathetic, fair, enthusiastic, and flexible (Richmond, Lane, & McCroskey, 2005).

Morris, Gorham, Cohen, and Huffman (1996) had four graduate teaching assistants (two males and two females) present a guest lecture in a section of the basic psychology course. The students were dressed one of three ways when they presented the lecture: formal professional (business dress), casual professional (for men, no jacket or tie; for women, a sweater and skirt instead of a suit), or casual (jeans, a T-shirt, and a plaid flannel shirt worn open). Following the presentation, the students rated the lecturer on scales measuring teacher competence, character, sociability, composure, and extroversion, as well as perceptions of how informed and how interesting the presentation was. Instructors who were dressed casually were rated as being less competent than those who dressed formally or in a casual but professional manner. But neither composure nor knowledge ratings showed any difference because of dress. Results indicated that casual dress resulted in higher ratings of sociability, extroversion, and making an interesting presentation; there were no differences on rating of character, however.

Students tended to favor presentations by the male instructors who wore the casual professional, or typical teaching assistant dress, over similarly dressed female instructors. Female students tended to rate male instructors more favorably if they dressed casually, but they rated female instructors more favorably if they dressed formally.

Children's names have been shown to be a boost or a barrier to their school success. Developmental psychology professor S. Gray Garwood (1983) of Tulane University asked teachers to list desirable and undesirable names. Garwood found sixth graders with those names and examined their achievement and self-concept scores. Students with desirable names had higher self-concept scores and, according to Garwood, had a better chance for higher achievement.

In a similar study, psychologists Herbert Harari and John McDavid (1983) gave a set of essays to eighty San Diego elementary school teachers. The teachers gave a higher grade to an essay written by David or Michael than to the same essay with the name Elmer or Herbert on it.

Kinesics

Kinesics is the study of body movement, gestures, facial expressions, eye contact, and so on. Ekman and Friesen (1969) classified kinesic behavior according to the following five categories:

- *Emblems* are nonverbal behaviors that have direct verbal translations. For example, "I don't know" may be communicated emblematically by a shrug of the shoulders and raised eyebrows.

- *Illustrators* are nonverbal behaviors that are tied directly to speech. During a geography lesson a teacher might illustrate where a city is located by pointing to that city on a map.
- *Affect displays* are facial expressions that communicate emotional states. Your frown may communicate displeasure with a student's answer. A confused expression or bored expression may communicate a certain emotional state in one of your students.
- *Regulators* are nonverbal behaviors used to control and maintain verbal interactions. Rapid head nods may communicate, "Yes, I understand. Go ahead with the next portion of the lesson."
- *Adapters* are nonverbal behaviors developed in childhood as adaptive behaviors to satisfy emotional or physical needs. When they feel anxious or bored, students may chew their pencils, bite their nails, click their pens, or tap their pencils on the desks. All of these are ways to adapt to their boredom or anxiety.

When we compare the nonverbal behaviors of effective and average teachers, we find that effective teachers use more motions than average teachers to facilitate student-to-instructor interaction, to focus student attention on key points, and to demonstrate and illustrate concepts to students. In addition, nonverbally active teachers elicit more positive perceptions from students than do inactive teachers.

Your kinesic behavior can communicate that you like or dislike your students. Liking, compared to disliking, is characterized by more forward leaning, more pleasant facial expressions, and more openness of arms and body. Teachers who are perceived as "warm" smile, use direct eye contact, and tend to lean toward the other person. Warmth cues, along with verbal reinforcers ("mm-hmm"), increase verbal output from the other person.

In addition to liking and disliking, kinesic behavior can communicate how much you trust your students. For example, when monitoring a test, do you walk around the room, watching what the students are doing, or do you sit at a desk and work, occasionally glancing up?

EYE CONTACT.   One important area of kinesic behavior is eye contact. Eye contact signals that communication lines are open—that you're willing to communicate with another. Think about what you do when a teacher asks a question and you don't know the answer. You look down at your book, doodle, rearrange materials on your desk—anything to avoid looking at the teacher and thereby risking being called on!

In addition to this signaling function, eye contact may also be used to seek feedback or to convey information about relationships—for example, dominance and submission or liking and disliking. Students indicate they are more comfortable with a person who, when speaking, listening, or sharing mutual silence, looks at them 50 percent of the time than one who looks at them 100 percent of the time. Thus, teachers who stare at students lengthily may create anxiety or even hostility.

Teachers who use moderate eye contact monitor and regulate their classrooms more easily. Have you ever received the "evil eye" from a teacher when you were being disruptive? Generally, when students feel teachers looking at them, they stop their disruptive behavior.

Although constant eye contact is discomforting, eye contact has been found to enhance comprehension. In addition, direct eye contact usually communicates interest and attention, whereas lack of direct eye contact communicates disinterest and inattention.

Studies reviewed by Beebe (1980) suggest that eye contact has a significant effect on student retention of information, attitudes toward the teacher, attention, and classroom participation.

FACIAL EXPRESSION.   A teacher can use facial expressions to manage interactions in the classroom (a "dirty look" may be enough to stop a student from whispering, for example), regulate communication, signal approval or disapproval, and reinforce or not reinforce. As teachers we need to consider what messages we are sending with our faces. Are we sometimes communicating messages we would rather not send? Learning to control our facial expressions may be a requirement of our profession. Sometimes we do not want to communicate what we're thinking. Increased sensitivity to and control over our display of emotions can improve the communication between teacher and students.

The teacher's facial expressions communicate much in the classroom. The teacher who smiles and has positive facial affect will be perceived as approachable and immediate. A teacher's dull facial expression may be perceived by students as indicating disinterest in them or the subject matter.

In theory, a teacher should be able to use student facial expressions and gestures to determine their understanding of material being discussed. However, neither novice nor experienced teachers are able to judge student understanding based on facial expressions and gestures alone. Sometimes we can read nonverbal kinesic cues incorrectly. Students are very adept at looking interested and awake when their minds are a million miles away!

Touch

Touch is a "touchy" subject in our society. Touch can communicate many things—emotional support, tenderness, encouragement—and is an important aspect in most human relationships. In his book *Touching: The Human Significance of the Skin*, Montagu (1971) indicates the importance of touch in the development of healthy, happy individuals:

> When affection and involvement are conveyed through touch, it is those meanings, as well as the security-giving satisfactions, with which touch will become associated. Inadequate tactile experience will result in a lack of such associations and a consequent inability to relate to others in many fundamental human ways. (p. 292)

The amount of touching between student and teacher declines steadily from kindergarten through sixth grade, but is still greater than most adults engage in. Junior high students engage in about half as much touching as do students in the elementary grades. Most touching occurs between same-sex pairs.

As teachers, we should be aware that touch in the elementary grades can be used as an effective means of communicating caring and understanding. Research indicates that children who are touched often have higher IQs than those who don't receive a lot of touch. However, we must be aware that as students grow older, they equate touch with intimacy. Thus, although a teacher's touch is usually inappropriate with older students and will probably create a barrier to effective communication, remember that a pat on the shoulder or back may be appropriate at times and may be very much appreciated by a student.

Reading Objectives and Discussion Prompts

4.4 Categories of Nonverbal Communication

What do you know?
List and describe the categories of nonverbal communication.

What do you think?
What are some things you can do to prepare an optimal nonverbal learning environment for your students? Think about a class where you have been a student. What are some examples of nonverbal communication categories that were evident?

NONVERBAL COMMUNICATION AND CULTURE

As we examine nonverbal communication in the classroom, it is important to remember that few nonverbal norms are universal. According to Samovar and Porter (2009), "many of your nonverbal actions are touched and altered by culture" (p. 164). These authors also point out three parallels between culture and nonverbal communication: both are invisible, omnipresent, and learned. First, most people are not consciously aware of their nonverbal behavior much like their culture. In addition, culture is all-pervasive (it is everywhere and in everything), as is nonverbal communication. Finally, both culture and nonverbal behavior need to be learned. That is, you are not born knowing the specific signals that constitute nonverbal communication, and you are not born knowing the norms or values associated with your culture. For example, Samovar and Porter (2009) clearly demonstrate how nonverbal communication and culture are inextricably linked in the following passage:

> In the United States people greet by shaking hands. Arab men often greet by kissing on both cheeks. In Japan, men greet by bowing, and in Mexico they often embrace. Touching one's ear is protection against the evil eye in Turkey. In southern Italy, it denotes jeering at effeminacy, and in India, it is a sign of repentance or sincerity. In most Middle and Far Eastern countries, pointing with the index finger is considered impolite. In Thailand, to signal another person to come near, one moves the fingers back and forth with the palm down. In the United States, you beckon someone to come by holding the palm up and moving the fingers toward your body. In Vietnam that same motion is reserved for someone attempting to summon their dog. The Tongans sit down in the presence of superiors; in the West, you stand up. Crossing one's legs in the United States is often a sign of being relaxed; in Korea, it is a social taboo. In Japan, gifts are usually exchanged with both hands. Muslims consider the left hand unclean and do not eat or pass objects with it. Buddha maintained that great insights arrived during moments of silence. In the United States, people talk to arrive at the truth. (p. 4)

Reading Objectives and Discussion Prompts

4.5 Nonverbal Communication and Culture

What do you know?
What are the parallels between culture and nonverbal communication?

What do you think?
Considering each of the categories of nonverbal communication, what are some possible differences for students from other cultures?

IMPROVING NONVERBAL COMMUNICATION

As stated in the introduction to this chapter, the impact of nonverbal cues on learning is not completely clear. Therefore, we cannot tell you the right nonverbal moves to make in the classroom. However, the following is an instrument used to record nonverbal behavior. The instrument was developed by two researchers, Love and Roderick (1971), after considerable observation of elementary and secondary teachers. Thus, these behaviors seem to represent some of the important nonverbal teaching practices. Studies using this instrument reveal two fairly consistent findings: (1) Teachers who are nonverbally active are more effective (perceived as more interesting and informative), and (2) teachers can be trained to improve their nonverbal behavior.

Love-Roderick Nonverbal Categories and Sample Teacher Behaviors

- *Accepts student behavior.* Smiles, affirmatively shakes head, pats on the back, winks, places hand on shoulder or head.
- *Praises student behavior.* Places index finger and thumb together, claps, raises eyebrows and smiles, nods head affirmatively and smiles.
- *Displays student ideas.* Writes comments on board, puts students' work on bulletin board, holds up papers, provides for nonverbal student demonstration.
- *Shows interest in student behavior.* Establishes and maintains eye contact.
- *Moves to facilitate student–student interaction.* Physically moves into the position of group member, physically moves away from the group.
- *Gives directions to students.* Points with the hand, looks at specified area, employs predetermined signal (such as raising hands for students to stand up), reinforces numerical aspects by showing that number of fingers, extends arms forward and beckons with the hands, points to student for answers.
- *Shows authority toward students.* Frowns, stares, raises eyebrows, taps foot, rolls book on desk, negatively shakes head, walks or looks away from the deviant, snaps fingers.
- *Focuses students' attention on important points.* Uses pointer, walks toward the person or object, taps on something, thrusts head forward, thrusts arm forward, employs a nonverbal movement with a verbal statement to give it emphasis.
- *Demonstrates or illustrates.* Performs a physical skill, manipulates materials and media, illustrates a verbal statement with a nonverbal action.
- *Ignores student behavior.* Lacks nonverbal response when one is ordinarily expected. (This is sometimes appropriate, particularly in classroom management.)

Reading Objectives and Discussion Prompts

4.6 Improving Nonverbal Communication

What do you know?
What are some important nonverbal teaching practices?

What do you think?
Can you think of specific classroom examples for each of these behaviors? Take into account the subject matter and age group you will be teaching.

In Sum

The areas of verbal and nonverbal communication are important ones for teachers. Our verbal and nonverbal communication affect students' perceptions of the classroom that, in turn, affect how students view the educational environment, the people in it, and how much they desire to communicate.

Finally, although we have isolated nonverbal communication from verbal communication, such an isolation distorts the process. Nonverbal communication can be used to reinforce, contradict, substitute for, accent, complement, or regulate the flow of verbal communication. Remember that the two systems—verbal and nonverbal—work together in the classroom.

Key Terms

Symbolic Language
Arbitrary Language
Triangle of Meaning
Language Creates a Social
    Reality
Verbal Communication
Teacher Clarity
Appropriate Language

Inclusive Language
Verbal Delivery (articulation,
    pronunciation, volume,
    rate, pauses, pitch,
    inflection, monoton,
    vocal variety)
Nonverbal Communication

Categories of Nonverbal
    Communication
    (proxemics, spatial
    arrangements, chrone-
    mics, monochromic,
    polychromic, kinesics)

5   Sharing Information

OBJECTIVES

After reading this chapter, you should be able to:

- Understand considerations for choosing a teaching strategy.
- Make appropriate decisions about when to lecture.
- Prepare a lecture using the five steps of lecture preparation.
- Use visual aids effectively.
- Identify communication barriers that often arise when lecturing.
- Understand the causes of teacher communication apprehension.

INSTRUCTIONAL STRATEGIES

Teachers can choose from a variety of teaching strategies—lecture, discussion, experiential activities, storytelling, independent study, small-group instruction, peer instruction, and so forth. During any one day, a teacher may use several of these strategies. None of these strategies has been found to be consistently superior to any other. How, then, can teachers choose the "best" strategy for their students?

Choosing a teaching strategy is not an easy task. However, there are certain guidelines a teacher should follow. Keep in mind that no teaching method is inherently good or bad. However, given the guidelines presented throughout this unit, you should be able to choose the appropriate strategy for your particular needs.

Factors to Consider When Choosing a Strategy

THE TEACHER. The first consideration in determining which teaching strategy to use is the personality and expertise of you—the teacher. Some teachers feel most comfortable when lecturing, others feel quite capable of facilitating a class discussion. A teacher's ability to tolerate high levels of ambiguity, willingness to relinquish some of the control over the classroom, and ability to tolerate low levels of organization and structure will influence that teacher's liking of the discussion method. To a certain extent, you should use the approach with which you feel most comfortable. However, we would encourage you to experiment with a variety of teaching strategies. You might find you enjoy and do well with several approaches.

THE OBJECTIVE.   A second important factor to consider is the instructional objective of the lesson. If the objective is information acquisition, the lecture method would be one appropriate method. If the objective is to have students develop their critical-thinking abilities, a discussion method would be more appropriate. It's imperative that you formulate objectives for each lesson and then use the teaching strategy that will best enable your students to meet those objectives. Your **instructional objectives** may be based on certain local, state, or national standards. For example, the American Diploma Project (ADP) in association with Achieve Inc. has a consortium of thirty-five states and has developed national standards for K–12 English Language Arts. These standards can be found at http://www.achieve.org/ADPNetwork. In the state of Illinois, there are a series of English Language Arts standards that address how students should perform in reading, writing, speaking, and listening skills. There are also speaking, listening, and media literacy standards published by the National Communication Association (NCA) for K–12 students. For example, one NCA standard states that competent communicators demonstrate knowledge and understanding of the relationships among the components of the communication process.

As teachers, it will be important for you to determine which standards your lessons will be expected to address because state funding and testing procedures are designed based on these standards.

Designing your teaching according to various standards means starting with the agreed-upon standards and designing content, lessons, activities, and assessments according to those standards. For example, one of the Illinois ELA Standards addresses the students' ability to read with understanding and fluency. Objectives, then, are written based on the students' ability to meet the benchmark for the standard. For early elementary students, this benchmark states that they should be able to apply word analysis skills (e.g., phonics, word patterns) to recognize new words.

Thus, your lesson objectives will specify what you want the students to be able to know or do once they complete the particular lesson. Objectives can be for knowledge gain, or skills/behavioral gain.

THE STUDENTS.   Students—their age, intelligence, motivational level, and previous learning of the subject matter—are an important consideration in choosing a particular teaching strategy. For example, the attention span of elementary schoolchildren is limited. Thus, the lecture method will not be as appropriate as some other teaching methods. Most researchers recommend only 10 to 20 minutes of lecturing for any age group.

Students differ in how well they use their senses in the learning process. In addition, any time we as teachers use a strategy that eliminates use of one or more senses by students to receive messages, we are further limiting their learning ability. Simply lecturing on how to dissect a frog is not nearly as effective as combining that lecture with student dissection of the frog.

TABLE 5.1 ELA Standard 1

STATE GOAL 1: Read with understanding and fluency				
Early Elementary	**Late Elementary**	**Middle/Junior High School**	**Early High School**	**Late High School**
1.A.1a Apply word analysis skills (e.g., phonics, word patterns) to recognize new words.	**1.A.2a** Read and comprehend unfamiliar words using root words, synonyms, antonyms, word origins and derivations.	**1.A.3a** Apply knowledge of word origins and derivations to comprehend words used in specific content areas (e.g., scientific, political, literary, mathematical).	**1.A.4a** Expand knowledge of word origins and derivations and use idioms, analogies, metaphors, and similes to extend vocabulary development.	**1.A.5a** Identify and analyze new terminology applying knowledge of word origins and derivations in a variety of practical settings.
1.A.1b Comprehend unfamiliar words using context clues and prior knowledge; verify meanings with resource materials.	**1.A.2b** Clarify word meaning using context clues and a variety of resources including glossaries, dictionaries, and thesauruses.	**1.A.3b** Analyze the meaning of words and phrases in their context.	**1.A.4b** Compare the meaning of words and phrases and use analogies to explain the relationships among them.	**1.A.5b** Analyze the meaning of abstract concepts and the effects of particular word and phrase choices.

As teachers, we should also consider the **emotional state** of our students. It's extremely difficult to acquire and process any information when students are tired, depressed, anxious, or experiencing some kind of conflict or personal problem. The more supportive you can make the climate in your classroom, the less tense and anxious students will be and the easier it will be for them to acquire the information you present.

As Maslow has told us for years, when lower-level needs (such as safety) are not met, students cannot fulfill higher-level needs. Maslow classified human needs into five hierarchical categories. An adaptation of his hierarchy for educational settings is shown in Figure 5.1. For example, many schools and districts now offer breakfast programs to ensure that all students enter the learning environment free from the physical need for food.

We should also consider a student's learning style as we create our lessons. **Learning style** refers to a student's preference for learning. For example, one student may be an auditory learner, another a visual or kinesthetic learner. **Cognitive style** refers to the way in which one processes information and is a part of a person's overall learning style (Vermunt & Verloop, 2000). Specifically, a cognitive style is a person's typical or habitual mode of problem solving, thinking, perceiving, and remembering (Riding & Cheema, 1991) and will determine the way in which a person goes about performing a task. One distinction should be made about learning or cognitive styles and ability. Simply because people possess a particular style does not necessarily indicate increased

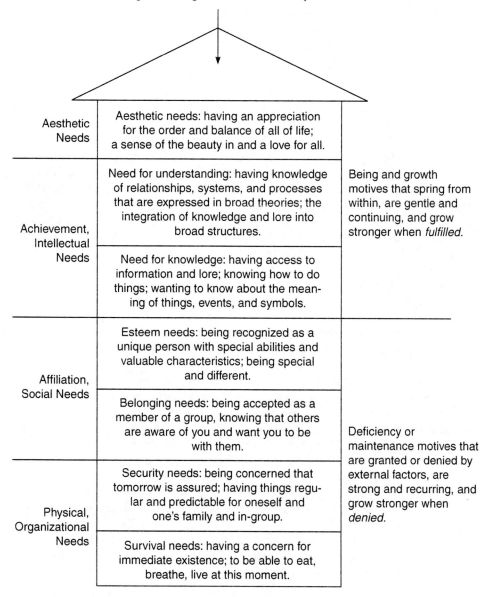

Self-actualization, displaying the needs of a fully functioning student or human being; becoming the self that one truly is.

Aesthetic Needs	Aesthetic needs: having an appreciation for the order and balance of all of life; a sense of the beauty in and a love for all.	
Achievement, Intellectual Needs	Need for understanding: having knowledge of relationships, systems, and processes that are expressed in broad theories; the integration of knowledge and lore into broad structures.	Being and growth motives that spring from within, are gentle and continuing, and grow stronger when *fulfilled.*
	Need for knowledge: having access to information and lore; knowing how to do things; wanting to know about the meaning of things, events, and symbols.	
Affiliation, Social Needs	Esteem needs: being recognized as a unique person with special abilities and valuable characteristics; being special and different.	
	Belonging needs: being accepted as a member of a group, knowing that others are aware of you and want you to be with them.	Deficiency or maintenance motives that are granted or denied by external factors, are strong and recurring, and grow stronger when *denied.*
Physical, Organizational Needs	Security needs: being concerned that tomorrow is assured; having things regular and predictable for oneself and one's family and in-group.	
	Survival needs: having a concern for immediate existence; to be able to eat, breathe, live at this moment.	

FIGURE 5.1   A Hierarchy of Needs.

Note: This hierarchy of needs is based on a formulation by Maslow (1954).

From *Educational Psychology,* by N. L. Gage and D. C. Berliner, p. 286. Copyright © 1974 by Houghton Mifflin Company. Used with permission.

ability to perform a particular task such as learning (Rickards, Fajen, Sullivan, & Gillespie, 1997). It merely indicates a preference for how to learn or process information.

As Dunn, Beaudry, and Klavas (1989) indicate, no style is better or worse than another. In fact, all learning styles are found within all ethnic groups to a varying degree but with a dominant style for each ethnicity (Hollins, King, & Hayman, 1994). What is important, however, is that when students are permitted to learn difficult academic information or skills through their identified learning style preferences, they tend to achieve statistically higher test and aptitude scores than when instruction is inconsistent with their preferences.

Teachers need to identify their students' learning styles. There are numerous commercially published instruments that measure one or many aspects of learning style (Kolb & Kolb, 2001). The Kolbs' learning theory sets out four distinct learning styles (or preferences) including diverging, assimilating, converging, and accommodating, which are based on a learning cycle that represents how the learner "touches all the bases" of experiencing, reflecting, thinking, and acting. The Kolbs' learning style instrument can be accessed at www.businessballs.com/kolblearningstyles.htm. However, even without formal instruments, it is possible to obtain assessment information from observations of students or discussing with students their own views by asking, "How, when, where, and what do you learn best?" Another technique is to ask students to write or tell about a learning or study situation in which they were either productive or nonproductive and to analyze the situation.

An example of cognitive style is **field dependent** versus **field independent**. Table 5.2 summarizes the differences in characteristics between field-dependent and field-independent learners. Field-dependent learners tend to "take elements or background variables from the environment into account . . . [and] perceive the event holistically, including the emotionality and the feelings associated with the entire event" (Lieberman, 1994, p. 179). By contrast, field-independent learners are analytical and use strategies to isolate elements of the field (Brown, 2006). Field-dependent learners prefer to work with others, seek guidance from the teacher, and receive rewards based on their relationship with the group. In contrast, field-independent learners prefer to work alone, are task oriented, and prefer rewards based on individual competition (Lieberman, 1994). To put it simply, some people see the forest; some see the trees. Field-dependent style is prevalent in group-oriented, high-context, collectivist societies. Field-independent styles predominate in low-context, highly competitive, highly industrialized societies (Lieberman, 1994).

It is important to note that cultural differences affect learning styles. Specific dimensions related to cultural diversity will be discussed at length in Chapter 10, but for now, we'll discuss how culture might affect learning styles. An example of learning style is a preference for groups versus individual learning. In Euro-American cultures, education typically emphasizes individual learning. Each student strives for her individual grade or praise. In many collectivist cultures, group learning is expected. For example, children of Hawaiian ancestry come under the guidance of their older siblings very early in life. Parents interact with their children as a group, not so much as individuals. As a result of this kind of upbringing, children learn best from siblings and peers in group situations, not from one adult, as is typical in Euro-American cultures as well as in the school setting (Cushner & Brislin, 1996).

In other words, some cultures emphasize cooperation while others emphasize competition. African Americans, Asian Americans, and Hispanic Americans raise their

TABLE 5.2   Cognitive Styles

Examples of characteristics exhibited by people who possess the field-dependent or field-independent cognitive style.

Field Dependent

Low tolerance for ambiguity
Less-developed sense of identity
Tend to have more social or interpersonal orientation
Have greater need for externally provided structure and benefit from teacher providing examples, charts, graphs, etc.
Respond well to teacher feedback
Desire to understand the social and personal meaning of the learning experience
Perform poorly on memory tests
Recall more information when provided with cues such as structural maps
Aspire to careers that require involvement with people such as teaching or counseling

Field Independent

High tolerance for ambiguity or uncertainty
Less-developed sense of identity and do not mind being alone
Perform better on short-term memory tests thought to involve extensive interference, underscoring ability to focus attention on relevant aspects of the field
Score better on reading and math tests
Able to encode more words than field-dependent learners
More likely to enroll in and flourish in distance education courses
More likely to work independently and less likely to ask teacher for assistance
Aspire to careers dealing with the subject areas of natural sciences, mathematics, and engineering

Data compiled by Steve Hunt (1998) from a number of sources (Jonassen & Grabowski, 1993; Witkin, 1976; Witkin et al., 1962; Bosacki, Innerd, & Towson, 1997; Witkin et al., 1977; Reiff, 1996; Rickards et al., 1997; Chmielewski, Kiewra, & Frank, 1988; Berger & Goldberger, 1979; Richardson & Turner, 2000; Mahlios, 1981). Used with permission.

children cooperatively, and the educational system perpetuates this cooperativeness. Peers offer help to one another. In contrast, U.S. students are encouraged to work alone. Even when they work in groups, each student is expected to "carry his own weight."

THE ENVIRONMENT.   Finally, the environment in which learning is to take place must be considered. The environment includes such variables as time, class size, and furniture arrangements. How much time will you have for the lesson itself? To adequately evaluate and respond to students' needs takes more instructional time with some teaching methods than with others. Class size is a factor to consider. For example, the larger the class, the more difficult it will be to use the discussion method. Some classrooms do not lend themselves to using small instructional groups. If chairs in a straight row arrangement are bolted to the floor (as was the case in a classroom in which one of the authors taught), it's impossible to rearrange furniture spatially in a manner conducive to small-group communication. Remember that the classroom is a system. All these factors—teacher, objectives, student, environment—interact to affect your decision on which teaching strategy is best for a particular lesson.

Keeping these general guidelines in mind, the next few chapters examine specific teaching methods—the lecture, discussion, use of small groups, storytelling, and communicative reading. It's important to remember that these methods are examined from a communication perspective. In other words, we'll be concerned with the communication interaction that occurs when each of these methods is used, as well as communication skills necessary for each of these methods. We'll begin with the most traditional teaching strategy—the lecture.

Reading Objectives and Discussion Prompts

5.1 Instructional Strategies

What do you know?
What are the factors to consider when choosing a teaching strategy?

What do you think?
Think about the classes and the students you want to teach. What are some possible instructional objectives for these classes? How will you monitor your students' emotional states? How will you consider their learning styles as you prepare your lessons?

ADVANTAGES AND DISADVANTAGES OF THE LECTURE METHOD

The major **advantage** of lecturing is that vast amounts of information can be presented in a relatively efficient manner. The major **disadvantage** is that the communicative interaction among students and between students and teacher is limited.

Although teachers of elementary schoolchildren will not use this method to the extent that teachers of older students will, the principles discussed can be used for any information-sharing function in the classroom—giving direction, providing explanations, and conducting reviews.

Lecturing is advantageous because:

- It presents a human model.
- It is inexpensive because the student–teacher ratio is quite large.
- It is flexible in that it can be adapted easily to a particular group of students, subject matter, and so on.
- It can cover vast amounts of information.
- It provides for reinforcement.

Lecturing is disadvantageous because:

- Lectures are usually used when class size is fairly large, thus prohibiting student–teacher interaction as well as student–student interaction. Students often feel they are "just a number." This depersonalization may impair learning.
- Students can become easily confused because a large amount of information is being covered. If, as a lecturer, you don't pay close attention to nonverbal feedback from students, you won't know which material needs to be clarified.
- It is a difficult method by which to probe deeply into material that is abstract or theoretical in nature.
- It is difficult for students to maintain attention in such an inactive role for more than 15- to 20-minute intervals.
- Lecture audiences are heterogeneous; therefore, it is difficult to gear material to all audience members.

These advantages and disadvantages of the lecture method suggest there are times when lecturing is appropriate and times when other methods are perhaps more advantageous. The following presents conditions under which the lecture is appropriate and inappropriate.

Lecturing is appropriate when:

- The basic instructional purpose is to disseminate information.
- The information is not available elsewhere.
- The information must be organized and presented in a particular way.
- It is necessary to arouse learner interest in a subject.
- It is necessary to introduce an area of content or provide directions for learning tasks that will be developed via some other teaching method.

Lecturing is inappropriate when:

- The basic instructional purpose involves forms of learning other than the acquisition of information.
- The instructional objective involves higher cognitive levels, such as analysis, synthesis, and evaluation.
- The learning task involves initiating or changing attitudes, values, beliefs, and behavior.
- The information acquired must be remembered for a long period of time.
- The information is already available, abstract, or detailed.
- Learner participation is essential to the achievement of the instructional objective.

Reading Objectives and Discussion Prompts

5.2 Advantages and Disadvantages of the Lecture Method

What do you know?
What are the advantages and disadvantages of the lecture method?

What do you think?
Think about a classroom lecture where you have been a student. What were some of the strengths and weaknesses of this lesson? How did you as a student learn from the lecture?

PREPARING A LECTURE

Teachers are often called on to give information. No teacher escapes giving directions, specifying procedures, providing demonstrations, making assignments, and reviewing. Although we focus on the lecture as sharing information, remember that the suggestions made concerning the lecture relate to other forms of information sharing as well.

> *The robins sang and sang and sang,*
> *but teacher you went right on.*
> *The last bell sounded the end of the day,*
> *but teacher you went right on.*
> *The geranium on the window sill just died,*
> *but teacher you went right on. (Cullum, 1971, p. 56)*

Too often, this poem describes students' reactions to lecturing. However, this doesn't have to be the case. When you use the lecture method, it doesn't excuse you from responsibility for getting students involved during the lecture. Rhetorical questions, handouts to be completed as the lecture progresses, previewing the lesson, and continually referring to the reading assignment are all means of enhancing student involvement in the lecture. As you read about how to effectively construct and use a lecture, keep in mind that the lecture is a communicative event and the give-and-take of communicative messages is a transactional process.

Lecturing is, essentially, sharing information. The major purpose is to secure clear understanding of the concepts you present. Perhaps the most important considerations as you prepare your lectures are the teaching objectives you want to accomplish. Everything you do in your lectures should relate to the objectives. As you go through the preparation process, continually ask yourself, "How will this help me meet my teaching objectives?"

There are five steps in lecture preparation: (1) choose a topic; (2) narrow the topic; (3) gather supporting materials; (4) organize the lecture; and (5) practice the lecture. We discuss each of these in detail.

Choose a Topic

The first step in lecture preparation is to choose a topic. What information do you want your students to know? Recall the factors for considering an instructional strategy provided earlier in this chapter. These factors also need to be considered here. First, you need to consider yourself. What do you know about the topic? Can you rely exclusively on your own knowledge or will you need to utilize the thoughts and research of others? What materials and resources do you have available to you? Is there a textbook that will serve as the framework for your content? Are there other teachers in your school teaching the same material? Are there curriculum guidelines or state and national standards that have to be addressed?

Your students must also be considered—their age and educational level are particularly important since most state standards and benchmarks are based on the academic level of the students (from early elementary to late high school). Is the topic of relevance to them? What knowledge do they already possess concerning the topic? What attitudes, past experiences, and unique characteristics do they have that might influence how the topic should be approached? Again, at this point you will want to consider their emotional states and learning styles as you choose your topic for the lecture.

The classroom environment is another important factor. Are the physical environment and the psychological environment of the classroom conducive to covering the topic? Is there enough time? Will visual aids be necessary to stimulate attention to and to clarify the topic?

Narrow the Topic

The next step in lecture preparation is to narrow your topic. You need to narrow your lecture topic until you have just one or two clear instructional objectives for your lesson. Recall that these objectives may need to be directly tied to local, state, or national standards. To begin the narrowing process, you may need step back and consider the broader picture.

Look at your curriculum. How does your course fit in with the rest of the curriculum in the school? Determine what expectations might exist by other faculty because the students take your course first. It's possible that later courses depend on certain knowledge and skills taught in your course.

Determine which standards and benchmarks and objectives match the course. You should know what you want the students to be able to do once they leave your course at the end of the term. Find those standards and benchmarks and make them your guiding principles.

Make a course plan. What units will you need to teach in order to obtain those standards and benchmarks? Determine what is logical for the amount of time you have so that the students, the parents, the school, and the state are satisfied with the knowledge and skills you are teaching to the students. Think about how long certain topics will take and leave enough time to accomplish. Be ready to cut material since it's better to over-plan rather than under-plan.

Develop your units. What kinds of things need to be covered or happen within each unit? Be thinking about what general content coverage is demanded because of the standards. Begin outlining each unit accordingly. Start with the relevant standards and benchmarks, and then break them into appropriate lesson plans. Identify the lessons that will need to occur.

As you narrow the topic of each lecture to one or two objectives, remember to ask yourself such questions as, "What do I want my students to know specifically about this topic?" "Are they at an age level at which they can understand this particular aspect of the topic?" "What do they already know and how can I use this prior knowledge in my lecture?" and "What material have I already taught them and how can I use this material in this lecture?"

Gather Supporting Materials

The third step in lecture preparation is gathering supporting materials that will make the ideas you're presenting "come alive." Supporting materials can be verbal or nonverbal. They are the materials that provide proof and explanation of what you say. **Supporting material** provides clarification for the content you are teaching and can include examples, statistics, personal stories, definitions, and visual aids. Table 5.3 presents a brief explanation of the most common types of verbal supporting materials used for clarification.

Examples are difficult to come up with off the cuff. To be sure that your supporting material is accurately connected to the concepts of your lecture, make sure that your material is planned in advance. As in every step of lecture preparation, you must consider yourself, your students, and the classroom environment when choosing supporting materials. What supporting materials do you have available already? For example, what personal experiences do you have that you can use as supporting materials? Based on your experiences with your students, what kinds of supporting material do they find particularly enjoyable and helpful? Finally, what constraints does the classroom environment place on you? Perhaps a limited budget prohibits the use of video, for example.

TABLE 5.3   Verbal Supporting Materials: Clarification Devices

Clarification Device	Function
Example	Expository or descriptive passage used to make ideas, process, and so forth, clear.
A. Illustration	Detailed narrative example.
1. Hypothetical	Tells what *could* have happened.
2. Factual	Tells what *did* happen.
B. Instance	An undetailed example.
Statistics	Uses quantification in order to make a complex situation clear, to substantiate a claim, or to make an abstract idea concrete.
Testimony	Uses the opinions or conclusions of others—can act as proof or add impressiveness to an idea.
Definition	Presents a meaning for a word—particularly important when the word is abstract or technical in nature.
Contrast	Points out the differences between two phenomenon, one of which is familiar to the students.
Comparison	Points out the similarities between something that is familiar to students and something that is not.
Restatement/ Repetition	Restatement is the reiteration of an idea in different words—repetition, in the same words. Both restatement and repetition are used to drive home an idea.

Adapted from Waldo W. Braden, "Beyond the Campus Gate," in *Principles of Speech Communication*, 7th ed., p. 121, by A. Monroe and D. Ehninger (Eds.). Published by Allyn and Bacon, Boston. Copyright © 1974 by Pearson Education. Adapted by permission of the publisher.

In addition to these considerations, you need to keep the basic purpose of the lecture—to create clear understanding—in the forefront. When choosing supporting materials, consider whether they help clarify your ideas and enhance student attention.

A nonverbal form of supporting material is the presentation aid. **Presentation aids** can make your ideas more concrete by presenting a pictorial or graphic representation of the idea being explained. Presentation aids can also help maintain your students' attention. However, these two purposes—clarification and maintaining attention—will be accomplished only if the presentation aids you use are appropriate to the subject matter and the students.

Many things can be used as presentation aids including written text, data graphics, photographs, illustrations, models, and objects. For more information on selecting and designing presentation aids, please see Box 5.1.

Many modern classrooms are now equipped with the technology to use computer-generated software programs (PowerPoint, Persuasion, or Astound) as a way of organizing and presenting a lecture. In addition, classrooms now have Internet connections to access the World Wide Web. However, there are a few pedagogical and presentational

BOX 5.1

Using Presentation Aids

This section will give you ideas about the types of aids that are available, how you can display these aids using various technologies, some tips on designing the aids, and finally how to integrate the aid gracefully into your lecture.

Presentation aids can come in many forms, but some of these forms may not be immediately obvious.

Typically, when most teachers think of presentation aids, they think of something that they will show the students. The most basic things you can show while speaking are written presentation aids represented in the textbooks you will be teaching from and certainly available to use for classroom purposes. Here are some of the things you may find or choose to create on your own.

A table brings visual organization to a lot of information in a fairly compact form.

Another common textual visual is the use of numbered or bulleted lists. Numbered lists can show the steps of a sequence, ratings, or hierarchy.

Bulleted lists illustrate membership in a set. Bullets may be very useful when previewing or reviewing the main points of your presentation. When your students can see your main points, it helps them create mental maps of what you are saying, which will help them organize the information. Try not to make the bullets too wordy and make sure that they are written in a parallel fashion. Many speakers often misuse or abuse bulleted lists since they are so easy to create. Typing up several slides full of bullets and reading them to your students is not a lecture—at best it's a poor representation of a chapter read out loud!

If you have statistics to explain, then consider a data graphic. These graphics can take many forms, but let's look at a few of the most common ones.

A pie graph shows how the various categories relate to the whole and are reported using percentages that add up to 100 percent. Typically, a pie graph is useful up to about seven or eight categories. This might be a great way to illustrate the budget of a particular organization or project.

Line graphs communicate changes over time or overall trends and are sometimes called times-series plots.

Column graphs are also known as vertical bar graphs and can include a time series, but they also allow viewers to make quick comparison between groups. Regular bar graphs that are situated horizontally don't include a time element but are still very useful for making comparisons.

Data maps show the location of the data that are often represented using various colors. These maps are often used to show voting and demographic patterns.

Diagrams are not used to show data, but instead excel at showing processes and relationships.

Another example of a diagram would be an organization chart that allows your students to see at a glance relationships that might otherwise be difficult to put into words.

Illustrations or paintings resemble what they represent and can be very useful if they are large enough to be seen by your audience. You will need to have some sort of easel available to hold the artwork or the print so that you can point out necessary details while you are speaking.

Photographs are extremely powerful and can show people, places, and things with immediacy and clarity.

Films, videos, and animation can also be a great way to engage the interest of your students.

Objects are often required when you wish to demonstrate something. Make sure that your object is large enough to be seen by your students. However, if your object is too large, it may not be feasible to use in a classroom. If the actual object cannot be brought to the classroom, perhaps a model of the object can be built or located.

While using models during a lecture, make sure that they are truly representative of the subject and that they are made to scale. The model must be easy to see and understand.

(Continued)

The kind of presentation aid you choose can be created and displayed using a variety of techniques. Typically your aid will be print or screen based.

Printed materials could include posters, paintings, or photographic enlargements.

Poster presentations are common at conferences and trade shows where presenters speak to small groups of people often in a question-and-answer format. If a poster, painting, or photograph is appropriate for your situation, make sure it is large enough to be seen by your students and that you avoid blocking their view.

Make sure your poster is designed carefully—a poorly designed poster will damage your credibility. Unless you are skilled at illustration or drafting, it is probably best to create your printed materials using computer-based tools.

Most of the time you will be creating and then presenting your visuals using a computer. Specialized presentation software like Microsoft PowerPoint and Apple Keynote make some of the most common visual forms relatively easy to construct.

Your electronic presentation can include text, data graphics, illustrations, photographs, and video—all in one integrated package.

You can choose a pre-designed theme that give you a head start on the design process and ensure that the look is consistent. From there, you can make choices about the basic layout of each slide in your presentation. Now, you add any textual content that you require such as a table. If you know in advance what your information is, it is easy to create just the right amount of table cells.

Bulleted lists are extremely easy to create—just be sure you don't overdo it.

Depending on which version of PowerPoint you are using you will be entering data into either Microsoft Excel or Microsoft Graph. When you enter data into the spreadsheet, the changes are reflected back in PowerPoint. If you use Apple Keynote on a Macintosh, the data is entered from within the program—though the process is very similar. Once the data is entered, you can try out different kinds of graphs. Make sure you are using the graph that is most appropriate for your content.

Both PowerPoint and Keynote have basic drawing tools that make it relatively easy to create diagrams. Depending on your software version, you may even have some pre-drawn templates that you can customize with your own text or photos.

As long as your photos are in digital form, they are very easy to include in your presentation. By clicking and dragging you can find just the right size and position for your photos.

The same is true for digital videos, though there are some pitfalls to be aware of. There are many different video formats and codes and it is possible that what plays on your machine will not play on another computer. Also, make sure your clips are relatively short. Most modern computers have rudimentary video-editing tools that will allow you to shorten longer clips. You could even shoot a video segment using your cell phone or digital camera to use in your presentation. Just make sure to hold the camera very steady and edit out any unnecessary footage.

Modern software allows you to integrate several visual forms with relative ease, but there are a few design principles to consider.

Contrast, repetition, alignment, and proximity are four things to keep in mind while you create your presentation aids.

Contrast means that if things are not similar, then make them very different. For example, color contrast. Black text on a dark blue background isn't very legible because there is not enough contrast. The color values are too similar. Likewise, size contrast—some information is more important than others and should thus be larger. Titles should be larger than bullets, which in turn are larger than captions. Font contrast—some information is of a different kind and could be represented using a different font. When Bryan is reviewing his speech, he refers back to his attention getter, which is a quote. Notice that he chose a script font to set it apart from his main points.

The next principle is repetition. This principle is about consistency. Consistent background colors as well as font choices and sizes are some of the things you should consider. Once you've chosen a font, size, and color for titles, bullets, captions, or quotes, then stick with your choices. If you suddenly change the look and feel of your presentation, it will be jarring to your students and chances are they will start thinking about the visual changes rather than your message.

Paying close attention to alignment means placing elements on the page or screen deliberately and not haphazardly. Text blocks such as captions should align with the strong lines of digital photos to create a connection between the two elements. Try to ensure that everything that gets placed aligns with something else in your design. This will clean up a messy visual in a hurry!

Proximity means placing things that belong together near one another. The physical closeness creates an association in the minds of your audience. If two or more elements don't belong together, then spread them out to avoid creating an association that should not exist.

After you have placed everything into your design, check to make sure that you have considered these principles. The more things you can point out and recognize, the better your visual will be.

Now that your lecture has been written and your presentation aids have been created, it is time to stand and deliver.

You should be able to maintain eye contact with the students and avoid obstructing their view of the presentation aid. In addition, you need to be able to point confidently to the presentation aid and explain the necessary concepts.

Timing is important. After you have used the aid, it should be removed. Do not display the next aid until you are ready to use it. If you are using an older technology such as an overhead projector, turn it off until you are ready to show your next overhead. If you are using PowerPoint or Keynote, you can hit "B" on the computer keyboard to "blank" or "black-out" the screen.

issues to consider when using such technology. First, technological advances "are resulting in pressure being placed on instructors to become technologically literate" (Hunt & Lippert, 1999, p. 65). To support faculty in their use of technology in the classroom, many educational institutions have computer labs with staff ready to assist in this area. Second, technology should be used as an aid to instruction, not as the instruction itself. In other words, teachers should not make a decision to lecture merely because they have the technology to do so. Rather, the technology should be used to supplement other forms of instruction, including the lecture. Researchers have found that students, especially students whose native language is not English, tend to react favorably to instructors' use of technology in the classroom (Atkins-Sayre, Hopkins, Mohundro, & Sayre, 1998; Downing & Garmon, 2001; Sammons, 1995) when it is used appropriately.

For more information on using presentation media effectively, instructors can consult texts such as *Looking Good in Presentations* (Joss, 1999), which are written specifically for these purposes. Finally, research has shown that the effective use of technology in the classroom helps teachers teach and students learn (Balli & Diggs, 1996; Hunt & Lippert, 1999). What more reason do we need to become more technologically literate?

Organize the Lecture

Most teachers agree that an organized lecture is better than an unorganized lecture. In her review of research on direct instruction, Anderson (1986) reports that several studies indicate the importance of organization to an effective lesson. Brophy and Good (1986) summarize principles for lesson organization:

> Achievement is maximized when teachers not only actively present material, but structure it by beginning with overviews, advance organizers, or review

of objectives; outlining the content and signaling transitions between lesson parts; calling attention to main ideas; summarizing subparts of the lesson as it proceeds; and reviewing main ideas at the end. Organizing concepts and analogies helps learners link the new to the already familiar. Overviews and outlines help them to develop learning sets to use rule-example-rule patterns and internal summaries tie specific information items to integrative concepts. Summary reviews integrate and reinforce the learning of major points. (p. 362)

A lecture has a general organization of introduction, body, and conclusion. The body can be organized according to several patterns. First let's examine the purposes and types of introductions and conclusions.

THE INTRODUCTION   of your lecture should accomplish the following four purposes:

Gain Student Attention.   If students are not attending to what's being said, they cannot learn it. Thus, the introduction must grab them and make them want to listen to the rest of the lecture. An **attention getter** is a strong opening statement that uses some kind of creative device to capture your student's attention and motivate them to listen. There are several creative strategies to choose from. You could ask a series of questions, provide a quotation, make a startling statement, describe a scenario, tell a story, use humor, or refer to a recent event. It is important to note that the attention getter should create interest and be relevant to your students and the content you are teaching.

Set the Scene.   The introduction should provide a framework for your lecture. Providing a framework (sometimes known as **set induction)** allows the students to understand how the current information fits in the context of the overall course. What did you cover last time that relates to the material you will cover today? What has been happening in class and how does this information build on previous skills or knowledge we have obtained? In addition, students should know why what you have to say is important—why they need to know the content you'll cover.

State the Instructional Objective.   What will the students be able to do when your lecture is complete? Remember that **instructional objectives** may be based on local, state, or national standards. It is important to state these objectives for your students so that they can self-assess their progress in the class. If, at the end of the lecture, they do not feel confident in having accomplished this objective, they will know to ask questions for clarification.

Preview the Lecture.   In addition to stating your instructional objectives, you will want to **preview** the information you will cover. What are your main points and in what order will you cover them? This will give students an overview of the material and allow them to mentally organize the lecture. This may also help students know how to take notes for study purposes.

THE CONCLUSION   The conclusion to the lecture should accomplish two purposes:

Give an Overview.   Too often we confuse coverage of content with learning. Student exposure to the subject and student learning of the subject are not synonymous. Students need to be reminded of what it was they were to learn from the lecture. This is easily done by summarizing your main points and how they helped you accomplish the instructional objective.

Provide a Sense of Closure.   Avoid false endings. It is frustrating for students to believe that you're finished and then have you add "just one more point." In addition to a summary, you might also want to conclude your lecture with a quotation, an example, or any of the methods of introduction discussed earlier. One good technique is to refer back to your introduction. This helps tie your lecture together, making it a complete package. You may also want to explain how this content will provide a framework for what you will be doing next in class.

THE BODY   The main points of the **body** of your lecture can be arranged according to several patterns. You could organize your lecture using a time sequence, a spatial arrangement, or by subtopic. This organizational pattern will dictate the arrangement of your main points. Again, the instructional objective is directly supported by the main points in the body of the speech, which are bolstered by supporting material.

In this section we explore several strategies for organizing the main points in the body of the speech. Given that the main points will form the core of your speech, you must carefully select the key ideas you will focus on and arrange them in a logical fashion.

There are several factors that will influence your choice of an organizational pattern. Initially, you should pick a method of organizing the lecture that is consistent with your objective, your topic, and your students.

If you use a **chronological pattern**, your main points will follow a time sequence. This pattern is appropriate if you want to inform your students about a series of events as they occurred. You can organize your main points chronologically by either addressing events in time from present to past or from past to present. You can also use the chronological pattern if your goal is to demonstrate how to do something or explain a process.

Ideas can also be organized based upon spatial relationships. Specifically, the **spatial pattern** arranges ideas according to place or position. For example, if you teach music, you would use the spatial pattern for a lecture demonstrating the location of various parts on a guitar (e.g., headstock, fret board, bridge, pickups, etc.). This pattern is especially useful if your topic is geographical or involves the discussion of multiple physical spaces.

The **topical order** pattern organizes your speech by breaking your overall topic into smaller subtopics. In other words, each main point is a subtopic of a larger topic. For example, you may have categories of plants, types of tornadoes, or branches of government. Some additional ways that topics can be subdivided include lists, steps, functions, goals, dimensions, causes, effects, and so forth. Perhaps you can come up with some other ways to divide the topic you choose.

Remember, you can look at the textbook you are using to see how the authors have organized their thoughts with regard to your topic. Each time you think of a way to divide your topic to narrow it, you can take one of your divisions and narrow it even further until you come up with a focus to your topic that is manageable given your time limits.

Lectures using the causal pattern highlight the **cause-effect** relationships that exist among the main points. In this format, one of the main points is devoted to establishing causes and the other main point describes the effects. Given the versatility of this organizational pattern, you may also choose to proceed from effect to cause.

Finally, you may choose the **problem/solution pattern**. In this format, the first main point is devoted to establishing the problem. In the second main point, you'll introduce a specific plan and explain how it solves the problem.

The most often used organizational patterns are presented in Table 5.4. Examples of each are also provided. The important thing to remember about organizing the body of your lecture is that it should relate to the central idea of the lecture and the instructional objectives.

Now that we have discussed each of the elements of the lecture (the introduction, body, and conclusion), let's see how it all fits together. Table 5.5 shows a basic template for an outline of a lecture using all of the principles discussed so far in this chapter.

TABLE 5.4   Organizational Patterns for the Body of the Lecture

Type	Definition	Example
Chronological	A time sequence	In preparing a lecture, five sequential steps must be followed: choose a topic, narrow the topic, gather supporting materials, organize the lecture, deliver the lecture.
Spatial	Space relationships—moving systematically from east to west, front to back, center to outside, and so forth	Proxemic behavior differs across cultures. A "comfortable" distance between people as they converse differs. We'll examine this phenomena in the United States and Latin America. We'll then "fly across the ocean" and examine conversational distances of northern Europeans and southern Europeans. Finally, we'll examine the proxemic behaviors of Asians and Arabs.
Causal	Enumerating causes and moving to effects or enumerating effects and moving to causes	We all structure our own reality because we all perceive differently. Our perceptions differ because of differing environments, differing stimuli, differing sensory receptors, and differing internal states.
Problem-Solution	Describe the problem and present a solution	Researchers tell us that one of the major problems for people in the 1990s is developing and maintaining warm, personal relationships. The only way for us to solve this problem is to learn how to communicate effectively.
Topical	Topic provides its own organizational structure	Human communication consists of six components: interactants, message, channel, feedback, noise, and context.

TABLE 5.5 Template for Lecture Outline—Instructor Lesson Plan

I. Introduction
- **A.** Attention Getter—How will you capture the student's attention?
- **B.** Set Induction—What has been taking place in class prior to this lecture—Provide a framework or review here.
- **C.** Instructional Objective—What will the student be able to do when the lecture is completed? These may be based on local, state, or national standards.
- **D.** Preview—What are the major points to be covered?

II. Body (identify organizational structure here)
- **A.** Main point.
  - **1.** evidence (supporting material, could use any of these devices in any combination)
  - **2.** example
- **B.** Main point.
  - **1.** illustration of . . .
  - **2.** testimony of . . .
- **C.** Main point.
  - **1.** demonstration of . . .
  - **2.** example of . . .

III. Conclusion
- **A.** Summary of main points and instructional objective.
- **B.** Final closing sentence or preview to next class.

Practice the Lecture

In your first few attempts at presenting new content, you will want to be sure that the information is addressed in such a way that your students will not only listen but also understand. This might require that you practice the presentation to ensure that it is dynamic and meaningful. If you happen to have access to a trial audience that is similar in age to your students, you can ask them to give you feedback about your presentation. Did they understand the content, what questions would they ask, was it interesting, what other possible examples could be used that relate to this age group? Sometimes, a colleague who has taught the same age group may be willing to provide similar feedback. Having gone through a process such as this will give you the confidence you need to deliver content that is both interesting and appropriate to an intended audience.

Reading Objectives and Discussion Prompts

5.3 Preparing a Lecture

What do you know?
What are the steps to preparing a lecture?

What do you think?
Think of some ways that you can begin to collect content for your own classroom lectures. Where will you begin? Think of another lecture where you were the student. How was the lecture organized and developed?

DELIVER THE LECTURE

You're now ready to present your lecture. As we indicated earlier, a teacher's delivery can have a great impact on students' reactions to a lecture. If you are enthusiastic about your lecture material, that enthusiasm will come through in your delivery. An animated, enthusiastic delivery can greatly increase your students' desire to listen to you and, thus, enhance their learning.

Most classroom lectures are delivered extemporaneously, in other words, using brief notes so that you can maintain eye contact and a sense of connection with your students. This type of delivery is particularly effective for the lecture because it leaves you free to change your delivery in response to your students' reactions. You can rephrase and repeat ideas as necessary. In addition, your tone will be more conversational, because you must think about your ideas as you phrase them.

Effective delivery takes careful planning and practice. Five principles that should be useful to you are

1. *Think—really think—about what you're saying.* Speak ideas rather than simply reciting words.

2. *Communicate.* Think of your lecture as a dialogue, not a soliloquy. Talk with your students, not at them. This involves being direct and conversational and looking at your audience. Remember that it is not a group of empty chairs, but living students. Don't simply look at them—really see them and relate to them.

3. *Support and reinforce your ideas with your body, face, and voice.* Recall from Chapter 4 that we discussed the verbal and nonverbal characteristics of language. These principles can be applied to the delivery of your lecture. Studies indicate that a vocal variety is more effective for speaking than is a monotone. Your own experience no doubt supports this belief. A teacher who speaks in a monotone soon begins to make us weary. In addition, a monotone diminishes student comprehension and retention of what is said. To be an effective lecturer, then, you'll need to vary your verbal and nonverbal delivery. We'll provide a few reminders about verbal and nonverbal delivery as they relate to lectures here.

Vocal intensity refers to the loudness of your voice. A voice that is too loud or too soft is distracting. You should use loudness, just as you use pitch, to emphasize important thoughts. Remember too that a decrease in loudness can be just as effective for emphasis as can an increase in loudness. The important point here is that variety in intensity is important and you should strive for it.

Most beginning lecturers speak too fast or too slow. Their speech rate—the timing and pacing of their vocal delivery—is seldom varied. Research suggests that teachers who speak at a moderate rate are viewed by their students as more credible and clear than teachers who speak at a slow rate (Simonds, Meyer, Quinlan, & Hunt, 2006). One way to vary the rate of your speech is through the use of the pause. Pauses "punctuate" a speaker's thoughts just as commas, periods, and semicolons punctuate written discourse.

Oral punctuation—the pause—helps students accurately interpret the messages you send. Pauses also allow students time to reflect on what they have heard and how the previous statements relate to one another. Finally, pauses provide emphasis that will aid in student retention as well as comprehension.

As a lecturer, don't be afraid to use the pause as a means of providing yourself time to gather your thoughts. If you need to reflect on where you are, do so. Remember that pauses seem much longer to you than they do to your students. Don't feel a need to fill your pauses with "uhs" or "ahs." Such vocalized pauses are very distracting.

In addition to vocal factors in delivery, you should also be aware of the visual factors of effective delivery. Your interest in your topic can be communicated by your posture, gestures, and facial expressions. Stand erect, poised, and relaxed. You'll look better and feel better. It is also easier to move from that position in order to emphasize ideas or signal variations in thought. Gestures should flow from your thoughts. Don't force them. Most of us use gestures naturally in our conversations. Patterned or mechanical gestures distract from, rather than complement what you're saying. The key here is to be natural.

Facial expressions also communicate much about your interest in the topic presented. A deadpan expression does not enhance your presentation. As we've suggested before, look at your audience. Eye contact and animated facial expressions are very important for generating interest and enthusiasm in your students. If you fail to look at your students, they, no doubt, will suspect you are unconcerned or ill at ease. If you don't have visual contact with your students, there is no way you can adjust to their feedback.

4. *Adapt to your students.* Watch for cues indicating that you need to change some aspect of your delivery—pace, volume, pitch, gestures, and so forth.

An interesting study examined the way in which students signal a lack of comprehension. In lecture classes students often ignored the problem of lack of comprehension. In fact, ignoring was found to be more prevalent in the lecture than in discussion or small-group formats. Indicating confusion (with either a quizzical look or some short expression such as "Huh?") and asking for elaboration were used less in the lecture than in the other two formats (Kendrick & Darling, 1990).

5. *Practice your delivery.* Those of you who are beginning teachers should practice your delivery. Practice "on your feet" and aloud. If possible, you should practice in the room in which you'll actually present the lecture. You might want to practice before a mirror in order to get an idea of the visual image you present or you may want to get some friends to listen to you. The advantage to the latter is that they can comment on how they view you. You might videotape your lecture. Or, if videotaping is not possible, at least audiotape your lecture.

Reading Objectives and Discussion Prompts

5.4 Deliver the Lecture

What do you know?
What are some principles to consider when delivering the lecture?

What do you think?
Think of a lecture where you were the student. How was the lecture delivered? What were the strengths or weaknesses of the delivery? What could have made the delivery stronger?

COMMUNICATION BARRIERS TO EFFECTIVE LECTURING

If you decide the lecture method is the most appropriate method for your particular objective, you should be aware of some general communication barriers to effective lecturing. Although there are several, the most common have been outlined by Hart (1973) and are presented in Box 5.2. You will want to refer to this information as you prepare your own classroom lectures.

One particular barrier to effective lecturing may be that you, the teacher, are highly communicatively apprehensive. The following section addresses this concern.

Communication Apprehension

Practically speaking, **communication apprehension** is a serious concern for educators. What exactly is communication apprehension and how extensive is it? The teacher with high communication apprehension is one who attaches high levels of punishment to the communication encounter (McCroskey & Richmond, 1991). The individual is fearful of communication and will go to great lengths to avoid communication

---

BOX 5.2

Barriers to Effective Lecturing

1. *Too much or not enough information is presented.*
2. *Information is presented too factually or too inferentially.*
3. *Information is too concrete or too abstract.*
4. *Information is too general or too specific.*
5. *Communication is feedback-poor or feedback-rich.*
   a. *Selective feedback*—monitor the reaction of one or two representative members of the class and use these responses to guide ongoing changes in your lecture.
   b. *Overt feedback*—many lecturers use the "if you don't understand something, sing out" technique. This is probably the most desirable type of feedback, but an instructor who uses such a technique had better mean it.
   c. *Delayed feedback*—setting up a feedback committee (which makes daily or weekly reports to the lecturer) is often a practical device. If the feedback group is representative of the class and insightful, it can be very helpful to you despite the delay in the feedback.
   d. *Indirect feedback*—asking a fellow instructor to attend and critique your lectures can often be helpful, because he is in a position to know what to look for.
   e. *Self-feedback*—with the advent of audio- and videotaping equipment, the lecturer has a new ally. By reviewing your own lecture in such a fashion, many important insights can be derived if you make a conscious effort to keep bias at a minimum. In addition, teachers need to monitor students' nonverbal feedback throughout the lecture. Too often teachers lecture, assuming they are being understood. Monitoring student nonverbal feedback and adjusting accordingly (clarifying, slowing down or speeding up the pace, providing an example) will add to the teaching potential of the lecture.
6. *Information is presented too rapidly or too slowly.*
7. *Information is presented too soon or too late.*
8. *Information is presented with too much or too little intensity.*

Adapted from Hart (1973, pp. 10–14).

situations, and when by chance or necessity he is placed in them, the teacher feels uncomfortable, tense, embarrassed, and shy. Thus, lecturing becomes a problem for some teachers.

The specific causes of communication apprehension are not known. Four explanations have been posited: genetic predisposition, skills acquisition, modeling, and reinforcement (Daly & Friedrich, 1981).

The **genetic predisposition** explanation for communication apprehension holds that certain genetic components such as sociability, physical appearance, body shape, and coordination and motor abilities may contribute to the development of communication apprehension. However, as is true with many research findings concerning inherited characteristics, the environment can either enhance or decrease the hereditary predisposition toward communication apprehension.

One may also develop communication apprehension because she fails to **acquire** the necessary **skills** for effective social interaction at the same rate as her peers. The person with high communication apprehension is slow to develop such necessary social skills as reciprocity, language use, referential communication skills, sensitivity to verbal and nonverbal social cues, interaction management skills, and the use of verbal reinforcers. A vicious cycle emerges: As the apprehensive individual continues to fall behind her less apprehensive (more skillful) peers, she develops more communication apprehension because of her lack of skills.

A third explanation for the development of communication apprehension involves **modeling**. If we as teachers are communication apprehensive, students may observe our behavior and then imitate that behavior.

The explanation most often set forth for the development of communication apprehension relates to the theory of **reinforcement**. If an individual receives positive reinforcement, he finds communication a desirable, rewarding experience. He will develop little if any communication apprehension. If, however, the individual has been taught to be "seen but not heard"—if he has not been reinforced for communicating— he will find communication an unrewarding, undesirable experience, and communication apprehension may be high.

As individuals progress through life, communication apprehension is self-fulfilling. As you recall from Chapter 2, a self-fulfilling prophecy is a prophecy that comes true because we expect it to come true. Individuals with high apprehension fear they won't succeed in social interactions. Consequently, they avoid interaction, and the avoidance results in the loss of valuable practice time in communicating. As a result, when the individual is placed in an interaction, she performs more poorly than others. This failure then reinforces the individual's apprehension. In short, the individual expects to fail, shapes her environment so that she does fail, and is more convinced than ever that communication is punishing.

Obviously, no single explanation—genetic predisposition, reinforcement, skills acquisition, or modeling—is probably sufficient to explain why an individual develops communication apprehension. Instead, all four explanations work together to explain the development of communication apprehension.

Approximately one in three teachers at the lower elementary level suffers from communication apprehension (McCroskey & Richmond, 1991). Teachers who are communication apprehensive may gravitate to lower grades because teaching younger children may be less threatening to them.

Although little research has been conducted on the effect of communication apprehension on teaching effectiveness, one fact seems clear: Teachers with communication apprehension prefer instructional systems that reduce the amount of student–teacher and student–student communication (McCroskey & Richmond, 1991). Research does suggest that teachers may have an impact on the development of communication apprehension. Based on their findings that students increase in communication apprehension as they progress through elementary school, McCroskey, Andersen, Richmond, and Wheeless (1981) tested two hypotheses:

1. That there is a higher proportion of teachers with high communication apprehension in the lower elementary grades (K–4) than at other grade levels.
2. That there is a higher proportion of teachers with high communication apprehension in the lower elementary grades (K–4) than there are teachers with low communication apprehension in those grades (p. 30).

Both hypotheses were confirmed. Thus, the researchers concluded that highly communication-apprehensive teachers may have an effect on the development of communication apprehension in their students.

Because teacher communication apprehension may have an impact on the way an instructor prepares and delivers a lecture, the concept of communication apprehension and its causes were discussed here. In Chapter 6, we discuss communication apprehension from the student's perspective. Chapter 6 addresses leading classroom discussion and how student levels of communication apprehension may affect their abilities or willingness to participate in such discussions. In addition, Chapter 6 also addresses treatments for communication apprehension that teachers can use when faced with the anxiety associated with planning and delivering lectures.

Reading Objectives and Discussion Prompts

5.5 Communication Barriers to Effective Lecturing

What do you know?
What are some communication barriers to effective lecturing?

What do you think?
Will teacher communication apprehension affect your ability to lecture? If so, what strategies can you use to manage your apprehension?

EVALUATING YOUR LECTURE SKILLS

In Appendix A, we discuss teacher evaluation in depth. Suffice it to say here that evaluation of your lecture skills by you, colleagues, and students can increase your teaching expertise. A sample lecture evaluation form follows on page 131. After presenting a lecture, ask your students to complete the form. In addition, videotape one of your lectures. View the tape with a colleague. Using the evaluation form, discuss your lecture, and ways to improve it, with your colleague.

In Sum

Lecturing has been described as "the process whereby the notes of the professor become the notes of the student without going through the minds of either" (Walker & McKeachie, 1967, pp. 13–14). If you consider the principles of information exchange, clarity, and intercultural concerns as you go through the steps of lecture preparation discussed in this chapter—choose a topic, narrow the topic, gather supporting materials, organize the lecture, and deliver the lecture—you should be able to make your lecture a communicative transaction with your students. Not only will your notes go through your mind but your students' minds as well!

Key Terms

Instructional Objective
Emotional States
Learning Styles
Cognitive Styles
Field Dependent
Field Independent
Advantages of Lecturing
Disadvantages of Lecturing
Supporting Materials

Presentation Aids
Introduction (Attention
    Getter, Set Induction,
    Instructional Objective,
    Preview)
Conclusion
Body (Chronological, Spatial,
    Topical, Cause-Effect,
    Problem/Solution pattern)

Communication
    Apprehension
Genetic Predisposition
Skills Acquisition
Modeling
Reinforcement

CHAPTER

6
Leading Classroom Discussions

OBJECTIVES

After reading this chapter, you should be able to:

- Consider the advantages and disadvantages of the discussion method.
- List the characteristics of the discussion method.
- Prepare and facilitate a discussion.
- Consider strategies for motivating student preparation for participation in discussions.
- Explain how student communication apprehension might affect willingness to engage in discussion.

Dr. Cooper shares the following about leading classroom discussions:

> I have a love-hate relationship with the discussion method of teaching. It's noisy, messy, and sometimes unnerving. It's always hard work, but exciting. I can't always predict exactly where the discussion will lead, nor am I always sure how to keep the discussion on track. Yet I want my students to participate actively in the teaching–learning process—ask more questions of me, themselves, and one another—and think critically and creatively. I am left with my frustrations about the method and my love of its outcomes. Most teachers I talk with share my feelings. Like me, many of them also love the challenge and the excitement of the discussion method.

In this chapter we suggest ways to plan the discussion and examine characteristics of the discussion method, placing special emphasis on question-asking skills and response styles. We also present some tools to encourage student preparation for participation in discussion as well as ways to evaluate your discussion skills. Before we begin our presentation on leading classroom discussions, we refer to suggestions for choosing this strategy as well as the advantages and disadvantages.

CHOOSING THE DISCUSSION METHOD

As is the case with any teaching method, there are times when the discussion method will be appropriate and other times when it will not be. Some of the first considerations in determining the discussion method's appropriateness are those parts of the classroom discussed earlier—you, the teacher; your students; and the educational environment. In addition to these considerations, the discussion method is appropriate when the teacher is striving to do the following:

- Use the resources of members of the group.
- Give students opportunities to work out ways to apply the principles being discussed.
- Get prompt feedback on how well the teaching objectives are being reached.
- Help students learn to think in terms of the subject matter by giving them practice in thinking.
- Help students learn to evaluate the logic of, and evidence for, their own and others' positions.
- Increase students' awareness of class readings and lectures, and help them formulate questions that require them to seek information from the readings and lectures.
- Gain students' acceptance of information or theories counter to their previous beliefs.

The discussion method, like all teaching methods, has **advantages** and **disadvantages**, listed next. When considering using the discussion method, it's important to think about these advantages and disadvantages and their relationship to your particular teaching objectives.

The advantages of the discussion method include:

- Two heads are better than one—more ideas, resources, and feedback are generated.
- It provides students practice in expressing themselves clearly and accurately.
- It helps students gain skill in defending and supporting their views.
- Discussions expose students to a variety of ideas, beliefs, and information different from their own.
- There are motivational effects—students enjoy the activity and feedback discussion provides.

The disadvantages of the discussion method are:

- It takes considerable time.
- Successful discussion requires that teachers and students possess discussion skills.

This strategy views the students as active agents in the learning process. With the discussion strategy, teachers must be willing to relinquish control and realize that students can share in the teaching responsibilities. Their experiences, examples, and knowledge may offer insights into the material to the teacher and other students. For example, in the course of the discussion, a student may offer a personal example of a certain concept that the teacher could not. This example, in turn, may help another student to internalize the information that might otherwise have been misunderstood.

Reading Objectives and Discussion Prompts

6.1 Advantages and Disadvantages of the Discussion Method

What do you know?
What are the advantages and disadvantages of the discussion method?

What do you think?
How will you decide when to use the discussion method in your own class? Are there certain subjects that lend themselves to the discussion method?

CHARACTERISTICS OF THE DISCUSSION METHOD

The discussion method is characterized by (1) experiential learning, (2) an emphasis on students, (3) a focus on critical thinking, (4) the use of questions, and (5) reactions to student responses. Let's examine each of these.

Experiential Learning

One of the major characteristics of the discussion method of teaching is that it is based on experiential learning. The underlying assumption of **experiential learning** is that students learn best when they are actively involved in the learning process—when students "discover" knowledge through active participation. Many scholars have discussed theories of active learning through involvement (Cegala, 1981; Chickering & Gamsen, 1987; Astin, 1984). Their view of learning depicts students as active participants, who must spend time preparing for class by relating the course material to themselves, and then ultimately sharing their knowledge and experience with others. In using the discussion method, a student's concrete, personal experiences are followed by observation, reflection, and analysis of these experiences. Cegala (1981) further suggests that students who are highly "involved" in the classroom also display higher levels of communication competence and should be rewarded for their participatory efforts.

Emphasis on Students

The second characteristic of the discussion method, and one that flows directly from the experiential learning characteristic, is the **emphasis on students**. Students are the focus of this method. It is their experiences that serve as the basis for the discussion. Although you—the teacher—must have specific objectives in mind and a general framework for reaching your objectives, student input determines the specific direction the discussion takes.

Focus on Critical Thinking

Much has been written recently about the importance of teaching **critical-thinking** skills. One can hardly pick up an education-related journal or magazine without coming across an article on the topic. A growing consensus reflected in these writings is that, although "the basics" are extremely necessary, students must also be competent thinkers (Mazer, Hunt, & Simonds, 2008). Too often, testing and accountability drive the educational system so that the main message communicated to students is that they should provide "the right answer." Paul (1986) contends that the right answer should not be the end product of education, but rather that an inquiring mind should show:

> A passionate drive for clarity, accuracy, and fair-mindedness, a fervor for getting to the bottom of things, to the deepest root issues, for listening sympathetically to opposite points of view, a compelling drive to seek out evidence, an intense aversion to contradiction, sloppy thinking, inconsistent application of standards, a devotion to truth as against self-interest—these are essential components of the rational person. (p. 1)

Use of Questions

The discussion method involves a questioning strategy. In advance of the discussion, you must prepare carefully sequenced questions in order to organize the discussion. In addition, you must be flexible and adapt your questioning strategy to the needs of the students as the discussion evolves. Student responses must be integrated into the discussion and student questions should be elicited.

You may be asking yourself, "What's so important about questions?" **Questioning** is, perhaps, the single most influential teaching practice because teacher questions promote student involvement and are central to the analysis and synthesis of ideas (Dillon, 1988, 1990, 2004). For example, notice that in this textbook there are a series of **reading objectives** and **discussion prompts** at the end of each major section. The first set of questions *(What do you know?)* are knowledge-level questions that ask about the content of the section. The second series of questions *(What do you think?)* are higher order in that they ask the students (in this case, you) to think about and prepare a contribution for class discussion. While the answers to the knowledge-level questions will all be the same, the answers to the higher-order questions will all be different based on the students' (yours and your classmates) experiences.

When we vary question levels, probe, rephrase, prompt, wait for student responses, ask process questions ("How did you get that answer?"), and stress students' understanding of meaning, we promote critical thinking. We challenge students to think, not simply to parrot back to us what we've taught or what they've read in the textbook.

Most educators agree that questioning skills are very important, but teachers in training receive little instruction in either the theory or the art of questioning (Collins, 1993). So, where do we begin? The best place is to return to **Bloom's Taxonomy**. Your questions, depending on how they are phrased, can require different levels of thinking. Table 6.1 indicates the levels and examples and typical question terms for each level.

TABLE 6.1   Levels of Cognitive Skills You Can Require of Your Students with Your In-Discussion Questions (Based on Bloom's *Cognitive Domain of the Taxonomy of Educational Objectives*)

Level	Key Words	Typical Question Terms
A. Knowledge: Questions that require simple recall of previously learned material Example: What are the components of Berlo's communication model?	Remember	1. Name 2. List, tell 3. Define 4. Who? When? What? 5. Yes or no questions: "Was . . . ?" "Is . . . ?" 6. How many? How much? 7. Describe, label, match, select
B. Comprehension: Questions that require students to restate or reorganize material in a literal manner to show that they understand the essential meaning Example: Explain Berlo's model in your own words.	Understand	1. Give an example 2. What is the speaker's most important idea? 3. What will the consequences probably be? 4. What caused this? 5. Compare (What things are the same?) 6. Contrast (What things are different?) 7. Paraphrase, rephrase, translate, summarize, defend
C. Application: Questions that require students to use previously learned material to solve problems in new situations Example: A Democrat and a Republican are discussing foreign policy. Where in Berlo's model of communication would you predict their communication will break down?	Solve the problem	1. Solve 2. Apply the principle (concept) to . . . 3. Compute, prepare, produce, relate, modify, classify
D. Analysis: Questions that require students to break an idea into its component parts for logical analysis Example: Here are four models of the communication process. How are the components of these models similar? How do they differ?	Logical order	1. What reasons does the author give for his conclusions? 2. What does the author seem to believe? 3. What words indicate bias or emotion? 4. Does the evidence given support the conclusion? 5. Break down, differentiate, distinguish

If one of our goals as teachers is to help students develop their cognitive abilities, we need to ask them questions that require higher-level cognitive processes than mere recall. In addition, higher-order questions require more student talk to answer, so student participation increases. Finally, we need to ask higher-order questions because such questions appear to have a positive effect on achievement. Deethardt (1974) and Redfield and Rousseau (1981) cite research indicating that a teacher's asking of higher-order questions has been linked to greater student achievement.

When you are structuring your classroom questions, remember that there's nothing inherently wrong with the lower-level questions of Bloom's Taxonomy. We need them to help guide students' thinking patterns and to help eliminate comprehension problems. Notice the questioning sequence in the following example and the role of lower-level questions in creating the sequence (Duke, 1971, p. 470).

Knowledge: When was *Lyrical Ballads* published?

Comprehension: Compare a poem by Wordsworth with one by Coleridge. What differences you find? What similarities?

Application: Does this particular poem show the characteristics of poetry as indicated by Wordsworth and Coleridge in the "Preface" to *Lyrical Ballads?* If so, how? If not, what are the differences?

Analysis: What would some journalists and writers of the nineteenth century attack in *Lyrical Ballads?*

Synthesis: From studying Wordsworth's poetry, what conclusions can you make about his beliefs?

Evaluation: Do you feel that the concepts of romanticism as expressed by Wordsworth and Coleridge are still affecting our modern literature? Explain.

Although the taxonomy is helpful in determining the level of cognitive process you are requiring of your students, it is not without limitations. Several important types of questions are omitted. For example, the taxonomy does not include questions that cue students on an initially weak response, in other words, the probing question. Questions such as "Why?" "Could you elaborate?" "Can you think of any other examples?" and "Doesn't that contradict what you said previously?" are all examples of probing questions.

Probing questions are important. A positive relationship exists between the frequency of teacher probing questions and the amount of student oral participation. In addition, a positive relationship exists between a teacher's probing and pupil achievement. Finally, probing questions are important in fostering critical thinking (Kurfill, 1988).

Also missing from the taxonomy are questions that stimulate a discussion atmosphere. For example, a question such as "Johnny, do you agree with _____?" encourages students to question one another—an idea we'll return to later in this chapter.

In Box 6.1, Davis (2004) suggests teachers develop an inventory of questions in order to balance the kinds of questions asked. As you begin to develop questions for your own classroom discussions, you may want to refer to this inventory as a model.

BOX 6.1

Inventory of Questions

Exploratory questions probe facts and basic knowledge: "What research evidence supports the theory of a cancer-prone personality?"

Challenge questions examine assumptions, conclusions, and interpretations: "How else might we account for the findings of this experiment?"

Relational questions ask for comparisons of themes, ideas, or issues: "What premises of *Plessy v. Ferguson* did the Supreme Court throw out in deciding *Brown v. Board of Education?*"

Diagnostic questions probe motives or causes: "Why did Jo assume a new identity?"

Action questions call for a conclusion or action: "In response to a sit-in at California Hall, what should the chancellor do?"

Cause-and-effect questions ask for causal relationships between ideas, actions, or events: "If the government stopped farm subsidies for wheat, what would happen to the price of bread?"

Extension questions expand the discussion: "How does this comment relate to what we have previously said?"

Hypothetical questions pose a change in the facts or issues, "Suppose Gregg had been rich instead of poor; would the outcome have been the same?"

Priority questions seek to identify the most important issue: "From all that we have talked about, what is the most important cause of the decline of American competitiveness?"

Summary questions elicit syntheses: "What themes or lessons have emerged from today's class?"

From Davis (2004, pp. 83–84).

Improving Classroom Questions

Let It Live
Never kill a question;
it is a fragile thing.
A good question deserves to live.
One doesn't so much answer it as converse with it,
or, better yet, one lives with it.
Great questions are the permanent
and blessed guests of the mind.
But the greatest questions of all
are those which build bridges to the heart,
addressing the whole person

No answer should be designed to kill the question.
When one is too dogmatic, or too sure,
one shows disrespect for truth
and the question which points toward it.
Beyond my answer there is always more,

more light waiting to break in,
and waves of inexhaustible meaning
ready to break against wisdom's widening shore.
Wherever there is a question, let it live!   (Frost, 1974, p. 31)

Your success in the discussion method of teaching will depend greatly on your ability to let questions "live." Listed in Box 6.2 are several guidelines to help you develop and improve your questioning skills. These guidelines will be extremely useful to you throughout your teaching career. You will want to reflect on them each time you decide to use the discussion method. As seasoned instructors, your authors still reflect on these guidelines to help keep students at the center of instructional discussions.

BOX 6.2

Guidelines for Questions

Have a commitment to questions.   Developing questioning skills is difficult. In order to really master the art, you have to be willing to give the time and effort required.

Write out a sequence of "major" questions.   Begin with knowledge-level questions and progress to evaluation level questions.

Have a clear purpose.   Why are you asking the question? What's the response you want?

Phrase questions clearly.   If students are unfamiliar with the words in the question, they cannot answer it even if they know the information being requested. In addition, teachers should ask only one question at a time.

Know your subject matter.   When you do, you can direct your energies to observing and directing students' mental processes rather than having to focus on your notes.

Keep all students on-task.   Because only one student answers a question at a given moment, there is the chance that other students may get off-task.

Don't answer your own questions.   When students learn you'll answer your own questions if they simply wait long enough, they'll wait you out. Wait for students to answer. Silence seems very frustrating to teachers, yet it is not only desirable but also necessary:

There will be some silence in any class,
Sometimes it may be just dead silence
with nothing happening.
This is a terrifying thing;
one can only ask the spirit to brood over it,
creating again,
repeating the first miracle,
turning nothing into something.
But there are other silences,
the silence of reflection,
of confession, or reaffirmation,
or, the silence of recognition,
affection, opposition,
or even the silence of struggle
and decision . . . . (Frost, 1974, p. 72)

(Continued)

Seat students in a semicircle.   Remember our discussion of seating arrangements in Chapter 4. The semicircle or horseshoe (U-shaped) arrangement encourages participation.

Ask probing questions   in order to

initiate a discussion, change the subject, or modify the direction.

lead a member toward a particular statement or generate a logical sequence of steps toward a conclusion.

clarify a statement, help a member make a succinct statement, establish whether listening was accurate, or permit a member to amplify statements.

probe for more information, generate a more extensive response, or turn the discussion back to a member or the group.

Guide the flow of the discussion   by asking questions in order to

suggest that the discussion might be wandering.

encourage consideration of the personal significance of a discussion and to relate it to members' individual frames of reference.

avoid working over the same issues without fruitful results and to assess the group's position, if any.

elicit a response when a conclusion or consensus is near, but no one is willing to state it, or to suggest that it's time to move on.

suggest that a group is not ready to act.

get a student to take the initiative if the group is experiencing a momentary lull.

Finally, respond in a way that fosters the discussion process.

Reaction Styles

Much research suggests that how we **react** to students will stifle or enhance the discussion process. For example, students who perceived the greatest amount of support for their discussion efforts were more motivated and active in the learning process (Karabenick & Sharma, 1994; see also, Aitken & Neer, 1993; Andersen & Nussbaum, 1990; Auster & MacRone, 1994; Nadler & Nadler, 1990). Listed in Box 6.3 are several pragmatic suggestions to help you react appropriately to your students and thus encourage their participation. As with all the boxes provided in this text, you will want to visit these suggestions early and often throughout your teaching career.

BOX 6.3

Reacting to Student Responses

1. *React to student answers positively and constructively.*
2. *Accept and develop students' feelings.* Feelings are real. Demonstrate verbally and nonverbally that you are receiving the message and that you are interested in it. Gauge when to pursue students' feelings and when to take no action. Here, you as the professional must make the decision based on your knowledge of the student.
3. *Praise rather than criticize.*

4. *Encourage.* When you encourage, you are demonstrating your belief in the student and her ability.

5. *Use active listening.* How many times do we hear and not listen? (See Chapter 3.)

6. *Encourage student input.* First, don't talk most of the time. From our own experience, we have found this is a most difficult task to accomplish. Second, redirect questions to students, rather than simply answering questions directed toward you. Third, comments such as "What do the rest of you think about that?" or "Does anyone have something they'd like to add?" encourage student input.

7. *Metacommunicate.* Communicate about your communication. Make sure that you and the student both understand what's being said.

8. *Accept student mistakes.* Accept the mistakes without reprimanding, but focus on why the student made the mistake.

9. *Use a variety of responses.* Beginning teachers often ask, "What do I do if no one answers my question or if the answer given is wrong?" Too often beginning teachers give a one word response such as "Good" or "Right" if a student's answer is correct. The following list suggests a variety of responses for various situations.

   a. When the student's answer is correct:
      • Praise the student.
      • Restate the correct response as given by the student.
      • Modify the answer, if necessary, while maintaining the student's original idea.
      • Apply the student's answer to some situation.
      • Compare the student's response to something in the text, something already discussed, or some similar, concurrent event.
      • Summarize the response to draw a conclusion or to make a point.
      • Call on another student to agree, disagree, or build on the original answer.

   b. When the student's answer is incorrect:
      • Support the student's answer while saying the response is incorrect, as in, "Good try, John, but that's not the correct answer."
      • Rephrase the question.
      • Provide additional information for the student's use.
      • Probe the student's response for a route to the correct answer.
      • Consider the following:
        "What do you mean by _____?"
        "Can you give me an example of _____?"
        "How does that relate to the problem or issue?"
        "All of your answer depends on the idea that _____?"
        "Why did you base your answer on this rather than _____?"
        "What are your reasons for saying this?"
        "Can you be more specific?"
        "Let me see if I understood you. Do you mean _____?"
        "Could you explain your answer further?"
        "Can you rephrase you answer?"
        "What I heard you say was _____? Is that what you meant?"
        "Pattie, do you agree with the answer Bruce just gave?"
        "Let me rephrase the question. Now, what do you think?" (Eleser, Longman, & Steib, 1996, p. 3)

   c. When the student's response is "I don't know":
      • Urge the student to try to answer.
      • Restate the question.

(Continued)

- Rephrase the question.
- Redirect the question to another student.
- Ask the student what part of the question is unclear or if she can answer part of the question.

10. *Encourage quiet students.*

Assign a small specific task to a quiet student.

Reward infrequent contributors with a smile.

Bolster students' self-confidence by writing their comments on the board.

11. *Discourage students who monopolize the discussion.*
If only the dominant students raise their hands, restate your desire for greater student participation: "I'd like to hear from others in the class."
Avoid making eye contact with the talkative.
If one student has been dominating the discussion, ask other students whether they agree or disagree with that student.
If the monopolizer is a serious problem, speak to him after class or during office hours. Tell the student that you value his participation and wish more students contributed. Point out that learning results from give-and-take and that everyone benefits from hearing a range of opinions and views. (Davis, 2004)

12. *Provide wait time.* Wait time is the amount of time the teacher waits for a response after asking a question. When students are asked a question, they must go through a series of steps before responding. They must attend to the question, decipher its meaning, generate a covert response, and generate an overt response. To expect students to do this in 1 to 3 seconds is unrealistic.

Reading Objectives and Discussion Prompts

6.2 Characteristics of the Discussion Method

What do you know?
What are the characteristics of the discussion method?

What do you think?
Think about your own philosophy of teaching. How will these characteristics inform your philosophy?

PLANNING THE DISCUSSION

There are many reasons to engage in class discussion. You may want to discuss a class reading, debrief an activity, decide on a classroom or community policy, or solve social problems. What is important with this strategy is that students have something to discuss. That is, they have some shared content knowledge (class reading, experiential activity, current policies, or social issue) to serve as the impetus for discussion. Once you can determine that students share this knowledge, higher levels of learning can take place via the discussion. We will discuss ways to motivate students to come to class prepared to participate in the discussion later in this chapter.

A discussion, like a lecture, should have an **introduction**, a **body**, and a **conclusion**.

The Introduction

The introduction of the discussion should create attention in the students. It should motivate them to want to discuss the topic or idea. In addition, it should clarify the purpose of the discussion. In other words, it should preview the main points to be covered. Also, it should create a need to know in students by explaining the importance and relevance of the topic to them.

The Body

Planning the body of the discussion is somewhat different from planning the body of a lecture. The emphasis for the teacher should not be "What am I going to say?" but rather "What questions can I ask that will enable my students to meet the objectives?" Thus, the pattern will be developed by your (and your students') use of questions and responses rather than by your explanations, examples, and so forth. In other words, you and your students share in the development of the body of the discussion.

The Conclusion

The main purpose of the conclusion is to tie the entire discussion together. Often students leave a discussion session saying things such as, "That was interesting, but I'm not exactly sure what I was supposed to get out of it." As a teacher, you need to summarize the major ideas developed in the discussion. You might also preview how the knowledge learned will relate to topics to be discussed in upcoming lessons.

FACILITATING THE DISCUSSION

Dr. Simonds shares the following story:

> I remember a professor who asked us to read an article and come to class prepared to talk about it. He asked a question and a student answered. The professor responded, "No, you're wrong." The discussion halted and the professor continued to lecture about why the student was wrong. We never had another discussion in that class.

Figure 6.1 provides a **facilitation model** for leading classroom discussions developed by one of your authors, Dr. Simonds.

In general, start discussions with a **structure** move. That is, set the knowledge base for the question. What do students need to know in order to answer the question? This is when you reference answers to the reading objectives so that students can elaborate with their own ideas and experiences. For example, to start a discussion on the first reading objective in this chapter, you might say, "The text mentions several advantages and disadvantages of the discussion method." Next, **solicit** a student response by asking the question. To extend our example you might ask "How will you as a teacher decide when this method will be appropriate in your own

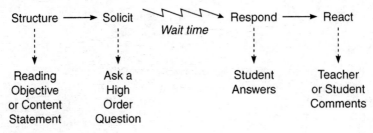

FIGURE 6.1 Facilitation Model.

From B. Simonds, C. Simonds, and S. Hunt. (2005). *Leading Instructional Discussions*—video. Prentice Hall.

class?" Remembering Bloom's Taxonomy, ask questions that require higher levels of thinking. Limit knowledge-level questions so that students do not feel that they are being quizzed. Try to ask questions that don't necessarily have a correct or incorrect answer. Rather, ask questions that require students to provide opinions, experiences, and so forth. **Wait**. One of the most difficult things for you to do will be to wait. After asking a question, silence can be quite uncomfortable, but if you think about it, a higher-order question requires time for students to prepare an answer. Hopefully, students will **respond** to your questions with extended and insightful answers.

Whatever you do, avoid answering your own questions. Students can become quite adept at waiting you out. Once a student has responded, **react** positively to the student's response. The nature of this reaction will determine the future success or failure of the discussion. As a student, how likely would you be to contribute to a discussion if your teacher reacted like the professor in Dr. Simonds's example earlier? Remember that you do not always have to be the one to react to a student response. Other students can build on contributions as well. Also, be sure that all students get to respond to a question. In other words, do not let questions die before all students get to contribute with a particular line of discussion.

Once you've reacted positively to a student's response, allow other students either to react to the student's response or to provide a response of their own. This process should continue until you believe that all students have had an opportunity to share with regard to the original question, or until the discussion gets off track, whichever comes first. Once this process is complete for the first question, move on to the next question.

Reading Objectives and Discussion Prompts

6.3 Planning and Facilitating the Discussion

What do you know?

What are the three major sections of the discussion? What are the steps in facilitating the discussion?

What do you think?
How is facilitating a discussion different from delivering a lecture? As a teacher, how will you prepare for this?

MOTIVATING STUDENT PREPARATION FOR PARTICIPATION IN CLASS

The success of the discussion depends not only on your use of questions and responses, but also on students being prepared to participate. How do we get them to do that? Rattenborg, Simonds, and Hunt (2005) discuss ways you can prepare students to become active members of class discussion using two particular tools: reading objectives and discussion prompts. These are modeled in this textbook. **Reading objectives** act as a framework for the daily instructional discussion. They serve as the content knowledge that students and the instructor share so that higher-order questions can be asked in a discussion. **Discussion prompts** challenge students to think beyond the text and allow them to plan possible contributions (ideas, examples, or questions) for the discussion. These instructional strategies are especially helpful for communicatively apprehensive students, because they can carefully plan out their contributions ahead of time. The strategies are also useful for students who may not be accustomed to taking an active role in class sessions.

Instructors should prepare higher-order questions that will go beyond the questions posed by the reading objectives and allow students to share their discussion prompts. In other words, class time should not be spent having students answer the reading objectives; rather, higher-order questions should be asked to extend the thinking of the class beyond the knowledge that reading-objective answers provide. Remember to start with reading objectives to form the knowledge base you want to extend. Given that the students know this information, what higher-order questions can you ask to get them to talk about it further? Once you ask the question and students respond, you now need to decide how to or who should react to those responses. In other words, you need to consider how you will facilitate the discussion.

Recall from the facilitation model in Figure 6.1 that discussions should start with a structure move. That is, set the knowledge base for the question. What do students need to know in order to answer the question? Again, this is where reading objectives and discussion prompts come in. Students consider the content of the reading objective and extend their thinking by planning a dialogue with the material, providing an example, or asking a question. They can then use these extensions to plan a contribution in class.

You should take time after the class session to review student answers to the reading objectives to ensure they are correct and to provide constructive feedback on the discussion prompts. This is an opportunity to dialogue with students about their personal examples and insights and to clarify any questions students may still have about the course material. In turn, students can use these materials as a review guide for their exams.

The discussion strategy focuses on student experiences as they relate to course content. In addition, reading objectives and discussion prompts allow students opportunities to practice communication in the classroom. They read the content, answer questions, think about the material, and prepare contributions for class. When they get to class, they have opportunities to contribute and articulate as well as defend their ideas. The goal of using these tools is to change the way students spend time out of class, which will have implications for what students do in class—talk rather than just listen. Hopefully, this will enable students to appreciate their responsibility in the learning process. To do so, students need to accept their role in the discussion process. Deemer (1986, p. 4) suggests teachers distribute a list of participation principles to students:

- I am critical of ideas, not people. I challenge and refute the ideas, but I do not indicate that I personally reject them.
- I focus on coming to the best decision possible, not on winning.
- I encourage everyone to participate.
- I listen to everyone's ideas even if I don't agree.
- I restate what someone has said if it is not clear to me.
- I first bring out all ideas and facts supporting all sides, and then I try to put them together in a way that makes sense.
- I try to understand all sides of the issue.
- I change my mind when the evidence clearly indicates that I should do so.

Tiberius (1990) also recommends several strategies students should follow in order to make discussions productive:

- Seek the best answer rather than trying to convince other people.
- Try not to let your previous ideas or prejudices interfere with your freedom of thinking.
- Speak whenever you wish (if you are not interrupting someone else, of course), even though your idea may seem incomplete.
- Practice listening by trying to formulate in your own words the point that the previous speaker made before adding your own contribution.
- Avoid disrupting the flow of thought by introducing new issues; instead, wait until the present topic reaches its natural end; if you wish to introduce a new topic, warn the group that what you are about to say will address a new topic and that you are willing to wait to introduce it until people are finished commenting on the current topic.
- Stick to the subject and talk briefly.
- Avoid long stories, anecdotes, or examples.
- Give encouragement and approval to others.
- Seek out differences of opinion; they enrich the discussion.
- Be sympathetic and understanding of other people's views.

In Chapter 5, we discussed how teacher communication apprehension might affect the lecture process. Because student communication apprehension may affect student participation in the discussion method, it is important to address at this point.

Reading Objectives and Discussion Prompts

6.4 Motivating Students

What do you know?

What are some strategies for motivating students to participate in class discussion?

What do you think?

Think of a discussion where you, as a student, participated. How did you feel? How did you prepare? How will you motivate your own students to participate?

STUDENT COMMUNICATION APPREHENSION

The presence of highly apprehensive students can baffle even the best teacher. There's nothing more disheartening than a student who has something worthwhile to contribute but, because of **communication apprehension**, is both unwilling and fearful of sharing that knowledge with others.

The low communication-apprehensive student presents quite a different picture. She is generally perceived as a high interactor, mature, independent, self-assured, assertive, competitive, talkative, determined, decisive, open-minded, and tolerant of ambiguous or uncertain situations. She enjoys people, is chosen for leadership, has a high need to achieve, sees herself as being in control of her own life, seeks occupations requiring a large amount of communication, and has high self-esteem.

Research indicates that highly communication-apprehensive students interact less frequently (Allen & Bourhis, 1996; Ericson & Gardner, 1992; Hawkins & Stewart, 1991; Neer, 1992; O'Mara, Allen, Long, & Judd, 1996). In addition, highly apprehensive students:

- Do not assume positions of leadership in groups.
- Do not volunteer to participate in classroom question-and-answer sessions.
- Drop classes requiring a large amount of communication.
- Are perceived by teachers as having less likelihood of success in almost every subject area regardless of intelligence, effort, or academic ability.
- Have low self-esteem.
- Express a preference for seating arrangements that inhibit communication interaction.
- Have lower grade point averages (GPAs) and score lower on student achievement tests than low communication-apprehensive students.
- Are more likely to drop out of school.
- Generally avoid classroom discussions.

Identifying the Highly Communication-Apprehensive Student

The first step in identifying the highly communication-apprehensive student is observation. Reexamine the characteristics of this type of student. If you have a student who exhibits several of these characteristics, he may be a highly communication-apprehensive person. You might also use an independent observer, such as your principal, speech therapist, or another teacher, to share their observations of your students with you.

You can also administer the Shyness Scale (SS) to your students (see Table 6.2). The scale can be administered orally if students are in the lower elementary grades.

TABLE 6.2   Shyness Scale (SS)

The following fourteen statements refer to talking with other people. If the statement describes you well, circle "YES." If it describes you somewhat, circle "yes." If you are not sure whether it describes you or not, or if you do not understand the statement, circle "?". If the statement is a poor description of you, circle "no." If the statement does not describe you at all, circle "NO." There are no right or wrong answers. Answer quickly; record your first impression.

1. I am a shy person.
YES   yes   ?   no   NO

2. Other people think I talk a lot.
YES   yes   ?   no   NO

3. I am a very talkative person.
YES   yes   ?   no   NO

4. Other people think I am shy.
YES   yes   ?   no   NO

5. I talk a lot.
YES   yes   ?   no   NO

6. I tend to be very quiet and listen in class.
YES   yes   ?   no   NO

7. I don't talk much.
YES   yes   ?   no   NO

8. I talk more than most people.
YES   yes   ?   no   NO

9. I am a quiet person.
YES   yes   ?   no   NO

10. I talk more in a small group (3 to 6) than others do.
YES   yes   ?   no   NO

11. Most people talk more than I do.
YES   yes   ?   no   NO

12. Other people think I am very quiet.
YES   yes   ?   no   NO

13. I talk more in class than most people do.
YES   yes   ?   no   NO

14. Most people are more shy than I am.
YES   yes   ?   no   NO

Scoring:

YES = 1; yes = 2; ? = 3; no = 4; NO = 5.

To obtain your SS score, complete the following steps:

Step 1. Add the scores for items 1, 4, 6, 7, 9, 11, and 12.

Step 2. Add the scores for items 2, 3, 5, 8, 10, 13, and 14.

Step 3. Complete the following formula: Shyness Score = 42 (minus) total from Step 1 (plus) total from Step 2.

Your score should be between 14 and 70.

Scores above 52 indicate a high level of shyness. Scores below 32 indicate a low level of shyness. Scores between 32 and 52 indicate an average level of shyness.

Interpretation

If you scored above 52, it is likely that you are shy and perhaps do not talk a lot. The higher your score, the more shyness you experience, and the less likely you are to be talkative. This suggests that you are quieter than most people. A high score does not necessarily mean that you are afraid to talk, but only that you prefer to be quiet in many circumstances when others would prefer to talk.

If you scored below 32, it is likely that you are not shy and probably talk a lot. The lower your score, the less shy you feel, and the more likely you are to be talkative. This suggests that you are more talkative than most people. A low score means that your own oral activity will dominate the activity of quiet children. You will need to be particularly careful not to be verbally aggressive or to expect your children to become as talkative as you are.

Scores within the moderate range (32 to 52) indicate that some situations might cause you to be shy. In other words, in some cases you might be quiet, and in other cases you might be verbally active.

Your score on the SS should give a fairly good indication of your normal oral activity level. If your score is incongruent with your own perceptions of your behavior, however, do not necessarily accept it at face value. Talk to someone whom you trust and who knows you well to see if your acquaintance thinks that the scale is accurate. If you teach above the kindergarten to fourth-grade level, discuss shyness with your students to see if their perceptions of you confirm your score.

The SS can indicate which students will be highly verbal. Although little research has examined overly talkative children, they can be very frustrating to the classroom teacher. In addition, teachers must be careful when "toning down" overly talkative students in order to avoid causing communication apprehension (McCroskey & Richmond, 1991).

Helping the Highly Communication-Apprehensive Student

Although clinical approaches to reducing communication apprehension (systematic desensitization, cognitive modification, skills training, and visualization) have been found to reduce apprehension, such methods are rarely at the classroom teacher's disposal (see, for example, Ayres, Hopf, & Ayres, 1994; Whitworth & Cochran, 1996). Reinforcement—a method in which individuals are conditioned to talk more by a series of reinforcing events—has also been found to reduce apprehension and is more readily available to the classroom teacher.

Vary the task assignments for students with high and low communication apprehension. Booth-Butterfield's (1986) research suggests that students with high communication apprehension need more structured tasks than students with low communication apprehension. The more concrete the assignment for highly communication-apprehensive students, the better their performance will be.

In addition, some research suggests that students may benefit from working in small-group or interpersonal settings with acquaintances (Booth-Butterfield, 1988). If you are having a difficult time getting some students to participate early on, then you might consider grooming them by getting them to participate in smaller groups before reporting back to the class as a whole.

When talking to highly communication-apprehensive students about getting help for their apprehension, teachers should attempt to be private and personal, provide positive feedback before negative feedback, be specific rather than general about what needs to be worked on, and note that they are encouraging other students to seek help also (Proctor, Douglas, Garera-Izquierdo, & Wartman, 1994).

One of the best ways to help the communication-apprehensive student is to provide a friendly, nonthreatening classroom climate (Cooper & Galvin, 1983; Ellis, 1995). On the first day, make clear to students exactly what is expected of them. Set ground rules that foster communication (for example, "you don't 'cut down' another student's comment"). Engage in get-acquainted exercises (Friedrich & Cooper, 1999).

For example, you might use an exercise in which you and your students share your full name and the significance of it. The point is that the more practice students get participating in discussions, the more comfortable they will feel in doing so. Some students will need a little more encouragement and the suggestions provided in this chapter may help them along the way.

Finally, recent studies have examined communication apprehension and culture (see, for example, Bolls & Tan, 1996; Klopf, 1984; McCroskey & Richmond, 1990; Olaniran & Roach, 1994; Olaniran & Stewart, 1996; Richmond & Andriate, 1984). One general caution these studies suggest is that what appears to be communication apprehension in U.S. culture may not actually be communication apprehension when seen in students from other cultures. For example, Klopf (1991) suggests, "With a low inclination to talk, the [Japanese] student relies more on nonverbal behavior to communicate feelings . . . the student will be rated low as a friendly, attentive, contentious, animated, impression-leaving communicator" (p. 137). In general, Asians exhibit relatively low verbal output, cautious and indirect speech, periods of silence, low expressiveness, and lack of eye contact (Barnlund, 1975; Chou, 1979; Elliott, Scott, Jensen, & McDonough, 1981; Hall, 1977; Kendon, 1967; Kindaichi, 1975; Nakane, 1970; Schneider & Jordan, 1981), whereas persons in the United States tend to exhibit high verbal output, self-assertion, verbal and nonverbal expressiveness, and frequent, sustained eye contact (Barnlund, 1975; Elliott et al., 1981; Hall, 1992; Kindaichi, 1975; Suzuki, 1973).

Reading Objectives and Discussion Prompts

6.5 Student Communication Apprehension

What do you know?
How can you identify and help students with communication apprehension?

What do you think?
Does the discussion method make students more or less apprehensive?

EVALUATING YOUR DISCUSSION SKILLS

If we want to improve our discussion skills, we need to honestly evaluate ourselves. Several types of evaluation are available. First, make your own informal evaluation of the discussion. Did everyone contribute to the discussion? How much did you dominate the session? What was the quality of students' comments? What questions worked especially well? How satisfied did the group seem about the progress that was made? Did students learn something new about the topic (Davis, 2004, p. 72)?

Second, ask your students to make an informal evaluation of your discussion skills (see Table 6.3). Third, video record one of your lessons. View the recording and complete the evaluation form that follows. Have a colleague view the recording with you and also complete the form, and discuss.

TABLE 6.3   Evaluating Your Discussion Skills

I. Introduction to the lesson
    A. Attention gaining strategy was
       Successful _____ _____ _____ _____ _____ Unsuccessful
    B. Motivating strategy was
       Successful _____ _____ _____ _____ _____ Unsuccessful
    C. Preview was
       Successful _____ _____ _____ _____ _____ Unsuccessful
    Comments:

II. Questioning strategy
    A. Most questions were asked on the _____ level.
    B. Any probing questions asked?
    C. Did students ask questions of me? Of one another?
    Comments:

    Generally, my questioning behavior was
    Effective _____ _____ _____ _____ _____ Ineffective

III. Wait time
    A. Appropriate to question level
       Usually _____ _____ _____ _____ _____ Never

IV. Reaction style
    A. What did I do to create a supportive, responsive climate?
    B. What types of responses did I get?
    Comments:

    Generally, my responses were
    Effective _____ _____ _____ _____ _____ Ineffective

V. Conclusion
    A. Summary was
       Successful _____ _____ _____ _____ _____ Unsuccessful
    Comments:

In Sum

In this chapter we have examined the discussion method of teaching. We have stressed not only the mechanics of this method but also the attitude toward teaching necessary to use this method effectively. Gerhard Frost summarizes that attitude:

Deliver Us!

From classrooms	*rather than the needs of children;*
that creak and squeak	*from prison-houses*
rule-ridden and constrictive	*of artificiality and anxiety,*
defensive and rigid,	*where nothing breathes,*
reflecting the neuroses	*Good Lord,*
of adults	*deliver us!*

(Frost, 1974, p. 71)

Much research suggests that when students interact with one another in a cooperative way, achievement increases, student attitudes toward learning and teachers are more positive, and self-esteem and motivation increase. Discussion that encourages students to work together to solve problems and to talk through ideas fosters positive results (Johnson & Johnson, 2002).

If you follow the guidelines presented in this chapter, two phenomena will occur in your classroom.

- Student participation will increase. You'll foster a positive attitude toward discussion.
- Students will become questioning beings. Postman and Weingartner (1971) suggest, "Children enter school as question marks and leave as periods"

(p. 3). They'll remain question marks in an atmosphere that fosters their curiosity and creativity—in a classroom in which questions are encouraged.

One teacher describes the effect of following guidelines such as those presented here:

Since I changed my method of questioning, I've found that my students have changed their attitudes toward learning. This change, very subtle at first, is now quite startling. Students pay attention. They listen to each other and give answers that show they're thinking about what they're going to say. The quality of their questions has also improved. They seem to have a better understanding of concepts and are showing improvement on tests and written work.

Since I have become used to this new style, the amount of material I cover seems to be about the same now as it was in the past, although I must admit that when I was learning to use good questioning techniques, the process did take longer. (Schumaker, 1986, p. 37)

Perhaps the determinant of commitment to the discussion method is your self-concept as a teacher. You must feel comfortable enough to relinquish your control as the teacher and become a learning facilitator. When you encourage students to question you, themselves, and other students, everyone becomes a teacher. If you are a person who has a low tolerance for ambiguity and a high need for control, the discussion method is probably not for you.

Key Terms

Advantages of the
  Discussion Method
Disadvantages of the
  Discussion Method
Experiential Learning
Emphasis on Students
Critical Thinking
Questioning

Reading Objectives
Discussion Prompts
Bloom's Taxonomy
Probing Questions
Reaction Styles
Introduction
Body
Conclusion

Facilitation Model (structure,
  solicit, wait, respond,
  react)
Reading Objectives
Discussion Prompts
Student Communication
  Apprehension

CHAPTER

7

Small-Group Communication

OBJECTIVES

After reading this chapter, you should be able to:

- Discuss the advantages and disadvantages of the small-group method.
- Define small group.
- Discuss the teacher's role in small-group communication instruction.
- Describe various tasks that can be completed in small groups.
- Discuss the students' role in small-group communication.

> *No man is an Island, intire of itselfe; every man is a peece of the*
> *continent, a part of the main: if a Clod bee washed away by the Sea,*
> *Europe is the lesse, as well as if a Promonttorie were, as well as if a*
> *Mannor of thy friends or of thine owne were: any man's death diminishes*
> *me, because I am involved in Mankinds: And therefore never send to*
> *know for whom the bell tolls; It tolls for thee.*
>
> —JOHN DONNE

Much of our lives is spent in groups—family, peer, and professional groups. We are socialized and obtain our identity through our communication within groups. Much of what we learn about ourselves is learned through interaction in groups. We see our image of self mirrored by others in the small groups to which we belong. Because of the pervasiveness of groups in our lives, it's important that teachers provide their students with experiences in small-group communication. The more opportunities we provide students to "try out" behavior in small groups and to internalize the mirrored reactions of others to these behaviors, the more effective communicators our students can be.

In addition, research suggests that small-group work can enhance higher cognitive levels of analysis on the part of students (see research reviewed in Dougherty et al., 1995; Smagorinsky & Fly, 1993). Small-group work also helps students acquire content knowledge and persistence (continuing study of the content area) as well as motivation (Bruffee, 1998; Tinto, 1993). Before we proceed with this chapter, we'll discuss the advantages and disadvantages of using small-group communication as a teaching method.

The advantages and disadvantages of the small-group teaching method are similar to those of the discussion method. When considering use of the small group as a teaching method, keep these advantages and disadvantages in mind. Consider your students and your objectives, making sure that the method is appropriate to both.

Some **advantages** of the small-group method are:

- It enhances student motivation and fosters positive attitudes toward the subject matter; students enjoy working together in small groups.
- It develops students' problem-solving and decision-making skills.
- It enables students to share their ideas with other students for critiquing and comparison.

Some **disadvantages** of the small-group method include:

- It is time consuming.
- Students need to understand small-group communication processes for the method to be effective.

Reading Objectives and Discussion Prompts

7.1 Advantages and Disadvantages

What do you know?
What are the advantages and disadvantages of working in small groups?

What do you think?
Think of a small group that you have been a member of as a student. Was this group effective or ineffective? Why or why not?

DEFINITION OF A SMALL GROUP

Numerous definitions of **small group** exist. Most of these definitions stress the interactional nature of small groups: persons who communicate with one another often over a span of time and who are few enough that each person is able to communicate with all others, not indirectly, but face-to-face.

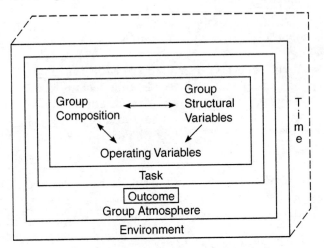

FIGURE 7.1   Rosenfeld's Model of the Small-Group Process.

From *Human Interaction in the Small Group Setting* by Lawrence Rosenfeld, p. 7. Copyright © 1973. Reprinted by permission of Prentice Hall, a division of Pearson Education.

After reviewing theories of small-group communication, Rosenfeld (1973) developed a general model of the small-group process that presents the relationship among the basic components of a small group. This model is presented in Figure 7.1.

According to the model, small-group processes occur across time and also change across time. Thus, small-group processes are dynamic, and the relationships among the components are constantly changing. **Group composition** consists of the members in the group—their attitudes, personalities, self-concepts, needs, and perceptions. Included also are group interaction variables, such as size and compatibility. **Group structural variables** are communication and attraction networks in the group. In other words, how do each of the members of the group interact with and cooperate with one another to get the task done? **Operating variables** are the roles, norms, and operating procedures of the group. The group—composition and structural and operating variables—exists within a framework consisting of four more variables: task, outcomes, group atmosphere, and environment. The **task** is the primary purpose of the group, the reason for the group's existence. The **outcome** is what the group accomplishes (quality, quantity, appropriateness, and efficiency of outcomes) and the group's satisfaction with the outcomes. This outcome, regardless of whether it's positive or negative, affects subsequent group interactions. **Group atmosphere** is the emotional climate of the group. The **environment is** both physical and social. It places limitations on the group that can either facilitate or hamper task accomplishment.

Note that Rosenfeld (1973) takes a transactional approach to examining groups. The model indicates that every component interacts with every other component. In addition, the perceptions and meanings of group members are considered important to the functioning of the group.

Reading Objectives and Discussion Prompts

7.2 Small Groups

What do you know?

What is a small group? What are the components of Rosenfeld's model of small-group processes?

What do you think?

Think about the subject and students you will be teaching. Do you think your students will need opportunities to work in small groups? Why or why not?

TEACHER ROLES

As we discussed previously, active learning has numerous positive outcomes. Yet, despite these, small-group work can be disastrous if the teacher does not set the stage for this work very carefully. Keep in mind that small groups can be used for the simple purpose of allowing students the opportunity to practice working in teams. Small-group tasks do not always have to be graded tasks. The remainder of this section focuses on the teacher's concerns and issues in using small-group instruction.

When using small groups as an instructional strategy, the teacher needs to understand that his role becomes one of an academic counselor and consultant (Joyce, Weil, & Calhoun, 2003). After initially presenting the small-group task, the teacher "responds to, rather than directly orchestrates, student activity" (Darling, 1990, p. 274). Darling also notes, what is "key here is the idea of **collaborative learning**—the 'heart and soul' of small group instruction" (p. 274).

Collaborative Learning

I was brought up in a traditional school setting, in which the roles of the teacher and students were clearly defined. The teacher bawled into our ears for fifty minutes, perhaps on the fox-hunting outfits in Silas Marner, and we took notes. Or the teacher demanded a 485-word essay—no fewer words—on "roadside beauty," and we students obliged. Later, when I began to teach, I did exactly the same thing. It was "teach as I was taught": the lessons were ground out, the desks were evenly spaced, a feet-on-the-floor atmosphere was maintained at all times. . . . About this time, I came upon the gospel of James Moffett. I was appalled. The man advocated a student-centered language arts curriculum, one in which students generated the ideas to be used in the classroom; one in which students taught each other through cross-teaching techniques; one in which the emphasis was on student cooperation and collaboration. The man was obviously a kook. Wouldn't my kids hoot and take advantage of the ensuing chaos? Wouldn't they tear each other up much worse than in their daily battles on the playground and in the halls? Terms like *cooperation* and *collaboration* weren't part of their vocabulary. And as for their teaching each other, wouldn't it be a case of the blind leading the blind? They didn't know a comma from a semiquaver. (Whitworth, 1988, p. 13)

In the preceding quotation, Richard Whitworth describes his trepidation about using collaborative learning. His description will be familiar to many teachers who "teach as they were taught." However, collaborative learning, the grouping and pairing of students for the purpose of achieving an academic goal, has been widely researched and advocated throughout the educational literature.

The collaborative learning method has been characterized as "a form of indirect teaching in which the teacher sets the problem and organizes students to work it out collaboratively" (Bruffee, 1984, p. 637). One of the basic features of collaborative learning is student talk. In fact, students are supposed to talk with one another as they work through various classroom activities and projects. Students assimilate their ideas and information through their talk. Thus, collaborative learning is a deliberate attempt to take advantage of differing viewpoints and perspectives through interaction of individuals and their ideas in a reciprocal or alternating action (Sills, 1988, p. 21). Merely putting students into groups, however, does not mean that collaborative learning is taking place. Specifically, "students put into groups are only students grouped and are not collaborators, unless a task that demands learning unifies the group activity" (Weiner, 1986, p. 55). They need guidance. As Golub indicates, the role of the teacher changes from "information giver" to "guide on the side" (1988, p. 5). The teacher is a facilitator whose role involves questioning, suggesting, and directing the discussion.

In sum, as Bruffee (1997) so aptly describes,

> The basic idea of collaborative learning is that we gain certain kinds of knowledge best through a process of communication with our peers. What we learn best in this way is knowledge involving judgment. We can sit by ourselves and learn irregular French verbs, benzene rings, the parts of an internal combustion engine, or the rhetorical devices which are useful in eloquent or effective prose. But when we want to know how to use this discrete knowledge—to speak French, to combine organic compounds, to find out why an engine won't start and then to fix it, or actually to write eloquent prose—we have to learn quite differently. . . . The best way to learn to make judgments is to practice making them in collaboration with other people who are at about the same stage of development as we are. (p. 103)

Johnson and Johnson (2002, p. 243) outline four elements necessary for effective collaborative learning:

- *Positive interdependence.*   There must be a clear structure to ensure that the group works together. In other words, the group must understand exactly what it is to accomplish.
- *Face-to-face interaction.*   The Johnsons refer to this as "eye-to-eye and k-to-k (knee-to-knee)." Students must sit looking at and facing one another.
- *Individual responsibility.*   Although the entire group learns collectively, each student must be responsible for some task. Too often, if this is not the case, one or more students may "go along for the ride," but not really contribute.
- *Appropriate interpersonal skills.*   The teacher should not assume that students know how to communicate in groups. Students need to be taught interpersonal skills such as paraphrasing, clarifying, listening, responding, agreeing, disagreeing, and so forth.

The values of collaborative learning are well established (see research in Bruffee, 1997; Dougherty et al., 1995; Qin, Johnson, & Johnson, 1995; Tinto, 1993). Collaborative learning promotes higher mastery, retention, and transfer of concepts. It promotes a higher quality of reasoning strategies than do competitive and individualistic structures. It promotes healthier cognitive, social, and physical development and higher levels of self-esteem. It results in more positive student–student relationships that are characterized by mutual liking; positive attitudes toward one another; and mutual feelings of obligation, support, acceptance, and respect.

The teacher may find that the collaborative learning method is not "neat and tidy" either in practice or in ease of assessing its outcomes. It is somewhat chaotic. However, as Berthoff (1981) suggests, the learning is well worth the chaos:

> Now, chaos is scary: the meanings that can emerge from it, which can be discerned taking shape within it, can be discovered only if students who are learning to write can learn to tolerate ambiguity. It is to our teacherly advantage that the mind doesn't like chaos; on the other hand, we have to be alert to the fact that meanings can be arrived at too quickly, the possibility of other meanings being too abruptly foreclosed." (pp. 70–71)

Classroom Climate

In addition to clearly understanding the teacher role and collaborative learning, the teacher also needs to create a supportive classroom climate. As we have discussed throughout this text, students are more likely to participate when a climate of respect and trust has been established in the classroom.

Reading Objectives and Discussion Prompts

7.3 Teacher's Role

What do you know?
What are the teacher's roles in small-group work?

What do you think?
How are these roles different from the lecture or discussion methods discussed earlier? How will you encourage collaborative learning in your classroom?

TASKS

Defining the Task

The real key to effective use of small instructional groups in the classroom is the planning and organizing of the task. Simply telling students to "get together and solve this problem," or "work in groups to complete the assignments," or "get together in small groups and discuss *Romeo and Juliet*," will make their learning experience frustrating at best! You must take considerable time to "set the scene." Any unfamiliar terms or concepts should be defined and clarified. The goal of the small-group task should be clear to students as well as the time allotted for them to complete the task. As groups work, you will need to observe them and provide immediate corrective feedback of student errors and positive reinforcement for on-task behavior. In short, teachers structure, guide, encourage, inform, and evaluate small groups all along the way to the conclusion of the task. Allen, Brown, and Sprague (1991) suggest

> For example, if the teacher observes that a small group of students, working cooperatively on a play-reading assignment, is floundering in its discussion of the play's meaning, the teacher should provide additional information regarding the author or the period in which the play was written. In independent or group study projects, teachers often must provide information regarding available resources, methods of gathering data, and intellectual methodologies. When students stumble in their learning tasks, teachers must provide information to enable them to regain their balance. (p. 286)

When groups have completed the task, you must process the experience; that is, answer the question students always ask: "What were we supposed to get out of this?" The class as a whole should discuss the major themes and subtopics their individual groups discussed. This material should be related to previous topics and readings, and implications of the new material for students should be identified.

Types of Tasks

A wide variety of tasks for small groups exist. In his text *Learning in Groups,* Jaques (2000) outlines several. As you examine the list in Box 7.1, think of ways you could use some of them in your own classroom.

Perhaps small groups are most often used as problem-solving task groups. Students are given a problem, and the task is to solve it. For example, you might divide your math class into "families." Each family is provided a monthly income and a list of fixed expenses such as lodging, car payment, department store credit charges, and so on. Each family must determine how the remainder of their monthly income is to be spent—how much should be budgeted for recreation, food, clothing, and so forth.

Before attempting to solve a problem, either real or hypothetical, students should be familiar with problem-solving patterns. For example, students could be taught the following problem-solving pattern:

1. *Identify the problem*—its limits and specific nature.
2. *Analyze the problem*—its causes and consequences.
3. *Set up standards for possible solutions.* What criteria would a good, workable solution have to meet?
4. *Suggest possible solutions.*
5. *Choose the best solution.* Which one of the solutions suggested in step 4 meet the most criteria outlined in step 3?

In a **problem-solving task** group the members are requested to come to an agreement on a decision concerning the case study. This agreement can be reached in several ways—majority vote, minority vote, consensus, compromise, or an expert's decision.

BOX 7.1

Types of Tasks

Argue with the instructor or students

Discuss presentation

Discuss misunderstandings

Draw up a list of similarities and differences

List items from experience

List items from observation in the group

List items from reading

Mark their own or each other's essays

Set criteria for marking essays

Generate ideas

Make categories

Clarify a problem, solve it, and evaluate it

Enact

Discuss critically

Diagnose

Argue relative merits

Share anxieties

Share essay plans

Share study methods

Watch videos

Read and evaluate text

Report back on the previous session

From Jaques, 1992, pp. 77–78.

Majority vote assumes that although 51 percent of the group members agree on the decision, dissenting (minority) views have been heard. Minority vote can occur when a subgroup determines the decision. Perhaps the entire group has difficulty meeting, and so members agree to abide by the decision of those members who do meet. The main problem here is that the total group may not be really committed to the decision, and conflicts remain unresolved. Decision by consensus occurs when all group members support the decision. Every student must feel he has had a chance to influence the decision. Although this type of decision making requires the most time, it has the strongest commitment of group members. Decision by compromise occurs when group members cannot agree on a decision.

Another common task for small groups is **research**. Students can be divided into small groups and asked to research a topic area. Groups enable students to develop research skills and critical thinking. For example, a social studies teacher might want students to study Mexico. Small research groups could be formed, one to research the history of Mexico, one to research the geography, one to research relations between Mexico and the United States, and so forth. Each group could then report its findings to the class.

Small groups can also be used in **debate**. Students are presented with a current issue being debated in their city, county, nation, or even internationally. A teacher assigns small groups to research the issue, discuss the issue in their groups, and finally, based on the research and discussion, have each member prepare a short speech that articulates a position. Each student is then placed with a partner who holds the same position. In teams of two, students debate one another using the following format:

Constructive Speeches	Affirmative Speaker 1	5 minutes
	Negative Speaker 1	5 minutes
	Affirmative Speaker 2	5 minutes
	Negative Speaker 2	5 minutes
Rebuttal Speeches	Negative Speaker 1	2 minutes
	Affirmative Speaker 1	2 minutes
	Negative Speaker 2	2 minutes
	Affirmative Speaker 2	2 minutes

Students who are not debating vote for the side they think won the debate. Small groups can decide which two members of their group will debate, or all students can have a turn at debating. Class discussions following the debates should focus on the issues and arguments presented, helping students to think critically. Small groups can also be used with other experiential learning methods—the case study, role-plays, and games or simulations.

The **case study** method has been described as an "active, discussion-oriented learning mode, disciplined by case problems drawn from the complexity of real life" (Christensen, Hansen, & Barnes, 1994, p. 16). More specifically, a case is a partial, historical, clinical study of a situation that has confronted a practicing administrator or managerial group. Presented in narrative form to encourage student involvement, it provides data—substantive and process-oriented—essential for an analysis of a specific situation, for the framing of alternative action programs, and for their implementation recognizing the complexity and ambiguity of the practical world (Christensen et al., 1994, p. 27).

The major goals of the case method are to teach students to solve problems and to select important factors necessary to solve the problem from a tangle of less important factors. As McKeachie (1986) suggests

> Teachers attempting to help students learn complex discriminations and principles in problem solving need to choose initial cases in which the differences are clear and extreme before moving to more subtle, complex cases. (p. 173)

Small groups may be used in **role-play** situations as a means of learning to solve problems and relate to others. Group members are presented with a real-life situation and asked to assume roles and act out the situation. Observations are made by other class members. These observations are then compared to the reactions and observations of the role-players.

Role-plays enable students to experience the learning objectives rather than simply reading and studying them. Role-plays, to be effective, must be carefully planned and executed. Following are five ideas to keep in mind when using role-plays:

1. Role-plays are more than entertainment. Although students enjoy role-plays, they should never lose sight of their major purpose—to act out real-life situations and analyze their own behavior and that of others.
2. Role-plays are most effective when the classroom climate is supportive. To begin, you might have students role-play in small groups rather than in front of the class. As students become more comfortable with this instructional technique, they can role-play in front of the entire class.
3. Role-plays have no scripts. In other words, the situation and characters are clearly defined for students, but students create the words and actions.
4. Role-plays, to be effective, require observers. Assign some students to act as observers who will describe what they observed in relation to the objective of the role-play. For example, what did they observe that contributed to the effectiveness of the communication in the role-play?
5. Role-plays should always be followed by an evaluation session. Both observers and participants should take part in the evaluation session. Questions such as the following should be discussed:
   a. What happened during the role-play?
   b. What helped make the communication effective or ineffective?
   c. How did the participants feel during the role-play?
   d. What did we learn that we can apply to similar situations?

You might present your class with a **simulation**, a **game**, or a **simulation game** task that could involve several small groups. A simulation models reality, whereas a game is an activity in which participants agree to abide by a set of rules. A simulation game, then, is an activity that models reality in which participants agree to "follow the rules." A simulation game often portrays adult society. Thus, students are encouraged to make responsible decisions in complex situations they may well come across in later life. If your goal as an educator is to prepare students for life in society, simulation games may be one of the most effective means of accomplishing your goal.

Facilitating the Task

Throughout this chapter, we have discussed the importance of setting the scene for group work. In other words, teachers need to carefully plan how to lead and facilitate a task. Gray (1998; 2007) provides clear direction for what teachers should consider before, during, and after the task. These considerations allow for efficient facilitation of group work and can reduce the chaos that sometimes results from ineffective planning. We have adapted this advice in the steps that follow.

BEFORE THE TASK

- Decide on the goal(s) and objective(s) for the activity. Make sure that participating in the task will accomplish the goal.
- Decide on the grouping you need. How many groups of how many students will you need given the task? How will students be divided into groups? Will you

have them "number off" or will you use some clever mechanism for breaking students into groups?

- Decide on any materials needed. What do you need to bring to class? What will students need to take with them when they disperse into their groups?
- Decide on the placement of students. Are there any noise or privacy issues? Is the classroom big enough to accommodate all discussions within each group?

DURING THE TASK

- Capture attention to engage student interest in the task.
- Give an overview of what students can expect during the task. Be sure not to give too much information away. What do students need to know to participate versus what do you want students to discover on their own?
- Provide relevance so students understand the value of participating in the task.
- Provide details. Do students need to review certain terminology? What specific directions do they need? How much time will they have? What is the expected outcome? What are the rules for participation?
- Answer students' questions before they disperse into groups. This will save time for the task once they get into their groups.
- Monitor work to keep students on task. This will also allow you, the instructor, to manage class time more efficiently.
- Focus back up front. Be sure that you have some sort of attention-getting device when you want students to focus back up front.
- Set up the environment for sharing. Be sure that all groups are finished with their task and are ready to listen to other groups share results of the task.

AFTER THE TASK.   Whenever case studies, role-plays, games, or simulations are used, debriefing by the teacher becomes extremely important. During the debriefing process, the real learning of the activity occurs as students analyze, draw conclusions, and discuss implications. Covert (1978) suggests an **EDIT system** for debriefing. Students **experience** the game, simulation, or role-play; **describe** what happened to them during the activity; **infer** from the descriptions what general principles, theories, or hypotheses might be developed about communication; and then **transfer** these principles to a usable form in their own lives. Table 7.1 provides an outline template for a small-group task that instructors can use to form lesson plans for these kinds of activities based on this facilitation system.

Weaver (1974) suggests that debriefing consider four areas: the awareness created of concepts and principles, the expressions of feeling brought out in the activities, the details of what happened during the interaction, and the success or failure of the exercise as a whole. Whatever method of debriefing you choose, the emphasis should be on what students learned and how that learning can be related to course objectives and content. As Nyquist and Wulff (1990) indicate, "The job of the instructor, then, is to choose a structure for debriefing and to develop the questions that will assist in the debriefing process. When reasonable, debriefing should also address the strengths, limitations, and overall usefulness of the activity to provide feedback for future use" (p. 354).

TABLE 7.1 Template for Small-Group Task Outline—Instructor Lesson Plan

I. Introduction
  A. Attention Getter—How will you capture the student's attention?
  B. Set Induction—What has been taking place in class prior to this small-group activity—Provide a framework or review here.
  C. Instructional Objective—What will the student be able to do when the task is completed? These may be based on local, state, or national standards.
  D. Content—What do the students need to know to complete the task?
II. The Task or **Experience**
  A. What will they need to take with them to their group? How will the groups be formed?
  B. Provide a list of step-by-step instructions for completing the task.
III. Conclusion
  A. Describe what happened (ask the student's questions in order to stimulate discussion about the task experience).
  B. Infer the results (how did it meet the objective).
  C. Transfer principles (to other situations).

Reading Objectives and Discussion Prompts

7.4 Tasks

What do you know?
What are the various tasks that can be completed in small groups?

What do you think?
Think about your subject and students. Which of these tasks might work in your classroom? Can you think of any others that weren't mentioned in the text?

STUDENT ROLES

Often students are hesitant about working in small groups. Perhaps past experience has suggested that small groups don't often work well or efficiently. Perhaps they have never been taught about the processes that affect group productivity. Whatever the case, students will need information and guidance about the task, the expected outcome, the procedures to be followed, as well as their role in the whole process. Thus, as Nyquist and Wulff (1990) suggest

> Active participation in small groups requires interpersonal skills that all students may not possess. Each person within a group brings to the task a variety of personality variables that create interpersonal relationships and affect the levels of participation, the satisfaction, and ultimately, the outcomes of the group. It behooves the instructor, then, to think about the kinds of roles that emerge within small groups and ways to help groups to function with those roles. Instructors may want to talk to students about the various task,

maintenance, and personal roles that group members might assume and about the stages through which a group will progress as a result of those roles. It is also helpful to clarify for students what the use of small groups requires from them in terms of preparation, participation, and debriefing. (p. 347)

Two variables are important for students' understanding of effective small group discussion: roles and group development.

Roles

Roles may be formal or informal. **Formal roles** are assigned and identify a position, such as president, chair, or secretary. Formal roles are independent of any person filling the role. The role of president has certain duties regardless of the person in that role. Thus, formal roles do not emerge naturally from communication transactions.

In most classrooms the roles of small groups are informal. **Informal roles** emphasize functions, not positions. For example, a group member may act as a leader without having been formally appointed as "the leader." Leadership, simply put, is the ability to influence others (Gamble & Gamble, 2001). Leadership can be either a positive or negative influence. In other words, a positive leader is someone who facilitates task accomplishment, whereas a negative leader inhibits group productivity. In this respect, any and all group members can become leaders. Whether their contribution is a positive or negative one "depends on individual skills, on personal objectives, and on commitment to the group" (p. 293). Some groups will assign the role of leader, whereas other groups will let that person emerge. It is important to note that there is a difference between being appointed as leader by other members of the group and exhibiting leadership. A positive leader will facilitate group meetings, keep the discussion on track, and make sure that all group members contribute to the discussion and tasks. Leadership must be exhibited by one or more members of the group to successfully accomplish group goals.

The duties expected from a group member playing an informal role are implicitly defined by the communication transactions among group members. In other words, the group members don't tell an individual what to do in order to be a good leader. Rather, members show their approval or disapproval as the person acts as a leader.

Informal roles are generally of three types: task, maintenance, and disruptive. Examining the role types in relationship to their communication function, Rothwell (2003) tells us that

> **Task roles** move the group toward the attainment of its goal. The central communicative function of task roles is to extract the maximum productivity from the group. **Maintenance roles** focus on the social dimension of the group. The central communicative function of maintenance roles is to gain and maintain the cohesiveness of the group. Self-centered or **disruptive roles** serve individual needs or goals (Me oriented) while impeding attainment of group goals. Individuals who play these roles often warrant the tag "difficult group member." The central communicative function of self-centered, disruptive roles is to focus attention on the individual. This focus on the individual can diminish group productivity and cohesiveness. Competent communicators avoid these roles. (p. 129)

Table 7.2 provides samples of each of the three informal role types. As you read these samples, remember that a student may fulfill many of these roles during a small-group interaction. A competent small-group communicator

- *Demonstrates flexibility.* This person plays a variety of maintenance and task roles, and adapts to the needs of the group. Fighting for roles perceived to be more prestigious and desirable may leave vital group needs unattended.
- *Avoids disruptive roles.* This person shows a commitment to group effectiveness, not self-centeredness at the expense of group success.
- *Is experimental.* This person tries different roles in different groups, and doesn't get locked into playing the same role in all groups. (Rothwell, 2003, p. 133)

Group Development

Although there are several theories of **group development**, Fisher's (1970) theory will be used here because it focuses on verbal interaction. In addition, it is a clear way to explain to students what to expect in terms of communication in small groups. Four phases, each with a characteristic interaction pattern, emerged from Fisher's analysis of groups:

- The **orientation phase** is primarily concerned with social interaction—with getting acquainted, clarifying, and tentatively expressing attitudes. There's a great deal of agreement during this phase as people work toward interpersonal understandings of one another. Opinions are expressed in tentative and qualified terms.
- The **conflict phase** is filled with dissent and dispute. Statements are less ambiguous than in the orientation stage. Polarization occurs as coalitions of group members advocating similar views appear.
- **Emergence** is characterized by cooperation. People become less polarized. Favorable comments are followed by more favorable comments until a group decision emerges. Unfavorable comments become more ambiguous.
- In the **reinforcement phase**, dissent is almost nonexistent. The group is concerned with affirming its unity as each member reinforces the decision. The ambiguity so prevalent in the emergence phase tends to disappear. This is the "pat ourselves on the back" phase.

Any small task group will progress through these stages. It's helpful for you to become aware of these phases so you can gauge how groups in the classroom are progressing toward task completion.

Reading Objectives and Discussion Prompts

7.5 Student's Role

What do you know?
What are some possible student's roles (formal and informal) in small-group work?

What do you think?
Think about your subject and students. What are some additional student responsibilities you may need to discuss before assigning a small-group task? Think about how you will manage the classroom climate and how students can help in this process.

TABLE 7.2 Sample of Informal Roles in Groups

Task Roles

1. *Initiator-Contributor:* Offers lots of ideas and suggestions; proposes solutions and new directions.
2. *Information Seeker:* Requests clarification; solicits evidence; asks for suggestions and ideas from others.
3. *Opinion Seeker:* Requests viewpoints from others; looks for agreement and disagreement.
4. *Information Giver:* Acts as a resource person for the group; provides relevant and significant information based on expertise or personal experience.
5. *Clarifier-Elaborator:* Explains, expands, and extends the ideas of others; provides examples and alternatives.
6. *Coordinator:* Draws together ideas of others; shows relationships between facts and ideas; promotes teamwork and cooperation.
7. *Secretary-Recorder:* Serves group memory functions; takes minutes of meetings; keeps group's records and history.
8. *Director:* Keeps group on track; guides discussion; reminds group of goal; regulates group activities.
9. *Devil's Advocate:* Challenges prevailing point of view for the sake of argument in order to test and critically evaluate the strength of ideas, solutions, or decisions.

Maintenance Roles

1. *Supporter-Encourager:* Bolsters the spirits and goodwill of the group; provides warmth, praise, and acceptance of others; includes reticent members in discussion.
2. *Harmonizer-Tension Reliever:* Maintains the peace; reduces tension through humor and by reconciling differences between members.
3. *Gatekeeper-Expediter:* Controls channels of communication and flow of information; encourages evenness of participation; promotes open discussion.
4. *Feeling Expresser:* Monitors feelings and moods of the group; suggests discussion breaks when mood turns ugly or energy levels flag.

Self-Centered or Disruptive Roles

1. *Stagehog:* Seeks recognition and attention by monopolizing conversation; prevents others from expressing their opinions fully; wants the spotlight.
2. *Isolate:* Deserts the group; withdraws from participation; acts indifferent, aloof, uninvolved; resists efforts to include him in group decision making.
3. *Clown:* Engages in horseplay; thrives on practical jokes and comic routines; diverts members' attention away from serious discussion of ideas and issues; steps beyond the boundaries of mere tension reliever.
4. *Blocker:* Thwarts progress of group; does not cooperate; opposes much of what group attempts to accomplish; incessantly reintroduces dead issues; makes negative remarks to members.
5. *Fighter-Controller:* Tries to dominate group; competes with members; abuses those who disagree; picks quarrels with members; interrupts to interject own opinions into discussion.
6. *Zealot:* Tries to convert members to a pet cause or idea; delivers sermons to group on state of the world; exhibits fanaticism.
7. *Cynic:* Displays sour outlook (a person who "smells flowers [and] looks around for a coffin"—H. L. Mencken); engages in fault finding; focuses on negatives; predicts failure of group.

OBSERVING AND EVALUATING SMALL GROUPS

If students are to learn effectively from small-group interaction, they must increase their small-group interaction skills. One of the best ways to help students increase these skills is to have them evaluate themselves and their group, and to observe and evaluate other groups.

Through observation and evaluation, students can reduce their errors, build on their strong points, and correct weak points. Following every small-group experience, students should discuss their own experience in the group. Each of the components of the small group should be analyzed—the group composition, the structural and operating variables, task, outcome, group atmosphere, and environment. You might ask students to evaluate their experience in a small group on an evaluation form such as the one shown in Table 7.3.

In addition to evaluating your students, you will also want to evaluate your ability to use small groups as a teaching strategy. To do that, you could use the evaluation form in Table 7.4. Ask your students to complete it.

TABLE 7.3   Small-Group Evaluation Form

Instructions: Circle the number that best indicates your response to the following questions about the discussion in which you participated.

1. *Adequacy of Communication:* To what extent did you feel members understood one another's statements and positions?

0	1	2	3	4	5	6	7	8	9	10

Much talking past each other, misunderstanding   Communicated directly with each other, understanding well

2. *Opportunity to Speak:* To what extent did you feel free to speak?

0	1	2	3	4	5	6	7	8	9	10

Never had a chance to speak   All the opportunity to talk I wanted

3. *Climate of Acceptance:* How well did members support one another, show acceptance of individuals?

0	1	2	3	4	5	6	7	8	9	10

Highly critical and punishing   Supportive and receptive

4. *Interpersonal Relations:* How pleasant and concerned were interpersonal relations?

0	1	2	3	4	5	6	7	8	9	10

Quarrelsome, status differences emphasized   Pleasant, empathic, concerned with persons

5. *Leadership:* How adequate was the leader (or leadership) of the group?

0	1	2	3	4	5	6	7	8	9	10

Too weak ( ) or dominating ( )   Shared, group-centered, and sufficient

6. *Satisfaction with Role:* How satisfied were you with your personal participation in the discussion?

0	1	2	3	4	5	6	7	8	9	10

Very dissatisfied   Very satisfied

(Continued)

TABLE 7.3 *Continued*

7. *Quality of Product:* How satisfied were you with the decisions, solutions, or understandings that came out of this discussion?

0	1	2	3	4	5	6	7	8	9	10

Very dissatisfied   Very satisfied

8. *Overall:* How do you rate the discussion as a whole, apart from any specific aspect of it?

0	1	2	3	4	5	6	7	8	9	10

Awful, waste of time   Superb, time well spent

TABLE 7.4 Small-Group Teaching Evaluation

	Never				Always
			Usually		
1. The teacher clearly defined the objective of the small-group task.	1	2	3	4	5
2. The teacher encouraged our group.	1	2	3	4	5
3. The teacher allowed us enough time to complete the task.	1	2	3	4	5
4. The group task stimulated my interest.	1	2	3	4	5
5. The teacher's debriefing was clear.	1	2	3	4	5
6. The teacher created a classroom environment conducive to small-group work.	1	2	3	4	5

In Sum

In this chapter we have set forth the concerns that teachers and students have in small-group communication. The types of tasks, group development issues, and issues in observing and evaluating small-group communication were also discussed.

Key Terms

Advantages of Small-Group Work
Disadvantages of Small-Group Work
Small Group
Group Composition
Group Structural Variables
Operating Variables
Task
Outcome

Group Atmosphere Environment
Collaborative Learning
Problem-solving Task
Research
Debate
Case Study
Role Play
Simulation
Game

Simulation Game
EDIT System (Experience, Describe, Infer, Transfer)
Formal Roles
Informal Roles (Task, Maintenance, Disruptive)
Group Development (Orientation, Conflict, Emergence, Reinforcement)

8 Communicative Reading and Storytelling

OBJECTIVES

After reading this chapter, you should be able to:

- Define the components of communicative reading.
- Prepare a selection for communicative reading.
- Present the selection.
- Discuss the value of storytelling.
- Use storytelling techniques to tell a story.

After supper she (the Widow Douglas) got her book and learned me about Moses and the Bullrushers, and I was in a sweat to find out all about him.

—MARK TWAIN

No teacher should pass up the opportunity to read and tell stories to students. Reading aloud and storytelling can be used to introduce a unit of instruction, to help explain a concept, to motivate students, and to simply provide enjoyment and appreciation of literature. Here is a fond remembrance of one of your authors.

One of my favorite teachers was Mrs. Nicholson, my fourth-grade teacher. Every day after lunch she would either read to us or tell us a story. How I looked forward to that time each day! In addition, during our lessons, it was not uncommon for Mrs. Nicholson to use a story to demonstrate some factual information or to read us a passage from a book or newspaper relevant to the topic under discussion. I remember Mrs. Nicholson was always ready to hear our stories as well. Often she would ask us to share our own experiences that related to the concept she was teaching. She also encouraged us to bring in materials we could read to the class. Both of these teaching tools—communicative reading and storytelling—made learning fun as well as relevant.

In this chapter we explore communicative reading and storytelling. Both of these teaching tools can be used to make your teaching creative and stimulating.

WHAT IS COMMUNICATIVE READING?

Reading aloud—**communicative reading**—involves more than simply vocalizing words. "It requires an appreciation of one's material as a work of literary art and the ability to communicate that work of art through voice and body. It demands full intellectual and emotional response from the interpreter, and a control and channeling of the understanding and emotion to elicit the appropriate response from the audience" (Lee & Galati, 1977, p. 3). Communicative reading is reading aloud to communicate meaning to an audience. As teachers, you may want to use communicative reading as an instructional strategy to illustrate class concepts. Think of a time in a classroom when something was read aloud either by the teacher or other students. What was the purpose of doing so? How powerful was it in helping students understand content? How effective was it in meeting course objectives? Additionally, as teachers you may want to assign communicative reading as an experiential activity as part of a larger unit. If so, what would be your goals? What skills would students learn in the process? How will you prepare students to use communicative reading effectively? Thus, the following section will help you as teachers use communicative reading as an effective teaching strategy.

In communicative reading, you want your audience to "see," in their minds, the images and ideas you create orally. To accomplish this, you need to be aware of three important characteristics of the material being read. First, you need to understand the content of the material. You cannot communicate the message of the material if you do not understand it. Second, you need to understand the emotional quality of the selection—the "feelings" in the selection. Finally, you need to be aware of aesthetic entirety, or the manner in which the parts work together to create the whole.

When we share literature with others, we want them to understand and enjoy the selection. Thus, a **triadic relationship** exists among the **communicative reader** (you), the **literary selection**, and the **audience** (your students). This relationship can be diagrammed as a triangle and, like all communicative relationships, is dynamic (Figure 8.1). Each component influences and is influenced by every other component.

Components of Communicative Reading

We discuss each of the three components important in communicative reading—the communicative reader, the literary selection, and the audience—separately. Remember, however, that this separation is for analysis only. In actuality, the components cannot be

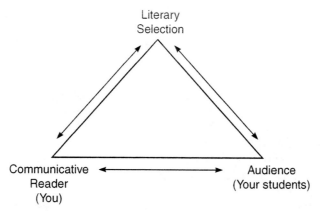

FIGURE 8.1   The Three Interactive Components of the Communicative Reading Relationship.

separated; they work together to create the "aesthetic entirety" discussed earlier. In addition to these three components, some techniques of oral presentation are discussed.

THE COMMUNICATIVE READER.   Think back to our discussion of self-concept in Chapter 2. We indicated that we each reveal ourselves every time we communicate. The literature you choose to share with your students reveals a lot about you—your feelings, beliefs, and attitudes. It's important to choose material that you enjoy. Beginning public speakers are often told to choose a topic of interest to them. The same can be said of communicative reading. If you're not truly interested in the material, your students won't be either. Have a genuine desire to communicate with your students. Never read to your students simply to "fill up time." Communicative reading should be used because it can help students with motivation, learning, or attitudes.

Consider your skills as an oral communicator. Consider your voice, gestures and bodily movements, eye contact, facial expressions, and so forth. Do you have any habits that might be distracting? Many things can distract your students from what you're reading, such as the time of day, noises outside as well as inside the classroom, and their internal states. You may not be able to control these factors, but you can eliminate the elements in yourself that could be distracting. Remember, the focus of your students should be on the thought, emotions, and attitudes of the selection, not on you as a reader.

THE LITERARY SELECTION.   You have a variety of literature from which to choose— poetry, prose fiction, nonfiction prose, and drama. Regardless of the type of literature, several guidelines should be followed when choosing literature for communicative reading.

Perhaps the first consideration when choosing literature is whether it's worth your time and effort. Does it have literary merit? Does it have unity and harmony of theme and style? Does it have sufficient variety and contrast to hold interest? Is the plot clear? Are the characters well developed? Does it have aesthetic qualities?

Having determined that the selection has sufficient literary merit to warrant your time and effort, your next consideration should be its appropriateness. Is it appropriate for your students? Will the selection hold their interest? Is it appropriate for their age level? Can they understand and appreciate it on the first reading?

Is the selection appropriate for the classroom situation? What are the physical limitations, such as time allotted for a particular subject or unit? Similarly, is the selection appropriate for your educational purpose? For example, suppose you want to instill an appreciation for poetry in your students by reading some poetry to them. It will be very important to choose poetry that they will enjoy. Although you may find *Beowulf* extremely exciting, it's probably not the best poem to choose for instilling an appreciation of poetry, at least not initially.

Finally, is the selection appropriate for reading aloud? Some selections are too complex for your students to understand when hearing them read aloud. They may contain too many words the students don't understand. The style could be too complex. For a variety of reasons, some literature is simply not appropriate for oral presentation.

> *The Audience—Your Students*
> *It's June, and it's over*
> *The quizzes, the tests—*
> *they passed them all.*
> *But I never found time to get to know them. (Cullum, 1978, p. 60)*

Too often we fail to really get to know our students. If we want to be effective communicative readers, we must know our audience—their attitudes, beliefs, likes, and dislikes. Only when we really know our students can we accurately determine what selections are appropriate for them. In addition to analyzing your students prior to the actual oral reading, you'll need to analyze them as you are reading and adapt accordingly. For example, if students are straining to hear you, you'll need to talk louder. If the oral reading is to be successful, it will be necessary to monitor the reactions of your students. This will be difficult if you never look up from your material! Finally, post-analysis is important. Ask for reactions from your students. Did they enjoy the reading? What did they learn? Ask them questions to determine if you fulfilled your purpose.

Reading Objectives and Discussion Prompts

8.1 Communicative Reading

What do you know?
Define communicative reading and describe its components.

What do you think?
Think in terms of the subject and audience you will be teaching. How might you be able to use communicative reading in your classroom?

PREPARING THE SELECTION

Now that you've chosen a selection that is suitable for you and your students, it's time to prepare the selection for reading.

Understanding the Selection

Preparation of the selection begins with a thorough understanding of it. What is the mood of the selection? What conflict exists? Who are the characters? What is the point of view of the selection? What is the theme? Does knowledge of the author's background or other works by the author help you to understand the selection? What images are created? What **literary techniques**, such as alliteration, metaphor, metonymy, hyperbole, or onomatopoeia, are used? Put yourself into the selection by considering such questions as, "How would I feel?" "What would I say?" and "What would my reactions be?"

Cutting the Selection

Sometimes you will find a selection that fits your purposes perfectly except that it is too long. If this is the case, the selection must be cut. **Cutting a selection** must not impair its purpose, attitude, atmosphere, or total impact. Follow these steps to cut a selection:

- When possible, cut whole incidents that are not essential to understanding the portion you will read.
- Cut out characters who are not essential to the part you will read.
- Cut any description unnecessary to the setting of the mood.
- Cut any repetition unless it is necessary for emphasis, or for some other obvious reason.
- Cut the "he saids" and descriptions of action or manner of speaking: "Gary looked up shyly." Imply the action with voice, movement, gestures, or facial expressions.
- Cut profanity or any element that may offend your audience.

Determining How the Selection Should Be Read

When you've completed any necessary cutting, you're ready to determine how the selection should be read. You'll use your voice and body to communicate the meaning of the selection. Voice changes can be used to communicate anger or joy. Posture and facial expression can help create a mood. Movement and gesture can help create a character.

Read the poem "Pam," which follows. To create images in your audience's mind you need to recall the smells and sounds of summer, the sights of a street you may have skipped along at age nine, the joy of your own childhood play pretending, the taste of a lollipop.

When you recall such things, your voice, facial expressions, gestures, movement, and so forth will reflect the images in your own mind. As a result, you will be better able to communicate these images to your audience.

Marking the Script

As a communicative reader, you should develop a system of **marking the selection** to indicate how you plan to read the material. Following are a few suggestions:

- A diagonal line to indicate a pause—the more lines between the words, the longer the pause.
- A curved line connecting words that should be read without stopping.

- Italics to indicate words to be stressed.
- Broken underlining to demonstrate a faster pace.
- A dash to indicate the continuation of a thought from one line to another.
- Notations to designate movement, gesture, facial expression, and others.

Examine the following selection by Beth Cooper (1956). Notice how the marking system is used.

> *Pam*
> *Her ponytail bounces—*
> *As moccasined feet/*
> Hop skip
> *And jump skip [make voice reflect movement]*
> The leaf shaded street.
> *Clad in checkered blue shorts—*
> *And a white midriff top/*
> *A band aided hand—*
> *Flaunts an iced lollipop. [raise hand up as if holding a lollipop]*
> *She has sun-blessed complexion.*
> *She has eyes trusting grey.*
> *She has a pert nose—*
> *And curved mouth/*
> *Enchantingly gay.*
> *She lives play pretending—*
> *This bewitched elf of mine/*
> *For the whole world*
> *Is magic/*
> *When a lady/*
> *Is nine.*

Introducing the Selection

To prepare your students for the communicative reading, you'll need to introduce the material you plan to read. The introduction to communicative reading has the same functions as any introduction. These are to (1) gain the attention of the audience; (2) tell the author and title of the selection; and (3) establish a favorable atmosphere for the performance.

Reading Objectives and Discussion Prompts

8.2 Preparing the Selection

What do you know?
What are the steps in preparing the selection?

What do you think?
How will these steps help you with your lesson?

DELIVERING THE SELECTION

You've done your job as a communicative reader of literature well so far. Now you arrive at the actual moment of sharing your material with your students. Perhaps the most important concept to remember is that you should interpret the material and not "act it out." It is fine to use gestures, movement, and voice variation as long as they do not distract from the reading itself. Anything that calls attention to the reader rather than to the reading should be avoided.

Facial expressions can be very effective in communicative reading. You can indicate that you expect a humorous response by a sly grin or twinkle in the eye, for example. The mood of the selection, be it sadness, joy, or confusion, can be communicated effectively through facial expressions representing these emotions.

Be direct. Although you are reading to your students, you need to maintain a great deal of eye contact with them. Eye contact allows you to gauge how your students are receiving the reading, and enables you to make any necessary adjustments. Obviously, there may be some selections, or parts of selections, that don't need direct eye contact. If seclusion or privacy is being communicated, for example, indirect eye contact is probably more effective than direct eye contact. Once again, the selection determines how much eye contact is necessary. However, more selections will profit from direct than indirect eye contact.

Don't leave your students hanging. We've all been in the situation of being unsure when a speaker has finished. Such experiences are frustrating. When you finish your reading, make a definite concluding movement so the listeners will know the reading is over. For example, pause and close your book.

Evaluating Communicative Reading

You can evaluate your communicative reading using the form in Table 8.1. You might also use this form to gather feedback about your communicative reading skills from your students.

Reading Objectives and Discussion Prompts

8.3 Delivering the Selection

What do you know?
What are some things to consider when practicing your selection?

What do you think?
How will you know if your communicative reading has been an effective part of your lesson?

In the next section of this chapter, we'll discuss storytelling as an additional instructional strategy that can be used in the classroom. Whereas, communicative reading involves a script usually written by someone else, storytelling is in the mind of the storyteller. It is an interpretation of events shared by the teller with an audience. In other words, storytelling is something that is told, not read.

TABLE 8.1   Evaluating Communicative Reading

Name _____

Type of Literature _____

Title of Selection _____

Author _____

	Excellent				Poor
1. Introduction	5	4	3	2	1
2. Appropriateness of vocal responsiveness	5	4	3	2	1
3. Appropriateness of physical responsiveness	5	4	3	2	1
4. Communication of mood, emotion, and thought	5	4	3	2	1
5. Appropriateness of selection	5	4	3	2	1
6. Clarity of ideas expressed	5	4	3	2	1
7. General effectiveness	5	4	3	2	1

Comments:

Total Score _____ (out of possible 35)

STORYTELLING

One dollar and eighty-seven cents. That was all. And sixty cents of it was in pennies. Pennies saved one and two at a time by bull-dozing the grocer and the vegetable man and the butcher until one's cheeks burned with the silent imputation of parsimony that such close dealing implied. Three times Della counted it. One dollar and eighty-seven cents. And the next day would be Christmas.

So begins O. Henry's story *The Gift of the Magi* (1982, p. 1). As a child I was mesmerized every time my mother read or told me this story. The **story** remains a favorite of mine. Perhaps it appeals to me because I am a romantic. Perhaps it appeals to me because I have always coveted beautiful, long thick hair, and so I can understand the sacrifice Della makes. Perhaps I love this story simply because it is a wonderful story.

We may not all be as eloquent storytellers as O. Henry, but we are all, nonetheless, storytellers. We tell stories every day. The parent asks the child, "What did you do in school today?" Husbands and wives ask each other, "How was work today?" The college student calls home, "You'll never guess what happened!" The point is, humans are storytelling animals. We tell stories to make sense of our lives, to share our experiences, and to share ourselves (Coles, 1989; Heilbrun, 1989; Kirkwood, 2000; Kramer & Berman, 2001).

As teachers, we tell stories every day. Stories often help us to explain otherwise difficult concepts. Sometimes we use personal stories (self-disclosure) to illustrate a point, and sometimes we tell hypothetical stories to support an idea. At other times, we pass on stories that have been shared with us. Additionally, we hear and listen to students tell us stories. In the following section, we'll discuss strategies for effective storytelling in the classroom. This information can help you as teachers prepare more effective lessons as well as help you prepare your students to engage in storytelling as an experiential activity.

Fisher (1984) indicates that the essential nature of human beings is that they are the **storytelling** animal—the "homo narran." In other words, we are all storytellers. We experience our world as a set of stories from which we choose among stories. We live life in a process of continual re-creation. A key concept in a narrative approach to communication is the definition of the word *narrative*. Often we think of narrative as fiction. This is a mistake, for as Fisher (1987) indicates, "When I use the term 'narration,' I do not mean a fictive composition whose propositions may be true or false and have no necessary relationship to the message of the composition. By 'narration,' I mean symbolic actions—words and/or deeds—that have sequence and meaning for those who live, create, or interpret them" (p. 58). Or put another way, "there is no genre, including technical communication, that is not an episode in the story of life" (Fisher, 1984, p. 347). Thus, for Fisher, all communication is narrative.

Narrative is not a specific genre (for example, stories as opposed to poems), but rather a mode of influence. Thus, listening to a class lecture, talking with friends, listening to a political speech or the evening news, and reading a book—all these comprise your hearing and shaping narratives. In Fisher's thinking, story is imbued in all human communication endeavors, even those involving logic. All arguments include "ideas that cannot be verified or proved in any absolute way. Such ideas arise in metaphor, values, gestures, and so on" (1987, p. 19). In short, Fisher bridges the divide we often have between logos (rational argument) and mythos (story or narration).

Because our lives are experienced through narratives, some standard for determining which stories to believe and which to disregard is essential. This standard is narrative rationality. This standard is different from the traditional one most Westerners have been trained in. Traditional standards of rationality ask questions such as:

- Are the claims supported by the facts?
- Have all relevant facts been considered?
- Are the arguments internally consistent?
- Does the reasoning used conform to the tests of formal and informal logic?

In contrast, **narrative rationality** is concerned with the principle of coherence and fidelity. **Coherence** refers to the internal consistency of the narrative and asks such questions as:

- Do the elements of the story flow smoothly?
- Is the story congruent with the stories that seem related to it?
- Are the characters in the story believable?

Fidelity, the second principle of narrative rationality, concerns the truthfulness or reliability of the story. Stories with a high degree of fidelity "ring true" to the listener. When the elements of a story "represent accurate assertions about social reality" (Fisher, 1987, p. 105), they have fidelity. Fisher proposes that we assess narrative fidelity through the logic of good reasons. If a narrative possesses fidelity, it constitutes good reasons for a person to hold a certain belief or act in a certain way. The logic of good reasons enables a person to judge the worth of stories by presenting the listener with a set of values that appeal to her and form warrants for accepting or rejecting a certain story.

The **logic of good reasons** consists of asking two sets of questions. The first set constitutes a logic of reasons:

- Are the statements that claim to be factual in the narrative really factual?
- Have any relevant facts been omitted from the narrative or distorted in its telling?
- What are the patterns of reasoning that exist in the narrative?
- How relevant are the arguments in the story to any decision the listener may make?
- How well does the narrative address the important and significant issues of this case?

The second set of questions transforms the logic of reasons into the logic of *good* reasons, by introducing the concept of values into the assessing of practical knowledge. The questions comprising this set are

- What are the implicit and explicit values contained in the narrative?
- Are the values appropriate to the decision that is relevant to the narrative?
- What would be the effects of adhering to the values embedded in the narrative?
- Are the values confirmed or validated in lived experience?
- Are the values of the narrative the basis for ideal human conduct?

Taken together, narrative rationality and narrative fidelity enable us to choose the stories we want to influence our lives.

Jack McGuire (1988) makes a strong argument for the educational value of storytelling:

> Within the necessarily artificial climate of a classroom environment, storytelling is alive, intimate, and personally responsible in a way that the majority of contemporary educational processes are not. In fact, it can be easily claimed that no other educational process comes as naturally to our species. Throughout humankind's preliterate history, storytelling remained the preeminent instructional strategy. By casting information into story form, ancient instructors accomplished several purposes: they rendered that information more entertaining and memorable (for themselves as well as their pupils); they made that information more relevant to their pupils' lives, because it was already grounded in a recognizably human context; and they expressed themselves not simply as experts but as creative, living beings, which helped their pupils to understand, trust, and emulate them more effectively. (p. 6).

This same idea is presented in the following:

In Defense of Telling Stories

I tell a lot of stories. Stories are nails that I hammer into the wall. On those nails I can hang up the whole, usually highly abstract, conceptual stuff of a philosophy course. If there are no nails in the wall, all the stuff falls down and will be forgotten. But if there are stories, illustrations, visualizations, they will not be forgotten; and contained in the stories there are the problems and the concepts. Years later students will remember the stories and because of the stories, still understand the concepts.

—Jacob Amstutz, philosophy professor emeritus,
University of Guelph (*Teaching Forum*, 1987)

Several researchers have examined the positive effect of using storytelling as a teaching strategy (see Collins & Cooper, 2005; Cooper, 2004; Engen, 2002; Ibarra & Lineback, 2005), and teachers are increasingly using this strategy (Carter, 1993; Chevalier, 1997; Engen, 2002). Why? No doubt the reasons relate to the value of storytelling.

Citing a decline of language skills over the past two generations, child psychologists and educators are actively championing storytelling as an ideal method of influencing a child to associate listening with pleasure, of increasing a child's attention span and retention capacity, of broadening a child's vocabulary, and of introducing a child to the symbolic use of language (see research cited in Collins & Cooper, 2005).

What Do Stories Do?

Storytellers Ellin Greene and Laura Simms (1982) asked children, "What would happen if there were no stories in the world?" The children gave some very perceptive answers as recorded in the *Chicago Journal*:

"People would die of seriousness."

"When you went to bed at night it would be boring, because your head would be blank."

"There wouldn't be a world, because stories make the world."

In his essay, "The Power of Stories," Sanders outlines nine functions of story:

stories entertain us; stories create community; stories help us see through the eyes of other people; stories show us the consequences of our actions; stories educate our desires; stories help us dwell knowingly in place; stories help us dwell knowingly in time; stories help us deal with suffering, loss, and death; and stories teach us how to be human.

In addition, storytelling introduces us to the symbols, artifacts, and traditions that characterize our culture and the cultural heritages of others. Stories are one of the best tools for cultural understanding. In some cultures storytelling was the major teaching tool. Because traditional cultures were not literate, they needed an efficient way to store and transmit cultural values. Their method was storytelling. Stories were not only for entertainment but they also could be used to model ideal values and behavior, define the place and purpose of people in the cosmos, and provide language models.

Even today some cultures still use storytelling as a major teaching tool. One of our Native American friends tells the story of growing up with her grandmother. Whenever the friend did something she shouldn't, her grandmother would tell her a story. The point of the story was always what happened to those who engaged in the behavior in which our friend engaged. Such learning stories are common among Native Americans and can communicate the values of Native American culture. In our families, much of the history and values are communicated through story. Storytelling is among the oldest forms of communication. It exists in every culture. Storytelling has a commonality among all human beings, in all places, at all times.

Storytelling is powerful. Michael Patterson (1999) provides a vivid description:

> Storytelling is the most powerful activity we can engage in to empower communities, because storytelling is how new empowering ideas are shared. Success stories are the best sales method there is. "War stories" are the most useful part of any training, because they animate the tools. Who would not listen closely, when it's time to get the "low down" on the higher ups? In Japanese art there's a term for the "space between"—the white space on this page, for example, the context for the text. Stories deal with and structure this "space between" in the human psyche, and give meaning and context to most of what we do. (p. 3)

In the classroom the quality of our relationships with students, how we teach, and how we feel about teaching are influenced by the nature of our stories. Jim Downton (2003) tells the effect our stories can have in the classroom. When he began teaching, he "lived in" a story that students would lie and cheat if he failed to keep his eye on them. Such a story of expecting deceit caused him "to live in a gloomy picture." When he changed his story to one of trust—believing that most students were trustworthy and that deceit was the exception, not the rule—he began to have a positive story to live in. His enjoyment of teaching increased. The stories we tell ourselves as well as those others tell us do indeed make a difference (Collins, 2003).

Perhaps most important, storytelling is fun. Storytelling is not a spectator sport. The listener and teller are united in the building of the story. The listener may engage in one or more types of participation: ritual, coactive, bantering, predictive, and eye contact. In addition, it is not only the teacher who tells stories. Students should be encouraged to tell stories as well. One of the authors asked her students at the Chinese University of Hong Kong to tell a folktale from their culture. They then discussed how cultural stories can help us to understand another's culture and to analyze cultural universals.

Reading Objectives and Discussion Prompts

8.4 Storytelling

What do you know?
What is storytelling? Describe the narrative approach to teaching.

What do you think?
How and when will you use storytelling in your own classroom?

STORYTELLING TECHNIQUES

Choosing a Story

Each of us lives by stories. The stories we "buy into" shape us, give our lives meaning and direction. It is not, however, merely the content of these stories that is important. Perhaps more important is the process of storytelling—the dynamic learning experience that the occasion of storytelling makes possible. This no doubt occurs because the process of storytelling is one human reaching out to another in a direct and positive manner.

When choosing a story, look for one that has:

- simple, yet colorful language (repetitions, rhymes, catch phrases)
- simple, well-rounded plot
- limited number of well-delineated characters
- single theme, clearly defined
- suspense
- fast tempo and excitement

Most important, tell a story you really like. If you choose a story you like, your ability to remember it and tell it convincingly are enhanced.

Learning a Story

Beginning storytellers often try to memorize a story word for word. This is neither necessary nor desirable (unless there is a repeated phrase or rhyme that is central to the story). Memorizing a story leaves no room for your individual additions and nuances. What should be remembered is the sequence of events and images created in your mind. Table 8.2 presents the steps in learning a story.

Tips for Telling

You've prepared well. It's now time to tell your story to an audience—your students. Following the guidelines in Table 8.3 will greatly enhance your chances for success (Collins & Cooper, 2005).

TABLE 8.2   Steps in Learning a Story

1. Read the story over several times.
2. Close the book and try to see the sequence of the story in your mind.
3. Read the story again, this time for the words that will add color to your telling (descriptive, concrete words that describe shape, color, design, etc.).
4. Repeat the same process of visualizing the story in your mind.
5. Now write out, draw, or outline the story (whatever suits you).
6. Retell the story in your own words, out loud so you can hear whether it pleases the ear.
7. Tell the story to a friend, or record it.
8. Retell the story until you are pleased with your "performance."

TABLE 8.3   Guidelines for Storytelling

- *Rapport* is everything! Eye contact is essential. Each listener should feel that the story is being told just for him.
- *Image!* The tale teller must create vivid images for herself if she wants listeners to see them too. See the pictures and people you are describing. Encourage your audience to imagine with all five of their senses.
- Use *vocal variety;* predictability is death. Be sure to vary tone, rhythm, pitch, volume, and intensity. Use silences and pauses that will give your listeners time to imagine.
- Whenever possible, give the telling a *sense of occasion.* Use ritual (light a candle, share an object, close your eyes for a moment) to transform an environment into a private place for storytelling.
- Capture your audience with a *well-baited hook.* Make them eager to hear the story before you begin the telling.
- Leave your listeners with a *"button."* Give your story a sense of closure.
- Relish the *language.* Find the characteristic words that give this story its special flavor. Enjoy the alliterations, the onomatopoeia, and the other devices of language.
- Be *selective.* The artist knows how little is needed to tell a story well. Choose words, characters, and events carefully.
- *Enthusiasm* is a key ingredient for effective storytelling. As Winifred Ward, a well-known teacher of storytelling, said, "Tell it with zest!"

TABLE 8.4   Evaluating Storytelling Skills

Name of Storyteller: _____ Date: _____

Name of Evaluator: _____

	Effective				Ineffective
Language Appropriate for the story; words pronounced correctly.	5	4	3	2	1
Voice Avoided a monotone; if accent used, was used effectively; not too fast or too slow; easily heard.	5	4	3	2	1
Gestures and Body Movement Used gestures, body movement and facial expressions to make the story "come alive"; avoided gestures, body movement and facial expressions that distract from the story.	5	4	3	2	1

Evaluating Your Storytelling Skills

As with any teaching method you use, you'll want feedback concerning how you did. Ask your students to complete a form such as the one presented in Table 8.4. Analyze their responses and determine your strengths and weaknesses as a storyteller.

Reading Objectives and Discussion Prompts

8.5 Storytelling Techniques

What do you know?
What are some strategies for using storytelling in your classroom?

What do you think?
How might your students use storytelling in your classroom?

In Sum

*On the mornings you tell us about the
     night before,
you're like one of us.
The dress you bought,
or a movie you saw,
or a strange sound you heard.
You're a good storyteller, teacher, honest!
And that's when I never have to be
     excused.*
(Cullum, 1971, p. 18)

Communicative reading and storytelling can
have a positive influence in the classroom.

They offer ways to "connect" with students.
As a result, they can enhance learning.

Storyteller's Creed
*I believe that imagination is stronger than
     knowledge.
That myth is more potent than history.
That dreams are more powerful than facts.
That hope always triumphs over experience.
That laughter is the only cure for grief.
And I believe that love is stronger than death.*
(Fulghum, 1988, p. viii)

Key Terms

Communicative Reading
Triadic Relationship
Communicative Reader
Literary Selection
Audience

Literary Techniques
Cutting a Selection
Marking the Selection
Story
Storytelling

Narrative
Narrative Rationality
Coherence
Fidelity
Logic of Good Reasons

CHAPTER

9

Influence

OBJECTIVES

After reading this chapter, you should be able to:

* Discuss the relationship between ethics and the role of the teacher.
* List the guidelines for ethical decision making.
* Discuss strategies for classroom management.
* Discuss the relationship between power and compliance in the classroom.
* Identify student challenge behaviors.
* Discuss the ways to handle disruptive students.
* Discuss strategies for handling crisis situations.

At his retirement dinner, a former professor of communication relayed to his audience that his one desire was to gather all the students from his first ten years of teaching into one large auditorium, stand out in the middle of the auditorium among them, and say . . . "I'm sorry!" Unfortunately, like this retiring professor, it is not until we have influenced many lives that we as educators realize the potential of our social influence. The classroom involves various forms of social influence. As teachers, we have great influence over our students—the knowledge they acquire, the skills they master, and their attitudes toward self, others, and learning. By the very nature of who we are, the way we communicate, and the teaching methods we employ, we wield a form of social influence toward a desired end. Richmond and Roach (1992) suggest that social influence is by definition inherent in the role of a teacher. In order to have a lasting impact on student learning, teachers must facilitate academic growth while creating an environment conducive to learning. That is, we must establish and maintain positive teacher–student relationships if we hope to have a positive influence on learning. Because the classroom is a place of social influence, it is important to consider the ethical responsibilities that accompany such a dynamic.

ETHICAL CONSIDERATIONS

In recent years there has been an increased interest in ethical issues. Educators should not only be concerned with their own ethical practices but also with instilling ethical awareness and practices in their students. The question is, What standard of ethics do we practice and teach? Before the answer to that question is addressed, we first discuss the nature of ethics and the relationship of ethics and the teacher. Next, we discuss those ethical standards, and then close this section with a discussion of student ethical obligations.

Ethics Defined

According to Andersen (1990), **ethics** is "the systematic study of value concepts such as good, bad, and right, and the application of such terms to actions, to intentions, and as descriptors of character" (p. 460). In this sense, ethics is concerned with how one ought to teach and what constitutes a good teacher, as well as with values such as power, fairness, honesty, trustworthiness, and knowledge.

In 1999, the National Communication Association's (NCA) governance board addressed the task of developing a code of ethics for scholars and teachers in the communication field (see Box 9.1). This **NCA credo** addresses the distinction between ethics and ethical communication. You may refer to this credo as you encounter the ethical dilemmas associated with your role as a teacher (Morreale & Andersen, 1999).

Ethics and the Teacher

Ethical issues are inherent in the teaching profession and, more specifically, in the classroom. Teachers must always be aware of questions concerning clarity of course requirements, evaluating students, grading standards, favoritism, enforcement of rules, and effects of bias or prejudice (Andersen, 1990). These ethical issues cannot be overlooked or avoided. Andersen (1990) elaborates that "many elements of classroom management (protecting students from harassment, limiting intrusions and disruptions, accommodating a range of opinions and points of view, encouraging active participation, avoiding ridiculing or embarrassing students for 'wrong answers') are important ethical goals" (p. 461). There are also **ethical dilemmas** when considering relationships with colleagues, administrators, parents, and the community. For example, important decisions will be made with regard to reviewing colleagues for merit raises, conducting research, student or parent favoritism, professional conduct, social pressure, professional preparation, and finally, individual conscience. Audi (1994) explains the ethical role of the teacher in saying, "One is never just a teacher. One is always—even if not consciously—an advocate of a point of view, a critic of certain positions, an exemplar of someone trying to communicate, a purveyor of images, a practitioner of behavioral standards, a person dealing with, and indeed responsible for, others in common tasks" (p. 35).

BOX 9.1

NCA Credo for Ethical Communication

Questions of right and wrong arise whenever people communicate. Ethical communication is fundamental to responsible thinking, decision making, and the development of relationships and communities within and across contexts, cultures, channels, and media. Moreover, ethical communication enhances human worth and dignity by fostering truthfulness, fairness, responsibility, personal integrity, and respect for self and others. We believe that unethical communication threatens the quality of all communication and consequently the well-being of individuals and the society in which we live. Therefore we, the members of the National Communication Association, endorse and are committed to practicing the following principles of ethical communication:

- We advocate truthfulness, accuracy, honesty, and reason as essential to the integrity of communication.
- We endorse freedom of expression, diversity of perspective, and tolerance of dissent to achieve the informed and responsible decision making fundamental to a civil society.
- We strive to understand and respect other communicators before evaluating and responding to their messages.
- We promote access to communication resources and opportunities as necessary to fulfill human potential and contribute to the well-being of families, communities, and society.
- We promote communication climates of caring and mutual understanding that respect the unique needs and characteristics of individual communicators.
- We condemn communication that degrades individuals and humanity through distortion, intimidation, coercion, and violence, and through the expression of intolerance and hatred.
- We are committed to the courageous expression of personal convictions in pursuit of fairness and justice.
- We advocate sharing information, opinions, and feelings when facing significant choices while also respecting privacy and confidentiality.
- We accept responsibility for the short- and long-term consequences for our own communication and expect the same of others.

From Morreale & Andersen, 1999.

In Box 9.2, several examples of potential ethical classroom dilemmas are presented that were born out of real-life situations. As you enter the teaching field, you may want to refer to these dilemmas and reflect on how you would handle each situation using the NCA credo or ethical standards provided in this chapter.

Why should we as teachers be concerned with ethics in the classroom? Because for many hours of a student's day, we are held responsible for what happens to them. Let's examine two examples of ethical issues that teachers deal with on a regular basis that might affect student learning or well-being. In the course of your teaching career, you will most likely be faced with the issue of cheating or plagiarism. It is interesting to note that the word *plagiarism* comes from the Latin word *plagiarius*, which means kidnapper. Thus, **plagiarism** occurs when someone presents another person's ideas or words as her own (Gibaldi, 2003). Whether intentional or unintentional, it is the ethical responsibility of a teacher to report and deal with plagiarism or cheating when it occurs.

BOX 9.2

Potential Classroom Ethical Dilemmas

- The daughter of your best friend of many years is a student in your class. Several students have reported to you that they have seen her bullying other students. You know that if you sanction the student or report it to her parents, it will most likely affect your relationship with them. What will you do?
- In your first year of teaching, you notice that a student is cheating on an exam. You promptly report this to the principal and are chastised for not creating a classroom climate conducive to "test-taking." After taking this into consideration and making proper adjustments (providing multiple copies of the exam, separating students, etc.), you see another student cheating on the next exam. What will you do?
- You notice several bruises on a student who comes from a very influential family in your community. What is your obligation?
- You overhear a couple of students making sexual or racial slurs in the back of the classroom. You're not sure if anyone else heard the comments. What should you do?
- During a discussion on classroom ethics, a student raises his hand and says he would like to post a list of the Ten Commandments on the wall to remind everyone in the class how to behave. You want to promote openness and tolerance of ideas. How will you respond?

Keep in mind that most educational institutions have formal written policies on such matters and it is incumbent on each teacher to enforce them. Another growing concern for educators with ethical implications is bullying. **Bullying** can be either physical or emotional and when it occurs between students will certainly have an impact on a student's learning and well-being. Most people can remember instances of bullying in their own lives that are quite vivid and universally painful (Beane, 2000), but it is important to note that "bullying is not normal, natural, or acceptable" (p. 1). In other words, it is a teacher's ethical responsibility to deal with instances of bullying in or out of the classroom. Beane (2000, pp. 43–44) provides seven suggestions for dealing with these conflicting situations:

1. Cool down. Make sure there is some time between the incident and any discussion of it.
2. Describe the conflict. Teachers should be sure not to take a position during this step.
3. Describe what caused the conflict. Again, no blaming allowed.
4. Describe the feelings raised by the conflict.
5. Listen. Refer back to the chapter on effective listening skills in this text.
6. Brainstorm solutions. Make sure all ideas are presented and that none are ridiculed.
7. Keep trying out solutions.

Another suggestion that we would like to offer is to have students develop a **classroom credo** of ethical behavior including any consequences for violation. Teachers can prompt students by providing a list of suggestions from the NCA credo (truthfulness, tolerance of ideas, respect for others, etc.) and then have students add their own ideas to the list. In this way, students take ownership of their own behavior.

Other ethical issues of concern include sexual harassment, sexism, and racism in the classroom. These issues are addressed in more detail in Chapter 10.

Andersen (1990) advises that ethical dimensions must be addressed in the classroom because "omission of the topic increases the likelihood of attacks on the teacher for failing to deal with value issues" (p. 467). If this is the case, then how do we as teachers decide what ethical standards to practice and teach? There are many ways to deal with ethical issues.

Ethical Standards

When thinking of the **ethical guidelines** that serve to resolve certain issues, one might assume that we rely on **religious or moral** criteria, but there are various standards that can be employed. Although there is little agreement on which standard to use, there are many strategies to consider (only a few of which will be highlighted here). First, there is the method of **audience analysis** for determining ethical guidelines. That is, one should consider the ethical position of the group to which the standards will apply (Andersen, 1990). For example, a teacher should consider the gender, culture, values, and background of the students in the class. One might also consider the **political system** of the group as the basis for ethical reasoning (Andersen, 1990; Johannesen, 2001). For example, are the standards being applied to a democracy or a dictatorship? However, one might consider that **human nature** should be respected when making ethical decisions (Johannesen, 2001). This perspective allows for the analysis of individual differences and perspectives within an overall political structure. The **dialogical perspective**, first articulated by Buber (2005), suggests that one should listen to all sides of an issue while remaining committed to one ethical decision. There is also a **situational perspective** that promotes the idea that rules cannot be applied to ethical decisions because the situational element will determine one's standards (Johannesen, 2001; Rogge, 1959). One could also rely on the judicial system or the **legal perspective** for determining ethical guidelines (Johannesen, 2001). Finally, there is a **personal code of ethics** that can be applied after systematically reflecting on various approaches (Andersen, 1990). There are many standards that guide the ethical decisions teachers make in the classroom. It is only when we become aware of these that we can begin to apply them to our own teaching practices and inform our students of the same.

Student Ethical Obligations

The previous discussion highlighted the role of the teacher and ethical decision making in the classroom. But teachers are not the only ones held responsible for ethical behavior. Reed and Hallock (1996) outline standards for **student ethical obligations** shown in Table 9.1.

To summarize, we as educators have a responsibility to reflect on our own ethical practices and to help our students to become aware of their own ethical behavior as it relates to the climate of the classroom. There are numerous inherent features of the classroom that require ethical decision making such as teacher–student relationships, evaluation procedures, and classroom management issues. Infante (1995) suggests that we have an ethical obligation to teach students to understand and control verbal aggression. These and other issues have an impact on the climate of the classroom and have the potential to influence learning. As such, it is our ethical responsibility to address them.

TABLE 9.1   Encouraging Ethical Behavior in Class

As a student in this class, your ethical obligations are to

1. Engage in the free pursuit of learning by:
   - Seeking help and clarification when needed.
   - Respecting fellow students', professor's, and guests' opinions without disparaging and dismissing them.
   - Seeing beyond "personality issues" with others to appreciate their contributions to the learning environment.

2. Model ethical scholarly standards by:
   - Avoiding plagiarizing and all other breaches of academic honesty.
   - Avoiding any seeming approval, acceptance, or encouragement of fellow students' academic dishonesty and bringing any such instances to the attention of the professor and/or university officials.
   - Engaging in discussions with other students and professors about ethical issues in academics.

3. Acknowledge, accept, and expect just assessment of your learning by:
   - Understanding the professor's methods and rationale for your assessment and asking for clarification if you don't understand.
   - Engaging in accurate, just, objective self-assessments of your own work.
   - Engaging in constructive, value-neutral discussion with the professor about discrepancies between your self-assessment and the professor's assessment of your work.
   - Refraining from comparing assessments and grades with classmates so as not to diminish classmates' self-esteem.

4. Avoid harassment, discrimination, and exploitation by:
   - Getting to know classmates and the professor as individuals rather than applying prejudices and stereotypes.
   - Contributing your full effort in team and collaborative projects.
   - Respectfully voicing your expectations of full participation in team and collaborative projects to fellow students.
   - Not discouraging, in any way, a member's full participation in a collaborative project.
   - Being careful not to make racist, sexist, and other types of discriminatory remarks during class.
   - Being careful not to monopolize class discussion time so that others do not have a chance to participate or are intimidated about participating.

From "Encouraging Ethical Behavior in Class," by JoyLynn H. Reed and Daniel E. Hallock, in *The Teaching Professor* (January 1996). Copyright © 1996. Reprinted by permission of Copyright Clearance Center on behalf of Magna Publications.

Reading Objectives and Discussion Prompts

9.1 Ethical Considerations and Standards

What do you know?

What are some ethical considerations for teachers? What are the ethical standards that can be used in decision making?

What do you think?

What ethical dilemmas do you think you will face in the classroom? Which of the ethical standards will you use to make decisions? Will you always use the same standard?

Our communication counts. It influences our students and our students' communication influences us. Some scholars have studied the impact of teacher influence in the classroom (e.g., McCroskey & Richmond, 1983; Richmond & McCroskey, 1984; Richmond & Roach, 1992), whereas others have examined forms of mutual influence in which the teacher influences students, students influence the teacher, and students affect one another (e.g., Simonds, 1997b; Staton, 1990). Whether you agree that the classroom is a place of teacher influence or mutual influence, it is important to explore the issues that have the potential to impact student learning.

CLASSROOM MANAGEMENT

One of the greatest fears reported by teachers is a feeling of being "out of control" (Cooper, 1985). Whether instructors are novices or seasoned teachers, they can be haunted by a fear of being unprepared and, consequently, unable to manage the climate of the classroom. **Classroom management** can be described as actions that create, implement, and maintain a classroom climate that supports learning.

Creating a Supportive Climate

Most scholars believe that classroom management actions should be **proactive** rather than **reactive** and that decisions regarding these actions should be done in advance of entering the classroom. These advance choices about the social climate have important implications for student behavior, learning, and discipline. According to Evertson and Harris (1992), effective management enhances instruction and time on-task by setting and conveying both procedural and academic expectations. Orenstein (1994) supports the notion that planning and preparation are the most effective ways to prevent problems and to provide a suitable climate for learning. He notes that "orderly classrooms are brought about by teachers' efforts to manage behavior in ways that reduce the occurrence and effects of student disruption" (p. 594). Krasnow (1992) found that teachers who use management programs report less time spent on conflict resolution and fewer distracting behaviors.

Meyer and his colleagues (2007, 2008) conducted a series of studies on the need for classroom management training for new instructors (specifically graduate teaching assistants). These instructors reported a need to emphasize classroom management early in the semester to prevent student misbehaviors from occurring later in the course. Specifically, these new instructors noted the importance of setting the tone of the classroom during the first day and first few weeks of the course. They stressed the necessity of reacting firmly and immediately the first time an instance of misbehavior occurs. These studies found that the instructors who received classroom management training reported fewer instances of student misbehavior, fewer instances of severe misbehaviors, greater confidence in the training they received, and greater confidence in their ability to manage misbehaviors in the classroom. These studies emphasized that opportunities to participate in discussions of classroom management prior to initial teaching experiences allowed participants to feel less defensive about misbehaviors when they actually occurred. This, in turn, allowed them to create a more supportive climate in the midst of misbehaviors.

Kounin (1977) studied how a teacher's handling of misbehavior influences other students who witness it but are not themselves participants. He called this the "**ripple effect**." Kounin concluded that it was not so much how effective teachers handled misbehavior that influenced other students as much as how they prevented problems from happening in the first place. Kounin described the most effective teachers as possessing the skills necessary to elicit high levels of work involvement and low levels of misbehavior. These strategies include "**withitness**"—communicating awareness of student behavior; **overlapping**—doing more than one thing at once; **smoothness and momentum**—moving in and out of activities smoothly and with appropriately paced and sequenced instruction; and **group alerting**—keeping all students attentive in a whole-group focus.

According to research studies, an approach to classroom management includes, but is not limited to, the following:

- organization of instruction and support activities
- housekeeping procedures and behavior rules
- techniques for conflict resolution (Brophy, 1983)
- setting the tone in the first class
- demonstrating mastery of subject
- demonstrating enthusiasm for subject
- reviewing skills
- assigning work carefully
- developing fair tests
- monitoring student involvement
- being aware of barriers to learning (Brodsky, 1991)

Implementing a Supportive Climate

Once teachers have planned a management system, they must consider how they will implement that system at the beginning of the school year. According to Evertson (1987), "The first day of school has special significance for both teachers and students. It is at this time that rules, routines, and expectation are established. Students' first impressions about their classrooms, their teachers, and what standards are expected can have a lasting effect on their attitudes and on the ways they will engage in classroom tasks" (p. 34). Evertson and Emmer (1982, p. 153) summarize advice about implementing a classroom management approach. Teachers should begin their year by:

- Preparing and planning classroom rules and procedures in advance.
- Communicating their expectations clearly.
- Establishing routines, procedures, and expectations for appropriate performance.
- Systematically monitoring student work and behavior.
- Providing feedback about academic performance and behavior.

Because the first day is so significant, it is important to provide students with information that will form positive first impressions and have a lasting impact. According to Friedrich and Cooper (1999), there are three categories of information that students wish to acquire on the first day of class: course coverage, course rules, and teacher personality.

In providing this information, instructors should discuss assignments, rules, expected behaviors, and issues related to grades. Friedrich and Cooper (1999) add that "more important than the specific choice a teacher makes on such issues is the fact that the teacher makes and consistently enforces a choice" (p. 288). Gordon (1974) also recommends discussion of rules at the beginning of the school year. He recommends that teachers not only communicate these rules but also that they explain how these rules can benefit students. In doing so, teachers should describe the rule, explain why the rule is important, and describe the consequences of violating the rule.

Maintaining a Supportive Climate

Teachers must not only plan and implement their management system, they must also maintain it as well. Rule violation is an important issue to consider in the overall scheme of classroom management. As the school year progresses, it is important to maintain classroom rules and procedures continually and consistently. There is a major program of research devoted to the issue of rule violation or misbehavior. Within this research program, issues of power, compliance gaining, and conflict have been addressed.

Reading Objectives and Discussion Prompts

9.2 Classroom Management

What do you know?
Describe each of the actions that help with classroom management.

What do you think?
What can you do to have a proactive classroom management strategy? Who can you talk to for help?

POWER AND COMPLIANCE

Barraclough and Stewart (1992) define **power** as the potential or capacity to influence the behavior of some other person or persons. A great deal of research in the communication field has focused on power in an attempt to determine the strategies teachers use to gain student on-task compliance. Borrowing from the work of French and Raven (1959), McCroskey and Richmond (1983) described five bases of teacher power: **coercive**, **reward**, **legitimate**, **expert**, and **referent.** This began a series of studies called "Power in the Classroom" that explored the patterns and influences of teacher power. This line of research has linked instructor power and compliance gaining to factors such as student cognitive learning, affective learning, and learning motivation (e.g., Kearney, Plax, Richmond, & McCroskey, 1984; Kearney, Plax, Richmond, & McCroskey, 1985; McCroskey & Richmond, 1983; McCroskey, Richmond, Plax, & Kearney, 1985; Plax, Kearney, McCroskey & Richmond, 1986; Richmond, 1990; Richmond & McCroskey, 1984; Richmond, McCroskey, Kearney, & Plax, 1987).

McCroskey et al. (1985) examined the types of **behavior alteration techniques** teachers and students perceive that teachers use in effective classroom management. The result was a twenty-two-item list of behavior alteration techniques (BATs) and representative behavior alteration messages (BAMs), shown in Table 9.2. Student behavior

TABLE 9.2   Behavior Alteration Techniques (BATs)

Technique	Sample Messages
1. Immediate Reward from Behavior	You will enjoy it. It will make you happy. Because it's fun. You'll find it rewarding or interesting. It's a good experience.
2. Deferred Reward from Behavior	It will help you later on in life. It will prepare you for college (or high school, job, etc.). It will prepare you for your achievement tests. It will help you with upcoming assignments.
3. Reward from Teacher	I will give you a reward if you do. I will make it beneficial to you. I will give you a good grade (or recess, extra credit) if you do. I will make you my special assistant.
4. Reward from Others	Others will respect you if you do. Others will be proud of you. Your friends will like you if you do. Your parents will be pleased.
5. Self-Esteem	You will feel good about yourself if you do. You are the best person to do it. You are good at it. You always do such a good job. Because you're capable!
6. Punishment from Behavior	You will lose if you don't. You will be hurt if you don't. It's your loss. You'll feel bad if you don't.
7. Punishment from Teacher	I will punish you if you don't. I will make it miserable for you. I'll give you an "F" if you don't. If you don't do it now, it will be homework tonight.
8. Punishment from Others	No one will like you. Your friends will make fun of you. Your parents will punish you if you don't. Your classmates will reject you.
9. Guilt	If you don't, others will be hurt. You'll make others unhappy if you don't. Your parents will feel bad if you don't. Others will be punished if you don't.
10. Teacher–Student Relationship: Positive	I will like you better if you do. I will respect you. I will think more highly of you. I will appreciate you more if you do. I will be proud of you.
11. Teacher–Student Relationship: Negative	I will dislike you if you don't. I will lose respect for you. I will think less of you if you don't. I won't be proud of you. I'll be disappointed in you.
12. Legitimate-Higher Authority	Do it, I'm just telling you what I was told. It is a rule, I have to do it and I will have to give you an "F" if you don't.
13. Legitimate-Teacher Authority	Because I told you to. You don't have a choice. You're here to work! I'm the teacher, you're the student. I'm in charge, not you. Don't ask, just do it.
14. Personal (Student) Responsibility	It is your obligation. It is your turn. Everyone has to do her share. It's your job. Everyone has to pull her own weight.
15. Responsibility to Class	Your group needs it done. The class depends on you. All your friends are counting on you. Don't let your group down. You'll ruin it for the rest of the class (team).
16. Normative Rules	We voted, and the majority rules. All of your friends are doing it. Everyone else has to do it. The rest of the class is doing it. It's part of growing up.
17. Debt	You owe me one. Pay your debt. You promised to do it. I did it the last time. You said you'd try this time.

(Continued)

TABLE 9.2 *Continued*	
18. Altruism	If you do this, it will help others. Others will benefit if you do. It will make others happy if you do. I'm not asking you to do it for yourself; do it for the good of the class.
19. Peer Modeling	Your friends do it. Classmates you respect do it. The friends you admire do it. All your friends are doing it.
20. Teacher Modeling	This is the way I always do it. When I was your age, I did it. People who are like me do it. I had to do this when I was in school. Teachers you respect do it.
21. Expert Teacher	From my experience, it is a good idea. From what I have learned, it is what you should do. This has always worked for me. Trust me—I know what I'm doing. I had to do this before I became a teacher.
22. Teacher Feedback	Because I need to know how well you understand this. To see how well I've taught you. To see how well you can do it. It will help me know your problem areas.

From "Power in the Classroom V: Behavior Alteration Techniques, Communication Training, and Learning," by J. C. McCroskey, V. P. Richmond, T. G. Plax, and P. Kearney, *Communication Education,* 34 (1985), p. 217. Copyright © 1985. Reprinted by permission of Taylor & Francis, Ltd. http://tandf.co.uk/journals.

can be either active or passive (Kearney & Plax, 1987), and teacher alteration messages can be either prosocial or antisocial (Sorensen, Plax, & Kearney, 1989).

More recently, Golish and Olson (2000) found that a teacher's use of reward power was related to students' use of prosocial BATs. Conversely, the use of coercive power by the teacher was related to the use of antisocial BATs by students. Finally, yet another link is made between immediacy (discussed in Chapter 2) and another important communication variable as Golish and Olson also found that teachers who are friendly encourage students to demonstrate their knowledge and take responsibility for their own learning.

Compliance gaining in the classroom has been investigated from a multicultural perspective. Lee, Levine, and Cambra (1997) found that students from a collectivist society were less likely to resist teacher influence than students from an individualistic society. They report that students from a collectivist view "should be more concerned with appropriate and polite behavior and should be more likely to see a teacher as an authority figure who ought to be obeyed" (p. 34). This suggests that power research reflects the assumptions of individualism and that teachers should take into account the cultural background of students before reacting to certain student behaviors. Not only can a student's behavior vary according to cultural boundaries, but the behaviors of teachers with differing backgrounds may vary as well.

Although previous research with U.S. teachers shows a preference for reward-based, prosocial BATs, Lu (1997) found that Chinese teachers said they were more likely to use punishment-oriented, antisocial BATs. Lu explains that Chinese teachers emphasized authority, morality, and modeling in their use of BATs and BAMs. The **authoritarian teacher** is always the symbol of respect and authority and the source of knowledge and wisdom. Authoritarian teachers have complete control over the classroom and should be obeyed at all times. The authoritarian classroom is a very formal place where students must raise their hands and stand at attention before speaking. Also, a student who comes to class late must get the teacher's permission to enter the classroom (Lu, 1997). The **moralist teacher** often informs students of the rules of moral conduct and reasons for such conduct. These teachers are not only responsible for intellectual education but also for cultivating a strong sense of societal and filial respon-sibilities. Students have a debt to their government and their families for the cost of their education. They must honor and bring glory to their families and to society. Finally, Lu (1997) describes **modeling teachers** as "gardeners" who teach students by example as if "raising seedlings." Students should follow the example of their teacher, their peers, or their group (the whole class). The modeling teacher will often use the col-lective as an example mainly for the purpose of correcting an individual student's behavior. Modeling teachers tend to demand uniformity and conformity of student be-haviors. This line of research allows us to make the claim that teacher influence and student resistance is a culturally bound phenomenon.

Reading Objectives and Discussion Prompts

9.3 Power and Compliance

What do you know?
Describe the five bases of teacher power. What are behavior alteration techniques and how do they work?

What do you think?
What do you think are the differences between prosocial and antisocial BATs? How will you decide which technique is best for a given situation? Do you think there is a differ-ence between what techniques teachers report using and what they actually use?

CHALLENGE BEHAVIOR

As stated previously, the power research examines issues involving teacher control or influence and offers suggestions for methods of controlling student behavior. Simonds (1995) provides an alternative for studying challenges in the classroom. Rather than looking at issues of teacher influence, Simonds explores the nature of teacher–student interactions from a relational perspective where classroom expectations are negotiated, transactional, and mutually influenced.

Simonds describes the classroom as a unique culture where the teacher is the only one who knows, in advance, what the expectations of that particular classroom are. Because the teacher, as such, is the only "native," students must identify the teacher's expectations and speculate about the strategies necessary to meet these expectations successfully. Students are likely to face uncertainty about the rules, norms, and expecta-tions of the classroom and may attempt to reduce uncertainty in a variety of ways. They can observe the culture to determine expectations, ask questions, or test the rules or norms in the form of a challenge. Simonds (1997b) states that **challenge behavior** occurs when students behave contrary to implicit or explicit classroom expectations. Such behaviors can be motivated by a lack of classroom understanding or the "cultural" expectations of the class. For example, if a teacher does not communicate a certain expectation (or if the expectation is implicit), students may want to know what will happen if they behave a certain way. However, if the teacher does communicate an explicit expectation, the students may want to know if the teacher will follow through with the consequences for violation. In this sense, challenge behavior is a strategy that students use to share ownership of the classroom culture. It may be motivated by uncertainty and is manifested by behaviors that are contrary to teacher expectations.

To test whether challenge behavior was motivated by student uncertainty, Simonds (1995) examined the relationship between teacher clarity and the frequency of student challenges and found that as a teacher's clarity increased, student challenges decreased. Note how these research findings have influenced the teaching philosophy presented by the same author in Chapter 1 of this text. This is an example of how theory influences research and research, in turn, influences a teaching philosophy. A philosophy of teaching should then be reflected in actual classroom practices.

Simonds (1997b) notes that challenge behavior, if addressed appropriately, can serve to foster a supportive relational climate. For example, if a student is uncertain about a classroom rule and challenges that rule, then the resulting communication between the teacher and the student can enhance their relationship and the climate of the class. Teachers need to be able to identify student challenges so that they can adapt their communication practices accordingly—that is, provide the information the student needs to know.

Simonds (1997b) describes four types of challenge behavior and provides an instrument with which teachers can identify the frequency of challenges in their classrooms (see Table 9.3). **Evaluation challenges** occur when students question the nature of testing procedures or grades received. **Procedural challenges** occur when students test the rules and norms, whether implicit or explicit, in the classroom. **Practicality challenges** occur when students question the relevance of the course or certain tasks. **Power challenges** occur when students try to influence the behavior of the teacher or other students in the class.

Several challenge behavior scenarios are provided in Box 9.3. You may encounter such situations in your own class. In considering how you would approach these situations in advance, you will be taking the first steps in your own classroom management efforts.

Challenge behavior research examines the role of the student, as well as the teacher, in the influence process. Simonds (1997b) would argue that communication between teachers and students plays a vital role in the culture of the classroom. Research from both the teacher influence and mutual influence perspectives provides educators with insight for managing classrooms. For example, scholars (e.g., Barraclough et al., 1992; Kearney et al., 1984; and McCroskey et al., 1983) from the power research perspective would suggest to teachers that they use prosocial statements to gain student compliance; whereas Simonds (1997b) would direct teachers to clearly communicate classroom expectations prior to the need for a student challenge. We close this chapter with a few more practical suggestions.

Reading Objectives and Discussion Prompts

9.4 Challenge Behavior

What do you know?
Define challenge behavior and describe the four types of challenges.

What do you think?
How can challenge behavior be avoided? How should it be handled when it happens? How is the research on challenge behavior different than the research on power and compliance?

TABLE 9.3   Critical Incidents Frequency Report

Complete the following information based on the course you attended just prior to the one you are currently in. **All responses will remain anonymous. Please answer as honestly as possible.** In this section you are asked to recall how often you have observed students in your class engaging in the following behaviors. Choose only one answer for each behavior.

Generally, students . . .	very often	often	sometimes	almost never	never
are absent excessively.	___	___	___	___	___
beg for higher grades in class.	___	___	___	___	___
question instructor's knowledge of content.	___	___	___	___	___
question the relevance of tasks to everyday life.	___	___	___	___	___
want to receive full credit for late work.	___	___	___	___	___
compare scores with other students.	___	___	___	___	___
attempt to control when a task will be done.	___	___	___	___	___
question the importance of subject matter.	___	___	___	___	___
offer "off-the-wall" examples in class discussion.	___	___	___	___	___
question fairness of grading.	___	___	___	___	___
don't want to participate.	___	___	___	___	___
complain that theories do not apply to real life.	___	___	___	___	___
come to class late.	___	___	___	___	___
question grades on assignments.	___	___	___	___	___
attempt to embarrass the instructor.	___	___	___	___	___
question why the class should be required.	___	___	___	___	___
talk during class.	___	___	___	___	___
argue over test questions.	___	___	___	___	___
interrupt instructor to reinforce their own opinion.	___	___	___	___	___
question relevance of concepts being discussed.	___	___	___	___	___

From "Critical Incidents Frequency Report" by C. J. Simonds, *Communication Research Reports, 14*(4) (Fall 1997), pp. 481–492. Copyright © 1997. Reprinted by permission of the Eastern Communication Association.

BOX 9.3

Challenge Behavior Scenarios

- Mario comments on the difficulty of an exam as he turns it in. Later, as you are going over the exam, Mario persists in questioning the validity of specific items.
- You are explaining an upcoming assignment. Sherry raises her hand to say, "I don't understand why we have to do this. How will I ever be able to use this in the real world?"
- Jung began the semester by coming to class late occasionally. As the semester progressed, his tardiness began to disrupt the class. Sometimes he would come in as late as 15 minutes after class started.
- As you are lecturing, Sally interrupts to state an opinion that is contrary to the position in the textbook. You diplomatically point out that there is little evidence to support Sally's view and continue the lecture. A few minutes later, Sally interrupts again to reiterate her original opinion.
- After you return presentation grades to your students, you notice that some of them are comparing scores. After class, Bill comes up to you to discuss his grade. Bill believes he should have received a higher score because he did as well as Cathy did and Cathy received a better grade than he did.
- You are lecturing when Pam asks, "How does this information relate to our lives? I mean, is this really important?"
- While you are lecturing, you notice that Christian and Tomaz are discussing matters irrelevant to class. After several nonverbal hints, you have to stop the lecture and ask them to please stop talking. A few days later, you notice Christian and Tomaz engaged in another conversation while a student is giving a presentation.
- During a class activity, you notice that Roberto is not participating. When asked to participate, Roberto says, "I don't feel like it." As the activity progresses, you notice that Roberto has drawn other students away from the activity.

HANDLING DISRUPTIVE STUDENTS

It's important to remember that you need not intervene every time a problem arises in your classroom. Some problems are minor. For example, if one student briefly whispers to another, there's no reason to call attention to it. When behavior continues or threatens to spread to other students, you can no longer ignore it.

Good and Brophy (2007) suggest that minor misbehavior is fairly easy to eliminate by any one or a combination of the following four interventions:

1. *Eye contact.* If eye contact can be established, it usually is enough by itself to return attention to the task at hand. To make sure the message is received, the teacher may want to add a head nod or other gesture such as looking at the book the student is supposed to be reading.

Eye contact becomes doubly effective for stopping minor problems when the teacher regularly scans the room. Because students will know that the teacher regularly scans the room, they will tend to look at the teacher when they are misbehaving (to see if they are being watched). This makes it easier for the teacher to intervene through eye contact. Teachers who do not scan the room properly will have difficulty using eye contact in these situations, because they usually will have to wait longer before students look at them.

2. *Touch and gesture.* When the students are close by, the teacher does not need to wait until eye contact can be established. Instead, the teacher can use a simple touch or gesture to get their attention. This is especially effective in small-group situations. A light tap, perhaps followed by a gesture toward the book, will get the message across without any need for verbalization.

Gestures and physical signals are also helpful in dealing with events going on in different parts of the room. If eye contact can be established, the teacher may be able to communicate messages by shaking the head, placing a finger to the lips, or pointing. These gestures should be used when possible, because they are less disruptive than leaving the group or speaking to students across the room. In general, touch and gesture are most useful in the early grades, when much teaching is done in small groups and when distraction is a frequent problem. Touching would be unwise with some adolescents who resent any attempt by a teacher to touch them.

3. *Physical closeness.* When the teacher is checking seat work or moving about the room, he can often eliminate minor student behavior problems simply by moving close to the students involved. If the students know what they are supposed to be doing, the physical presence of the teacher will motivate them to get busy. This technique is especially useful with older elementary students.

4. *Asking for responses.* During lessons or group activities, the simplest method of returning students' attention may be to ask them a question or call for a response. This request automatically compels attention, and it does so without mentioning the misbehavior.

Sometimes punishment is unavoidable. You, however, not the principal, should do the punishing. Sending a student to the principal may work on a short-term basis, but sooner or later you must come to grips with behavior problems in your classroom. You must take responsibility for them. Deferring to someone else should be a last resort.

When punishment becomes necessary, communicate to the student that you are punishing her only because she has left you no other alternative. Your actions and paralanguage should communicate concern for the student as well as regret that punishment must be used. In other words, it should be clear to the student that she has no one to blame but herself. Her own behavior is the cause for the punishment.

When punishing, several guidelines are important. Make the reasons for the punishment clear, as well as the type of punishment. Don't make threats or punishments you can't "make good." In addition, be sure the punishment "fits the crime." In other words, the punishment should be related to, and proportional to, the offense. If a student plagiarizes, he should receive no credit for that particular paper, but should not fail the course.

Curwin and Mendler (1999) suggest that teachers need to think in terms of consequences rather than punishment. Consequences are simple, direct, related to the rule that's been broken, and instructive. They also preserve a student's dignity. Punishment, however, is not related to a natural extension of the rule and tends to generate anxiety, resentment, and hostility in the student. Following are some examples of the difference between consequences and punishments:

Rule: All trash must be thrown in the basket.

Consequence	Punishment
Pick your trash up off the floor.	Apologize to the teacher in front of the whole class.

Rule: Tests and homework must be completed by yourselves unless group work is assigned. There is no copying other students' work.

Consequence	Punishment
Do the test or homework again under supervision.	Write 100 times "I will not copy other students' work."

Rule: No talking when someone else is talking. If you want to speak, wait until the current speaker has finished.

Consequence	Punishment
Wait five minutes before speaking.	Sit in the hall for the entire period.

Rule: You must be in your seat by five minutes after the bell.

Consequence	Punishment
You are responsible to get any information or make up any work that you missed by being late.	Miss entire class sitting in the principal's office, then make up work.

Whenever conflict arises, control your anger. Pause before you react to the disruptive behavior. Think for a moment so you don't overreact and designate a punishment you can't enforce. In addition, the momentary pause may give the student time to settle down—to get over her anger or resentment.

Reading Objectives and Discussion Prompts

9.5 Handling Disruptive Students

What do you know?
What are some suggestions for handling minor misbehaviors? What are some suggestions for handling disruptive students?

What do you think?
Try to think of the disruptions you may face in the classroom. What are some ways that you can prevent this? What are some consequences that you will use when disruptions happen?

HANDLING CRISIS SITUATIONS

Unfortunately, in recent years, schools have had to prepare teachers to deal with crisis situations in the classroom. As a result of tragic events that have happened at Columbine and Virginia Tech University, programs such as the National Association of School Psychologist (www.nasponline.org) have provided many guidelines to school administrators on how to handle these tragedies. They suggest that school personnel plan in advance so that they can respond to tragedy in a supportive manner. Specifically, they provide some suggestions for teachers. In such crisis situations, the teacher's role is to:

- Provide accurate information to students. Lead classroom discussions that focus on helping students to cope with the loss
- Dispel rumors
- Answer questions without providing unnecessary details
- Recognize the varying religious beliefs held by students
- Model an appropriate response
- Give permission for a range of emotions
- Identify students who need counseling and refer to building support personnel
- Provide activities to reduce trauma, such as artwork, music, and writing
- Set aside the curriculum as needed
- Discuss funeral procedures

Hopefully, as teachers, you will never have to implement these strategies. But in the event that you do, these suggestions may help you and your school district better prepared to be responsive to the needs of the students.

Reading Objectives and Discussion Prompts

9.6 Handling Crisis Situations

What do you know?
What is the teacher's role in responding to a crisis in the classroom?

What do you think?
What are the first steps you will take when a crisis happens on your campus? How will you talk with students about this?

In Sum

As teachers, we have great influence in the education environment. Because social influence is an inherent part of teaching, it is important to consider the ethical responsibilities that educators must practice and teach. Many features of the classroom require ethical decision making, such as teacher–student relationships, evaluation procedures, and classroom management issues. These and other issues have an impact on the climate of the classroom and have the potential to influence learning. Through critical reflection, we can make informed judgments of how to incorporate theory and research into our own classroom practices.

Key Terms

Ethics
NCA Credo
Ethical Dilemmas
Plagiarism
Bullying
Classroom Credo
Ethical Guidelines or
    Standards
Religious or Moral
Audience Analysis
Political System
Human Nature
Dialogical Perspective
Situational Perspective

Legal Perspective
Personal Code of Ethics
Student Ethical Obligations
Classroom Management
Proactive
Reactive
Ripple Effect
Withitness
Overlapping
Smoothness and Momentum
Group Alerting
Power
Coercive
Reward

Legitimate
Expert
Referent
Behavior Alteration
    Techniques
Authoritarian Teacher
Moralist Teacher
Modeling Teacher
Challenge Behavior
Evaluation Challenges
Procedural Challenges
Practicality Challenges
Power Challenges

10 Communication Concerns

OBJECTIVES

After reading this chapter, you should be able to:

- Describe the extent and effects of sexism in the classroom.
- Describe ethnocentrism as a barrier to intercultural communication.
- Describe the dimensions of culture.
- Describe how cultural diversity affects classroom communication.
- Describe the effects of racism and classism in the classroom.
- Define ableism and its effect on classroom communication.
- Discuss strategies for addressing these concerns in the classroom.

The teaching–learning process is primarily a communication process that relies largely on the interactive behaviors of students and teachers. Any variable that prohibits effective communication can adversely affect the learning process. In this chapter we discuss several communication concerns that influence the teaching–learning process—sexism, ethnocentrism, classism, racism, and ableism. Each of these concerns creates communication barriers in the classroom. Within each of these barriers, we will address information that will allow instructors to affect change and communicate more competently with students.

SEXISM IN THE CLASSROOM

As Wood (2009) tells us, "schools teach us, who is important and who is not; who influenced the directions of history, science and literature, and social organization . . . and contribute in major ways to the process of gendering individuals" (p. 221).

And despite several decades of research suggesting problems in our educational system in terms of gender bias, the dominant mode in education remains geared to males. The system stresses objectivity, separateness, competitiveness, and hierarchical structure (Palmer, 1998; Simonds & Cooper, 2001).

Schools teach us in a variety of ways—through curriculum, educational materials, and classroom interaction. We examine each of these in relation to **gender bias**, discuss progress made in each area, and consider areas that still need improvement. **Sexism** is discrimination based on gender. Before we begin, it's extremely important to remember that although the focus has been on females in recent years, sex discrimination in education affects males as well (NCWGE, 2002; Sadker & Sadker, 1994; Sommers, 2000). Research suggests that:

- From grade school to high school, boys receive lower marks on their report cards.
- More boys than girls drop out and repeat grades.
- More boys than girls get suspended from school.
- Boys are designated as learning disabled and labeled emotionally disturbed more often than girls.

Other investigations confirm these findings. For example, in 1992, the American Association of University Women (AAUW) Educational Foundation commissioned a comprehensive review of 1,331 studies of gender and educational practices. The result was the report *How Schools Shortchange Girls* (AAUW, 1992) in which evidence was amassed to show that female students continue to receive less attention, less encouragement, and less serious regard than their male peers.

And yet, the research suggests that female students are making gains in the gender gap. In March 2000, the National Center for Education Statistics (the primary federal entity for collecting, analyzing, and reporting data related to education in the United States) released *Trends in Educational Equity of Girls and Women* (U.S. Department of Education, 2000). The report suggests that

- Females consistently outperform males in reading and writing.
- There are no more gender differences favoring male students in mathematics and science.
- Achievement gaps appear more closely related to attitudes than to course taking.
- Females are just as likely as males to use computers at home and school (some researchers note that females are more likely to use computers recreationally to pursue hobbies and e-mail friends whereas males use the computer to further professional endeavors) (Cyber Dialogue, 1999).

Women have made substantial progress at the graduate level overall, but they still earn fewer than half of the degrees in many fields. Women's progress toward earning an equal share of first professional degrees has been notable. In 1970, 5 percent of the law degrees, 8 percent of medical degrees, and 1 percent of dentistry degrees were awarded to women. In 1996, the corresponding percentages were 44, 41, and 36.

The recent report *Title IX at 30: Report Card on Gender Equity* (NCWGE, 2002) suggests that the problem of gender inequity in education still exists. The report indicates that sex segregation persists in career education with more than 90 percent of females clustered in training programs for the traditionally female fields of teaching, graphic arts, and office technology. At the college level, 60 percent of computer science and business majors are male, 70 percent of physics majors are male, and more than 80 percent of engineering majors are male. Women continue to suffer from the gender wage gap—the careers males choose tend to lead to higher paying jobs than the careers females choose. In addition, equal pay for equal work is not a reality. Let's take education as an example. *Trends in Educational Equity of Girls and Women: 2004* (Freeman, 2004) reports that among full-time year-round wage and salary workers in 2000, the median annual income earnings of young adult females were generally lower than those of their male peers with similar educational backgrounds. Where does this gender bias and its resulting inequities come from? In terms of the educational environment, there are two major sources—curriculum materials and classroom interaction patterns.

Curriculum Material

In the 1970s, researchers examining the most heavily used elementary textbooks in first through sixth grades reported disturbing results (Weitzman & Rizzo, 1975). For example, in social studies textbooks, only 33 percent of the illustrations included females. In one series designed to teach reading, 102 stories were about boys and 35 were about girls. Mliner (1977) examined elementary and junior high school math and science texts. In these textbooks, females were pictured as Indian dolls or witches or as participating in activities such as skipping rope and buying balloons. Males were pictured as sailors, kings, bakers, circus performers, band members, and balloon sellers. Males were pictured fifteen times for every one female pictured. Purcell and Stewart (1990) and Tetenbaum and Pearson (1989) found that sex stereotypes such as these persist. Although many changes have been made since that time, comparing three decades of science material, Nilsen (1987) found that artists were still drawing three times as many pictures of males as females. In addition, in the majority of books examined in this study, the word *man* was used to describe people in general, and few books depicted women in scientific careers. Such discrepancies present negative images of females and reinforce gender stereotypes. Thus, although more females may be taking math and science classes, some curriculum materials still reinforce traditional gender stereotypes.

Discrepancies also exist in the number of male and female authors included in textbooks. In an early survey of English literature anthologies, the seventeen books examined included selections by 147 male authors and only 25 female authors (Arlow & Froschel, 1976). Carlson (1989) reports that a survey of high school–level anthologies revealed a preponderance of male authors. One anthology, for example, included more than ninety selections by male authors and only eight by female authors. Most anthologies dealing with speech communication feature more speeches by men (Campbell, 1991; Vonnegut, 1992), some history textbooks devote only about 2 percent of their pages to women (Sadker & Sadker, 1994), and some art textbooks discuss male artists rather than female artists (Sadker & Sadker, 1994).

Generally, gender stereotypes may be found in all types of textbooks (Carter & Spitzack, 1989; Cawyer et al., 1994; Ferree & Hall, 1990; Kramarae, Schultz, & O'Barr, 1984). The results of all these studies indicated that women and ethnic groups were underrepresented.

Gullicks and her colleagues (2005) examined the frequency of gender and ethnic groups represented in photographs in the top ten public speaking texts. Their results indicate that men are pictured in power positions more often than women. However, in photos displaying multiple ethnic groups (with or without Caucasians), people of other ethnicities were more likely to be shown in positions of power than were Caucasians.

With the adoption of nonsexist guidelines during the past decade, many textbook publishers have made substantial progress. Harwood (1992) notes that "a cursory look through any high school Spanish or French book will, for the most part, reveal an equal number of illustrations of men and women and a fair depiction of their roles" (p. 16). Nevertheless, some authors have made relatively few changes to increase the visibility of females and to decrease the stereotyping of males and females. For example, the "nonbiased" material is often added to the center or end of a textbook without any attempt to integrate it into the overall format of the book. Peterson (1994) quotes one student as saying, "You'll see women's pictures all put in one chapter—'great women in history'—rather than throughout the book" (p. 2D). And Harwood (1992) describes a popular high school Latin textbook that rarely uses the word *she* in practice sentences and depicts more than two-thirds of the characters in the reading lessons as male.

In addition to textbooks, educators are being encouraged to use other books to supplement the basic curriculum. The image of males and females in literature—from a child's first picture book to adult best sellers—can influence the way in which males and females see themselves and, thus, can influence their communication.

In many ways, children's literature reflects and reinforces gender stereotypes. Numerical disparities and stereotyped behavior patterns and characteristics reflected in children's literature may help teach girls to undervalue themselves and teach boys to believe that they must always strive to be stereotypically masculine.

Although the situation continues to improve, females are not included in children's books in numbers that reflect their presence in the general population.

It's important to note that other societal images, such as gender images in advertising, television, movies, and so on are also sexist. These images, although not often used as classroom curriculum materials, do influence students and reinforce the images contained in classroom materials (for a review of these images, see Stewart, Cooper, & Stewart, 2003).

Classroom Interaction

Numerous studies have shown that (1) boys get teachers' attention by being straightforward and unreserved, (2) teachers praise boys more often, (3) boys receive more academic help, and (4) teachers are more likely to accept boys' ideas or opinions during classroom discussion (see research reviewed in Condravy, Skirboll, & Taylor, 1998; Simonds & Cooper, 2001; Stewart et al., 2003). Most of these studies have focused on student participation. In general, these studies support the idea that males and females experience classroom interaction differently.

For example, Karp and Yoels (1976) found that male students accounted for a majority of interactions in classes even though the classes contained nearly equal numbers of female and male students. Hutchinson and Beadle (1992) observed the interaction of a group of twenty-six students who attended two seminars, one taught by a female and one taught by a male professor. These researchers found that women and men made proportionately equitable numbers of contributions in the female professor's seminar, but in the male professor's seminar, male students spoke more often and for longer periods of time than the women. The female professor achieved gender parity by more closely managing the discussion, designating specific students to speak. The male professor more often allowed students to initiate discussion at will.

This pattern seems to be consistent at all educational levels. Sadker and Sadker (1994) observed teacher–student interactions in fourth- through eighth-grade classrooms. Boys consistently outtalked and outparticipated girls, primarily because teachers allowed boys to call out, responded more positively to boys than to girls when they did call out, called on boys more frequently, and gave them more feedback on their answers.

The research studies on classroom interaction are not unequivocal. As the *Report Card on Gender Equity* (NCWGE, 2002) suggests

> At all levels of education, gender continues to influence instruction. From grade school to graduate school, more active and assertive males continue to attract more instructor attention, both positive and negative. Gender inequities in teaching present problems for all students. Female students continue to receive less individual encouragement and assistance and learn to accept a quieter, secondary role, both in school and in the adult roles that follow. While many males benefit from the additional instructional attention they receive, some find the glare of the classroom spotlight an uncomfortable education environment and would prefer to learn in a quieter, less public manner. The harsher disciplinary messages directed at males reinforce the notion that they are troublemakers and problem students (pp. 32–33).

Bachen, McLaughlin, and Garcia (1999) examined how students' stereotypes of gender roles affected how they evaluated their instructors. The researchers concluded that female students' identification with female faculty was strong and probably constituted a measure of educational success for those students. Male students did not rate female faculty differently from male faculty, but their qualitative comments indicated that males were more comfortable with female faculty when the females seemed to be adapting to a more male style in the classroom. Extant research indicates that female instructors are consistently rated as significantly less credible than male instructors (Anderson & Miller, 1997; Centra & Gaubatz, 2000; Hargett, 1999).

An interesting aspect of gender in the classroom that has only recently begun to be examined is sexual orientation. Russ, Simonds, and Hunt (2002) examined the influence of instructor sexual orientation on perceptions of teacher credibility. The purpose of their study was to determine if college students perceive gay teachers as less credible than straight teachers. In addition, the authors explored the role of teacher credibility in terms of perceived student learning. In order to examine these variables, a male confederate presented a 30-minute lecture on cultural influences to 154 undergraduate students enrolled in eight separate introductory communication courses. The confederate's sexual orientation was systematically manipulated. During half of the lectures, the confederate referred to his opposite-sex partner three times ("My partner Jennifer and I . . . "). During the other half of the lectures the confederate referred to his same-sex partner three times ("My partner Jason and I . . . "). Students perceived a gay teacher as significantly less credible than a straight teacher. Students of a gay teacher perceived that they learned considerably less than did students of a straight teacher. The researchers also asked open-ended questions such as, "If one of your teachers told you he/she was gay, how would you respond and why?" More than 70 percent of the participants said that they would react unfavorably. Only 11 percent indicated they would welcome a gay or lesbian teacher. Although the same speaker presented the same lecture, delivered in identical fashion for all eight classes (only the sexual orientation was manipulated), some interesting findings emerged. Sixty-seven percent of students disliked the gay speaker's topic and suggested he was pushing an agenda. Students described the gay teacher as "flamboyant" and as having "distracting hand gestures."

Sexual harassment is another issue for concern. *Hostile Hallways: The AAUW Survey on Sexual Harassment in America's Schools* (AAUW, 1993) represents the first national scientific study of sexual harassment in public schools. Based on the experiences of 1,632 students in grades 8 through 11, the researchers found that 85 percent of the girls and 76 percent of the boys surveyed had experienced sexual harassment. The survey also indicated that although both girls and boys experienced sexual harassment, sexual harassment takes a greater toll on girls; girls who have been harassed are more afraid in school and feel less confident about themselves than boys who have been harassed.

Specific studies bear out these findings. For example, Stepp (2001) surveyed college students and coaches involved in extracurricular speech and debate activities. She found that sexual harassment is widespread and that females are sexually harassed (defined as ranging from generalized sexist remarks or behavior to sexual assault) more than males.

The limited improvements in gender equity in the past three decades can be attributed in part to teacher education programs. Two decades ago teacher education textbooks devoted less than 1 percent of content coverage to the experiences of women, the issue of sexism in the school, and curricular resources or teaching strategies overcoming such bias; today that figure is only 3 percent (NCWGE, 2002).

Reading Objectives and Discussion Prompts

10.1 Sexism

What do you know?
What is sexism and how does it affect classroom communication?

What do you think?
Do you believe that these issues are still present? If so, how will you be mindful of this in your own classroom?

Another communication barrier in the classroom is ethnocentrism. The following section will first describe this barrier, then discuss principles of intercultural communication that will allow instructors to teach from a more global perspective.

ETHNOCENTRISM

The definition of **ethnocentrism** comes from two Greek words: *ethos*, meaning "people" or "nation," and *ketron*, meaning "center." Sumner (1906/1940) divided the concept of ethnocentrism into two parts: the belief that one's culture is superior to all others and the consequent belief that other groups are inferior. Thus, ethnocentrism is being centered on one's own culture—believing it to be the center of the universe. And because other cultures are judged by our own cultural values, we tend to judge other cultures as inferior to our own. We are all ethnocentric to some degree. The problem is not that we feel proud of our culture, but that we sometimes draw conclusions that another culture is inferior to our own. Thus, ethnocentrism is a hindrance to intercultural communication because it prevents us from understanding other cultures. We need to be diligent in terms of understanding our own ethnocentrism and the problems it can cause in the teaching–learning process. In this section we look at how culture can affect our communication in the classroom by examining cultural dimensions and cultural diversity.

Cultural Dimensions

In order to understand ethnocentism as a communication barrier, it is important to understand culture. Although there are several approaches to the study of culture, one that is helpful in the educational environment is Hofstede's (2005) work. In his view, four cultural dimensions affect what occurs in the classroom: individualism/collectivism, power distance, uncertainty avoidance, and masculinity/femininity. The first of these is **individualism/collectivism**. In an individualistic culture, the focus for an individual is on himself and his immediate family (spouse, children). Collectivist cultures assume that any person belongs to one or more tight "in-groups" from which she cannot detach. The "in-group" (family, clan, organization) protects the interests of its members and in turn expects their permanent loyalty.

In terms of classroom behavior, in collectivist cultures students expect to learn how to do things for themselves, speak up in class only when called on personally by the teacher, and believe education is a way of gaining prestige within the social environment and of joining a higher status group. Formal harmony is important and neither a teacher nor a student should ever be made to lose face. In contrast, in individualistic cultures, students expect to learn how to learn, will speak up in class in response to a general invitation by the teacher, and believe education is a way of improving economic worth and self-respect based on ability and competence. Confrontation in the classroom is not necessarily avoided. Conflicts can be brought into the open and face-consciousness is weak. In a collectivist culture the group is emphasized rather than the individual; harmony and circularity are emphasized. This explains why Native American children learn better in an environment that is noncompetitive, holistic, and cooperative. Similarly, an understanding of this dimension explains why Mexican children, because their culture emphasizes cooperation, allow others to share their homework or answers. This demonstrates solidarity, helpfulness, and generosity—all important characteristics of their collectivist culture (see research reviewed in Calloway-Thomas, Cooper, & Simonds, 2007).

The second of Hofstede's dimensions, **power distance**, defines the extent to which the less powerful persons in a society accept inequality in power and consider it normal. In terms of classroom behavior, the power dimension suggests that in small power distance societies, the educational process is student centered. Students initiate communication, outline their own paths to learning, and can contradict the teacher. Thus, in the United States, where the power distance is small, students are encouraged to challenge the teacher and one another. The teacher encourages students to discuss and debate issues, to learn how to solve problems, and to create their own answers to the questions posed. Students prefer to learn through personal discovery and problem solving rather than through memorizing facts presented to them by an authority figure.

In contrast, in large power distance societies, the educational process is teacher centered. The teacher initiates all communication, outlines the paths of learning students should follow, and is never publicly criticized or contradicted. The emphasis is on the personal "wisdom" of the teacher. Thus, in Asian societies the power difference between teacher and student is large. A Chinese student would never consider arguing with a teacher. The Asian student's role is to accept and respect the wisdom of the teacher. Asking questions is seen as a challenge to the teacher's authority or as an admission of the student's ignorance (Wallach & Metcalf, 1995).

Uncertainty avoidance is the third of Hofstede's dimensions. It defines the extent to which people within a culture are made nervous by situations that they perceive as unclear, unstructured, or unpredictable. Those in a strong uncertainty avoidance society try to avoid these situations by adhering to a strict code of behavior and a belief in absolute truth. In terms of the classroom, in a weak uncertainty avoidance society, students feel comfortable in unstructured learning situations (vague objectives, no timetable, and broad assignments) and are rewarded for innovative approaches to problem solving. Teachers can say, "I don't know," interpret intellectual disagreements as stimulating, and ask parents for advice concerning their children. As you might suspect, in strong uncertainty avoidance societies, students feel most comfortable in structured learning situations (precise objectives, strict timetables, and detailed assignments) and are rewarded for accuracy in problem solving. Teachers are expected to know all the answers, interpret intellectual disagreement as personal disloyalty, and consider themselves experts who do not need parents' ideas.

Students in weak uncertainty avoidance cultures, such as the United States, Great Britain, Ireland, and India, tend to be competitive, need fewer instructions, and see conflict as stimulating. Students in strong uncertainty avoidance cultures, such as France, Chile, Spain, Portugal, and Japan, tend to prefer clear instructions, avoid conflict, and dislike competition.

The final dimension is **masculinity/femininity**. Cultures labeled as masculine strive for maximal distinction between what men and women are expected to do. Men are expected to be assertive, ambitious, and competitive; to strive for material success; and to respect whatever is big, fast, and strong. Women are expected to care for nonmaterial quality of life, children, and the weak, and to serve others. Feminist cultures define overlapping roles for the sexes. Thus, men do not have to be competitive and women do not have to do all the caregiving. In feminine cultures, quality of life, interpersonal relationships, and concern for the weak are stressed as compared to masculine cultures, in which material success and assertiveness are stressed.

In terms of the classroom, in masculine societies, academic performance is rewarded. Teachers openly praise good students because academic achievement is highly regarded and competition is fostered. Teachers use the best students as the norm. In contrast, in feminine societies, the students' social adaptations are rewarded. Teachers avoid openly praising students because academic achievement is less important than successful interpersonal relationships, and cooperation among students is fostered. Teachers use average students as the norm.

These cultural dimensions help to explain differences in how students learn and the problems that can arise in the classroom when the teacher and students come from cultures that differ on these dimensions. The way students study a problem differs across cultures. For example, European American students tend to be topic centered.

Their accounts of events focus on a single topic or closely related topics and are ordered in a linear fashion and lead to a resolution (Au, 1993). African American students often use a topic-associating style in which the student presents "a series of episodes linked to some person or theme. These links are implicit in the account and are not stated" (Au, 1996).

These differences in cultural dimensions also affect classroom interaction. As the Rosenthal and Jacobson (1968) "Pygmalion" study suggests, a teacher's expectations for students affects how he communicates with students. In addition, if teachers communicate with different frequency based on a student's group membership, such as race or ethnicity, this difference in access to feedback or accessibility of the instructor can lead to differences in the quality of education. A teacher who interacts less with a student has less information about the student's performance, skill, knowledge, and progress. This lack of interaction might cause reduced levels of immediacy and less learning (Morreale & Jones, 1997; Neuliep, 1995).

Cultural Diversity

There is a wide diversity of cultural backgrounds in today's classrooms and every indication is that this diversity will continue to increase. Yet, the classroom culture is, to a great extent, an extension of mainstream American culture (Condon, 1986; Samovar & Porter, 2009). For example, the values of the classroom are those of mainstream America—independence, competition, individualism, and concern for relevance and application. As a result, students whose backgrounds are different from this dominant culture often have a difficult time adjusting to the classroom culture. For example, many Hispanics and Asian cultures expect students to learn by listening, observing, and imitating. Compare this to the U.S. educational system in which critical thinking, active discussion, and question asking are expected. In the United States students are taught to answer questions quickly. In contrast, Asian and Native American students are taught to consider all sides of an issue before answering a question. And, to compound the problem such differences make in classroom learning, teachers often aren't trained in how to teach to a multicultural student body (Cole, 1995).

Although we know quite a bit about teacher communication patterns and influence in the United States, less is known about classroom communication in other countries. However, studies are beginning to explore the role of culture in communication both as it applies within the borders of a specific nation and also how it is manifested in classrooms across the world (e.g., Asselin & Mastron, 2001; McCroskey, Richmond, Sallinen, Fayer, & Barraclough, 1996; Roach & Byrne, 2001). For example, Roach and Byrne (2001) compared American and German classrooms. American instructors were perceived to be higher in power use, affinity-seeking, and nonverbal immediacy than were German instructors. Roach and his colleagues (2001) compared French and American classrooms and found that American students perceived higher levels of affective learning, report liking their instructors more and report higher cognitive learning.

Culture influences both behavior and psychological processes. It affects the way we perceive the world and the way we communicate. Culture "forms a prism through which members of a group see the world and create 'shared meanings' " (Bowman, 1989, p. 118). One way to improve the possibility that communication will be effective is to be sensitive to the "stumbling blocks" to intercultural communication. The six stumbling blocks have been defined as the following (Barna, 1988):

1. *Assuming similarity instead of difference.*   There seem to be no universals of "human nature" that can be used as a basis for automatic understanding. Each of us is so unconsciously influenced by our own culture that we assume the basic needs, desires, and beliefs of others are the same as our own.

2. *Language.*   Even words as simple as *yes* and *no* can cause trouble. When a Japanese person hears, "Won't you have some tea?" she tends to listen to the literal meaning of the sentence and answers "no," meaning she wants some. Also, in some cultures it is polite to refuse the first or second offer of refreshment. Many foreign guests have gone hungry because their U.S. host or hostess never presented the third offer—another case of "no" meaning "yes" (Barna, 1988, p. 326).

3. *Nonverbal misinterpretations.*   When we enter into another culture, we need to be able to hear its "special hum and buzz of implication" (Frankel, 1965, p. 103). When we misinterpret or do not comprehend the nonverbal cues, communication will be ineffective.

4. *Preconceptions and stereotypes.*   These reduce the chance for effective communication because they interfere with our ability to objectively view the situation.

5. *Tendency to evaluate.*   When we approve or disapprove the actions or statements of another, rather than try to comprehend, effective communication is difficult. We need to remain open-minded. Otherwise, communication may be cut off before we really understand the other person. Because we are all ethnocentric to some degree, that is, we think our cultural ways are "right" or "best," we evaluate other cultures as "not as good" or "wrong."

6. *High anxiety.*   Going into new, unfamiliar, or uncertain situations is difficult for many of us. We become anxious, and as a result, may become defensive. Jack Gibb (1961) tells us that defensiveness prevents us from concentrating on the message. In addition

> Not only do defensive communicators send off multiple value, motive, and affect cues, but also defensive recipients distort what they receive. As a person becomes more and more defensive, he becomes less and less able to perceive accurately the motives, the values, and the emotions of the sender.(Gibb, 1961, p. 142)

It is impossible to outline the cultural characteristics of every ethnic group here. Teachers must identify the groups present in their classrooms and learn about the characteristics of each. In terms of our focus, the communication variables that "are identifiable as culturally determined, as constituting ethnic communication styles, and as being influenced in shaping interactions among members of different ethnic groups" (Gay, 1978, p. 52) are:

- attitudes
- social organization (status of people within the structure)
- patterns of thought
- role prescription (how people are supposed to behave)

- language
- use and organization of space
- vocabulary
- time conceptualizations
- nonverbal expressions

Thus, the preceding list constitutes the categories of knowledge you will need about a particular ethnic group in order to communicate effectively with that group.

Anderson and Powell (1988), in their article on cultural influences on education processes, review research that highlights intercultural differences. For example, there is virtually no classroom interaction in Vietnamese, Mexican, or Chinese classrooms. In contrast, in an Israeli kibbutz students talk among themselves, address teachers by their first names, and criticize when they feel teachers are wrong.

In Italian classrooms, children greet their teacher with a kiss on both cheeks, and students and teachers touch one another frequently. African American children may use back channeling—a vocal response that is meant to encourage or reinforce the speaker ("yeah," "go on," "right on," etc.). Often European American teachers view this interaction as an interruption rather than a reinforcer. Looking at the teacher is a sign of disrespect in Jamaican and some African cultures, but a sign of respect in the United States.

Whereas European American culture values punctuality and a monochronic view of time, other cultures do not. This can cause problems in the educational process. For example, Latino students are not conditioned to use every moment in a productive, task-oriented way. Native Americans have a polychronic view of time—things are done when the time is right, not by a time on a clock or a date on a calendar.

Cultural differences among students are important to understand for two major reasons: (1) Cultural differences may result in differences in learning style, and (2) understanding cultural differences can help us communicate more effectively with students.

Gay (1978) indicates that two **cognitive patterns** are evident from research on ethnic learning styles. The **analytic style** is detail specific, impersonal, requires sustained attention, and uses an elaborate syntactic code. This style seems to be characteristic of European and Jewish Americans. The **relational style** employs self-centered orientations, determines word meanings by situational contexts, focuses on global characteristics of stimuli, uses a descriptive mode of abstracting information from stimuli, and uses a restricted syntactic code. This style seems to be characteristic of Mexican Americans, Asian Americans, African Americans, and some Native Americans.

In general, the research supports the conclusion that Latino, Native American, African American, and female students respond better to teaching methods that emphasize holistic thinking, cooperative learning, a valuing of personal knowledge, a concrete orientation, the oral tradition, and a reliance on imagery and expressiveness. This learning style is quite different from that of most college instructors, Asian Americans, and the majority of students, whose learning style is characterized by an abstract, independent, written, technical orientation (see, e.g., Anderson, 1988; Banks, 1988; Calloway-Thomas et al., 2007; Hilliard, 1989; Pemberton, 1988; Samovar & Porter, 2009).

Remember that although general statements such as these can be made as a result of existing research, careful attention must be given to individual differences to avoid stereotyping. That is why it is imperative for teachers to understand the cultural differences of their students in order to communicate effectively with them.

Reading Objectives and Discussion Prompts

10.2 Ethnocentrism

What do you know?
What is ethnocentrism? How does it create a barrier in the classroom? What are the cultural dimensions described by Hofstede?

What do you think?
What are some specific ways that you can be sensitive to the needs of diverse students? How will you enact these in your own classroom?

RACISM AND CLASSISM IN THE CLASSROOM

Before we begin a discussion of race, class, and ethnicity, several terms need to be defined. First, *stereotypes*. **Stereotypes** are generalizations about some group of people that oversimplify the group. When we stereotype, we categorize others based on easily identifiable characteristics. We then assume that certain attributes apply to all or most members of the group. Finally, we assume individual members of the category have the attributes associated with the group.

How do stereotypes affect our communication? When we stereotype we often make errors in our interpretation of another's behavior. Kunda and Sherman-Williams (1993) tell us:

> Consider, for example, the unambiguous act of failing a test. Ethnic stereotypes may lead perceivers to attribute such failure to laziness if the person is Asian but to low ability if the person is Black. Thus stereotypes will affect judgments of the target's ability even if subjects base these judgments only on the act, because the stereotypes will determine the meaning of the act. (p. 97)

Stereotypes often lead to prejudice. **Prejudice** involves prejudging without knowledge or examination of the available data. When we say things such as, "Well, of course, Junmei always gets the highest grade. Asians study all the time," we are communicating our prejudices.

When a negative attitude toward a group is translated into action, discrimination results. **Discrimination** is the process of treating individuals unequally on the basis of characteristics such as sex, age, ethnicity, race, or sexual orientation.

An ethnic group is a group of people who share a common culture that is usually based on nationality or language. In the United States the terms used to categorize ethnic groups are as follows (Rogers & Steinfatt, 2009):

Asian American or Asian—people who trace their origins to the Asian continent or to the Pacific Islands (for example, Korea, Japan, China, Samoa).

African American or Black—people who trace their origins to the sub-Saharan part of Africa. In the United States, *African American* is often the preferred term by black citizens of the United States, whereas black citizens of the Caribbean and Latin America prefer *black*.

Latino/Latina—people who trace their origins to Latin America or to Spain. *Chicano/Chicana* refers to Mexican heritage. *Hispanic* is the term used by the U.S. Census Bureau for all of these individuals.

Native American—the native peoples of the United States.

White, Anglo American, and European American—persons of European background other than Spanish.

We in the United States consider ourselves a "classless" society. However, in truth, class affects our view of others. Class consists of a large group of people who occupy a similar economic position in society based on income, wealth, property ownership, education, skills, or authority in the economic sphere. **Classism** is the systematic assignment of characteristics of worth and ability based on social class. It includes individual attitudes and behaviors and systems of policies and practices that benefit the upper classes at the expense of the lower classes. These systems result in drastic income and wealth inequality. By this definition, classism has three components:

- differential treatment based on social class or perceived social class
- systematic oppression of subordinated groups by the dominant groups
- a system of beliefs and cultural attributes that rank people according to economic status, family lineage, job status, level of education, and so on

Middle-class and higher-class people (dominant group members) are perceived as smarter and more articulate than working-class and poor people (subordinated groups). In this way dominant group members define what is "normal" and "acceptable" for all people in a society. Where we live, how many and what kind of possessions we have, our language (vocabulary, dialect/accent, etc.), and nonverbal cues such as posture are all indicators of our class.

Class can be viewed on a continuum. There are no hard and fast divisions between groups. We move a little up or down the continuum during our lifetime. Class is relative, both subjectively (how we feel) and objectively (in terms of position or resources). Our felt experience often varies depending on whether we look up or down the continuum. However, it is clear that everyone on the top end is mostly dominant with respect to class and derives benefit and privilege, while everyone at the bottom of the continuum is subordinate and has limited access to benefits. Table 10.1 illustrates this.

What effect does classism have on education? Research demonstrates that student from working-class or impoverished backgrounds often experience alienation in the classroom. For example, Beagan (2005) explored the medical school experiences of students who self-identified as coming from a working-class or impoverished family background. Students reported that having (or not having) money, while the most obvious impact of social class difference, was not the only problem. Students reported more subtle signs of class. Students from working-class or impoverished backgrounds were significantly less likely to report that they fit in well and more likely to report that their class background had a negative impact in school (Beagan, 2005).

TABLE 10.1 Class Continuum of Position and Resources		
Term	**Position**	**"Goods"**
Dominants	Ruling Class	"Have Mores"
	Owning Class	
Mostly Dominants	Middle Class	"Haves"
Mostly Subordinants	Working Class	
Subordinants	Poor/Low Income	"Have Nots"

In order to understand our communication in today's diverse classrooms, we need to consider the following (adapted from Condon, 1986):

Our expectations for appropriate student behavior—we may, for example, expect students to use standard English in both speaking and writing.

Actual behavior—students may not use standard English.

Our feeling about the student's behavior as well as the basis for this feeling–"I'm angry because the student refuses to learn standard English."

Our explanations for the behavior–we must remember that these explanations reflect our cultural values ("The student isn't motivated to learn").

Our response to the student's behavior—we may reprimand the student, either publicly or privately. Again, our response reflects our cultural values and norms.

When we are aware of the cultural differences in our classrooms, understand our attitudes concerning them, and understand the five considerations previously outlined, we can begin to structure our classroom so that we communicate effectively with multicultural students. We can, for example, respect the ethnic background of our students. We can read stories with varied ethnic and racial content in literature class. We might have students study world events from different cultural perspectives in social studies class. However, multicultural education is not content alone. Your attitude toward culturally diverse students and how you communicate that attitude is extremely important.

When one of the authors of this text was teaching Chinese students at the Chinese University of Hong Kong, she learned that our American teaching strategies can be problematic for the Chinese. For example, never ask Chinese students, "Are there any questions?" To ask a question would show one's ignorance, and a loss of face would result. However, if a teacher asks, "Have I explained this clearly?" students are free to ask questions because it is the teacher's "fault" that they don't understand. If she explained clearly, there would be no need for questions.

In addition, because of the high status of teachers, Chinese students are very uncomfortable with the informality, common in college-level American classrooms, of referring to a teacher by first name. Interestingly, one of the Chinese words for disobedience consists of two characters, which roughly translated mean "mouth back." As one might expect, students show their respect by keeping quiet in class. Thus, Asian students may be uncomfortable with a teaching strategy such as discussion or small groups.

African American students, whose culture emphasizes verbal skills and expressiveness, show greater emotion and theatrical behavior; demonstrate faster responses, higher energy, and more animation; and are persuasive and more active in the communication process. European American teachers often view these behaviors as confrontational because they are more passive in their communication style (Shade & New, 1993). Problems arise because the African American student perceives the communication of the European American teacher as dissuasive and distancing, whereas the teacher sees the African American student's communication as disruptive or confrontational (Shade & New, 1993).

In their quantitative summary of fifteen studies concerned with the impact of student race on classroom interaction, Cooper and Allen (1998) found that race did indeed have an impact in the classroom. Specifically, African American and Latino students participate in less total classroom interaction with instructors and experience greater proportions of negative interactions and fewer positive interactions than European American students. According to these studies, teachers interact with students differently based on race.

Reading Objectives and Discussion Prompts

10.3 Racism and Classism

What do you know?
What leads to racism and classism? How does it affect the classroom?

What do you think?
Have you observed or experienced any of these issues in the classes you've been in? How will you address this in your own class?

Diversity comes in all forms. We have previously discussed sexism, ethnocentrism, classism, and racism as barriers to effective classroom communication. Another cause for concern and potential barrier to effective instruction can be based on the various abilities of the students.

ABLEISM

In his article in the *Harvard Educational Review,* Hehir (2002) defines **ableism** as "the devaluation of disability" that "results in societal attitudes that uncritically assert that it is better for a child to walk than roll, speak than sign, read print than read Braille, spell independently than use a spell-check, and hang out with nondisabled kids as opposed to other disabled kids." Rauscher and McClintock (1996) define *ableism* as a pervasive system of discrimination and exclusion that oppresses people who have mental, emotional, and physical disabilities. They note that "deeply rooted beliefs about health, productivity, beauty, and the value of human life combine to create an environment that is often hostile to those whose physical, mental, cognitive, and sensory abilities . . . fall out of the scope of what is currently defined as socially acceptable" (p. 198). Black disability activist Greg Smith (2001) captures the essence of definitions in his article

"Backtalk: The Brother in the Wheelchair": "I've faced unintentional discrimination, and it is just as damaging as racism. . . . It is called ableism, the devaluation and disregard of people with disabilities" (p. 162).

The National Organization on Disabilities reports that more than 49 million Americans have a disability (Cohen, 1998). These may range from a "hidden" disability, such as a learning disability, to a visible physical disability, such as being confined to a wheelchair.

Physical Disabilities

In terms of the classroom, students with disabilities, particularly those with visible physical disabilities, report negative attitudes of faculty as a primary reason they fail at the postsecondary level (see research reviewed in Bilke & Yasel, 1999). Indeed, the classroom climate does not seem to be a supportive one for students with physical disabilities. Beilke and Yasel (1999) report that these students often find faculty willing to make instructional accommodations but encounter less than a supportive classroom climate.

When able-bodied persons encounter a person with a physical disability, the able-bodied person often feels uncomfortable. They are not sure what to say or do (Braithwaite, 1990, 1991, 1996; Braithwaite & Eckstein, 2003; Higgins, 1992). In addition, able-bodied people hold many stereotypes about people with disabilities:

> For example, they often perceive them as dependent, socially introverted, emotionally unstable, depressed, hypersensitive, and easily offended, especially with regard to their disability. In addition, disabled people are often presumed to differ from able-bodied people in moral character, social skills, and political orientation.(Coleman & DePaulo, 1991, p. 69)

Braithwaite and Braithwaite (2000, p. 144) provide guidelines for communicating with persons with disabilities. These are presented in Box 10.1.

In addition to students from varying cultural and racial backgrounds, as well as students with physical disabilities, you will also have students who have "hidden" disabilities. These students have special needs. Space does not allow an in-depth discussion here of students with special needs; however, books have been written on these students, referenced throughout this chapter. Following is a brief discussion of several types of students with special needs and some suggestions for teaching these students.

Students with Learning Disabilities

Students with **learning disabilities** often have a poor self-concept and are less accepted and more overtly rejected than their peers without learning disabilities. They frequently have problems interacting with teachers and parents and exhibit problem behaviors in general. Many young people with learning disabilities exhibit negative verbal interactions and misinterpret nonverbal communications.

The National Longitudinal Transition Study (NLTS; Wagner, Blackorby, Cameto, & Newman, 1993) investigated the educational results of a large sample of students with disabilities who attended high schools in the mid-1980s. This study, the largest and most thorough of its kind, paints a less than satisfactory picture. Along with other data

BOX 10.1

Communicating with Persons with Disabilities

Do Not
- Assume persons with disabilities cannot speak for themselves or cannot do things for themselves.
- Force your help on persons with disabilities.
- Avoid communication with persons who have disabilities simply because you are uncomfortable or unsure.
- Use terms such as *handicapped, physically challenged, crippled, victim,* and so on unless requested to do so by persons with disabilities.
- Assume that a disability defines a person.

Do
- Assume persons with disabilities can do something unless they communicate otherwise.
- Let persons with disabilities tell you if they want something, what they want, and when they want it. If a person with a disability refuses your help, don't go ahead and help anyway. The goal is to give the person with the disability control in the situation.
- Remember that persons with disabilities have experienced others' discomfort before and understand how you might feel.
- Use terms such as *people with disabilities* rather than *disabled people*. The goal is to stress the person first before introducing the disability.
- Treat persons with disabilities as *persons first*, recognizing that you are not dealing with a disabled person but with a *person* who *has* a disability. This means actively seeking the humanity of the person you are speaking with, and focusing on the person's characteristics instead of the superficial physical attribute. Without diminishing the significance of a physical disability, you can selectively attend to many other aspects of a person during communication.

such as the performance of students with disabilities on statewide assessments as well as recent research, the NLTS confirms that the educational attainment levels of students with learning disabilities is less than adequate (Katzman, 2001). Students with learning abilities drop out of school at relatively high rates—about twice as frequently as disabled students (Wagner et al., 1993). These students also participate in higher education in relatively small numbers. The NTLS also documents that relatively large numbers of these students are not taking challenging academic subjects. Interestingly, college students with learning disabilities view their professors as less communicatively competent and are less willing to communicate with their professors than students without learning disabilities (Frymier & Wanzwer, 2003).

Students with learning disabilities usually exhibit discrepancies between their actual level of performance and their intellectual potential. These students have difficulty processing auditory and visual stimuli, the result of which is a faulty interpretive response. Learning disabilities can occur in the following areas:

Memory—inability to remember newly presented information

Visual-auditory discrimination—inability to see or hear likenesses and differences

Visual-auditory association—inability to associate visual and auditory stimuli

Perceptual-motor skills—inability of visual, auditory, tactile, and kinesthetic channels to interact appropriately with motor activity

Spatial orientation—inability to master temporal, spatial, and orientation factors

Verbal expression—inability to express ideas, communicate, or request information

Closure-generalization—inability to extrapolate beyond an established set of data or information

Attending—inability to attend selectively or focus on tasks

Generally, students who are learning disabled need a structured classroom environment that encourages cooperative efforts among students and teachers (Carnahan, 1994; Rothman & Casden, 1995). When working with learning disabled students, you will need to:

- Increase attention span by removing distractions, including any materials other than those necessary for the assigned task.
- Teach the student how to organize desk belongings and materials.
- Carefully structure the learning environment and tasks with specific standards, limits, and rules.
- Be consistent—in rules, directions, and so on. Make consequences for rule infractions clear.
- Assign one task at a time, at first using a step-by-step procedure. This means short, sequential assignments, with breaks between tasks.
- Use a variety of media to present content (films, tapes, printed material, etc.).
- Use active methods (simulation games, experiments, role-playing, etc.) in the instructional strategies.
- Employ materials for differing learning patterns (pictures, tapes, concrete objects, etc.).

Inclusion

Inclusion is the practice of integrating students into the regular classroom who had previously been enrolled in special education classes. Prior to these students entering your classroom, an Individualized Educational Program (IEP) must be devised for each pupil with a disability. According to law, each IEP should be prepared annually by a team of specialized personnel, parents, and classroom teachers. It should contain (1) a statement of the pupil's present educational levels; (2) the educational goals for the year; (3) specifications for the services to be provided and to what extent the pupil should be expected to take part in the regular program; and (4) the type, direction, and evaluative criteria for the services to be provided. You should have an active role in the preparation of these specifications for all students with disabilities assigned to your classes, because you will have the major responsibility for carrying them out.

Regardless of the nature of the disability, the following steps should prove helpful in working with students who are included in a regular classroom (Roe, Ross, & Bums, 2009, pp. 197–198):

- Build rapport with the student who has a disability. Let the student know you are genuinely interested in seeing that he overcomes his difficulties. A comfortable, relaxed atmosphere also enhances rapport (see, e.g., Hart & Williams, 1995).

- Formulate a plan appropriate for the student. Instruction must be tailored to meet the needs of the individual student. Skills to be taught must relate to the student's learning characteristics and potential. Different approaches will succeed with different students, so you must be flexible in your approaches and familiar with many different approaches.
- Adjust the length of the instructional session to fit the student's attention span and needs. In fairly long sessions you will need frequent changes of activities or rest periods.
- When necessary, identify the basic life skills and relate them to subject content. For example, in mathematics, note skills related to everyday areas of usage, such as newspaper advertisements, price tags, money values, the calendar, road signs, road maps, recipes, timetables, measurement units, thermometers, clocks, sales slips, making change, budgeting money, planning meals, and balancing a checkbook.
- The student's interests need to be utilized. A student interested in a particular topic (hobby, game, sport, or the like) will tend to put forth a great deal of effort to master a concept or skill that relates to that interest.

Students at Risk

In a very real sense, all of the groups discussed previously are at risk. However, for our purposes, the **at-risk student** is defined as "one who is in danger of failing to complete his or her education with an adequate level of skills" (Slavin & Madden, 1989, p. 4). Risk factors include low achievement, behavior problems, low self-esteem, lack of social skills, poor attendance, retention in grade, low socioeconomic status, and attendance at schools with large numbers of poor students (Richman & Bowman, 1997). According to, Slavin and Madden (1989)

> each of these factors is closely associated with the dropout rate; and by the time students are in 3rd grade, we can use these factors to predict with re-markable accuracy which students will drop out of school and which will stay to complete their education. (p. 4)

In their book on at-risk learners, Lehr and Harris (1988, p. 11) identify the necessary skills and competencies to teach students at risk. These fall into five categories: a teacher's personal skills and competencies, professional skills and competencies, use of teaching materials, use of appropriate teaching methods, and creation of a supportive learning environment. In terms of personal skills and competencies, teachers should be empathic, flexible, patient, enthusiastic, and caring and have a sense of humor and effective communication skills. Professional skills and competencies include being professional (reliable, punctual, dedicated), using resources from other teachers and the community, having a thorough content knowledge, and being trained in dealing effectively with at-risk students. The materials the teacher uses should be relevant and at an appropriate level for the student. In addition, a wide range and variety of materials should be used. A teacher who utilizes effective teaching methods sets realistic goals and objectives; uses a variety of methods and techniques; is able to diagnose, prescribe for, and evaluate students; and reteaches and gives students time to practice the skill or concept. Finally, teachers need to create a supportive learning environment by being a cheerleader (be positive, use motivational strategies, ensure successful experiences), being firm, consistent, and fair in classroom management, and considering the total student (mental, physical, emotional).

In addition, cooperative learning has been found to improve academic and social skills of at-risk students. Slavin (1986) summarizes the effectiveness of cooperative learning:

> The research on cooperative learning methods supports the usefulness of these strategies for improving such diverse outcomes as student achievement at a variety of grade levels and in many subjects, inter-group relations, relations between mainstreamed and normal-progress students, and student self-esteem. Their widespread and growing use demonstrates that in addition to their effectiveness, cooperative learning methods are practical and attractive to teachers. The history of the development, evaluation, and dissemination of cooperative learning is an outstanding example of educational research resulting in directly useful programs that have improved the education experience of thousands of students and will continue to affect thousands more. (p. 126)

Research suggests the importance of supportive communication for at-risk students (Richman, Rosenfeld, & Bowen, 1998; Rosenfeld & Richmond, 1999; Rosenfeld, Richmond, & Bowen, 1998). In general this research examines supportive communication and school outcomes. Supportive communication can take eight forms as described by Rosenfeld, Richman, and Bowen (1998, p. 311), as shown in Table 10.2.

Finally, teachers need to consider how to motivate at-risk students. According to Brophy (1987), research supports the following strategies for motivating students to learn:

- Providing essential preconditions of a supportive environment—appropriate level of challenge and meaningful learning objectives.
- Maintaining success expectations by teaching goal setting, performance appraisal, and self-reinforcement; helping students recognize linkages between effort and outcome.
- Supplying extrinsic incentives such as rewards for improved performance.
- Capitalizing on students' intrinsic motivation by allowing opportunities to make choices and decisions; providing opportunities for students to respond actively; providing immediate feedback to student responses; interacting with peers; incorporating novelty elements such as gamelike features, fantasy, and students' own interests.
- Stimulating student motivation to learn by modeling interest in learning, motivation to learn, task-related thinking, and problem solving; communicating desirable expectations and learning objectives; projecting intensity and enthusiasm; inducing task interest, appreciation, curiosity, and suspense; minimizing students' performance anxiety during learning activities; and making abstract content more personal, concrete, or familiar.

These strategies are particularly important in teaching at-risk students.

TABLE 10.2 Types of Support

Type of Support	Description Perception that the other is
Listening	Listening without giving advice or being judgmental
Emotional	Providing comfort and caring
Emotional challenge	Challenging the support recipient in order to encourage him to evaluate his attitudes, values, feelings
Reality confirmation	Helping to confirm the support recipient's perspective of the world
Task appreciation	Acknowledging the support recipient's efforts and expressing appreciation for the work she is doing
Task challenge	Challenging the support recipient's way of thinking about a task or activity in order to motivate the support recipient to greater creativity, involvement, or excitement
Tangible assistance	Providing the support recipient with either financial assistance, products, or gifts
Personal assistance	Providing services or help, such as running an errand

Note: In terms of at-risk students, Rosenfeld, Richman, and Bowen (1998) found that for middle school students, various types of support were related to school outcomes. Technical appreciation and reality confirmation were related to the student avoiding school problems (e.g., being "kicked out" of class, fighting). Emotional support and emotional challenge support were related to higher school engagement (e.g., finding school fun, looking forward to learning new things). Technical challenge was related to higher school satisfaction (e.g., liking classes, enjoying coming to school). High school students who received emotional support, emotional challenge support, and personal assistance support reported studying more hours than students who did not receive these types of support. In addition, higher school engagement was related to task assistance support, whereas task challenge support and emotional challenge support were related to higher attendance (Rosenfeld & Richman, 1999). Thus, it appears that teachers should strive to be as supportive as possible in their communication with at-risk students.

Students Who Are Intellectually Gifted

There is one more group with special needs—the intellectually **gifted student**. Intellectually gifted students often progress academically one and a quarter or more years within one calendar year. Usually gifted students possess some of the following characteristics:

- an interest in books and reading
- large vocabularies and an ability to express themselves verbally in a mature style
- a wide range of interests
- a high level of abstract thinking
- a curiosity to learn

Instructional materials and programs for the gifted are numerous. In general, the following instructional procedures (Roe, Ross, & Burns, 2009, p. 183) should prove helpful:

- Make use of trade (library) books in the program.
- Develop units of work that provide opportunity for in-depth and long-term activities, as well as library research.

- Use special tables and bulletin boards for interesting and challenging problems, puzzles, worksheets, and so on.
- Use special enrichment materials appropriate to the content areas.
- Encourage oral and written reports on topics under discussion and related topics.
- Challenge creative thinking by using games and simulation.
- Provide opportunities for participation in special clubs or groups designed to challenge gifted students.

In terms of teaching gifted students, several traits of effective teachers of the gifted have been identified (Martin-White & Staton-Spicer, 1987). These include building and maintaining interpersonal relationships with students, skill in problem-solving strategies, skill in conducting group discussions, using debate and controversy to involve students in discussion, communicating with children at their level of understanding, and asking questions to elicit higher-level cognitive responses.

The voluminous research on gifted and talented youth demonstrates that gifted students need accelerated, challenging instruction in core subject areas that parallel their special aptitudes; opportunities to work with other gifted students; and highly competent teachers (Feldhusen, 1989).

Reading Objectives and Discussion Prompts

10.4 Ableism

What do you know?
What is ableism? How does it affect the classroom? What are some concerns for students with special needs?

What do you think?
Do our current educational practices privilege the able-bodied student? How will you work with students with special needs?

STRATEGIES FOR CHANGE

Teachers are the primary agents for implementing change in gender, ethnic, class, and racial stereotypes. The government publication *Taking the Sexism Out of Education* (1978) emphasizes the role of the teacher: "Teachers' behavior is probably the most critical factor in determining whether what happens in the classroom will encourage the development of flexibility or the retention of old stereotyping practices" (cited in Koblinsky & Sugawara, 1984, p. 365).

Several authors have suggested the importance of developing teacher education programs that emphasize gender and ethnic issues in the educational environment. Surveying twenty-four leading teacher education textbooks, Sadker and Sadker (1981) report that

- None of the texts provide future teachers with curricular resources or instructional strategies to counteract sexism in the classroom.
- Twenty-three of the twenty-four texts give less than 1 percent of space to sexism in education.

- One-third of the texts fail to mention sexism at all. Most guilty of this are math and science education texts.
- An average of five times as much content space is allocated to males as to females in the education texts analyzed.
- In the science methods texts, an average of seven times more space is allocated to males than to females.
- Continued stereotyping is evident in language arts texts. For example, the Sadkers note one text that indicates girls will read boys' books, but boys will not read girls' books; the text concludes, therefore, libraries should buy two boys' books for every girls' book purchased.

The same can be said of race and ethnicity. For example, Hanson (1999) examined photographs included in public speaking texts in terms of ethnicity of the person pictured. The most frequently appearing ethnicity in all texts was Caucasian, followed by (in order of next most to least) African Americans, Asian Americans, Hispanics, international students, and Native Americans.

Some authors have suggested that teachers consider a **feminist perspective** in their teaching. A feminist educational perspective begins with the assumption that all students have equal abilities that need to be nurtured and challenged. Differential treatment of students is acceptable only if it is designed to maximize learning and opportunities for everyone. Wood (2009) says that a feminist perspective on teaching and learning is effective because feminism:

- is inclusive so that topics representative of both sexes' experiences and concerns are addressed;
- values diversity so that multiple ways of knowing are accepted and valued,
- values human relationships so that teaching becomes interactive rather than authoritative;
- values personal experience so that thoughtful consideration of how ideas and knowledge relate to personal experience is encouraged;
- emphasizes empowerment, not power, so that students have control over their own learning; and
- seeks to create change so that learners perceive themselves as agents of change. (pp. 4–5)

Such an approach to education means that the teacher places an emphasis on individual learning styles, variety in teaching strategies, student–student interactions, collaborative learning, and requesting and reacting to student feedback on course content and pedagogy.

Banks (1998) suggests that we need an **equity pedagogy**. Equity pedagogy exists when teachers use techniques and teaching methods that facilitate the academic achievement of students from diverse racial and ethnic groups and from all social classes, regardless of gender. Using teaching techniques that cater to the learning and cultural styles of diverse groups and using the techniques of cooperative learning are some of the ways that teachers have found to be effective in teaching both male and female students from diverse racial, ethnic, and language groups.

Synthesizing recommendations from several researchers, Vernay (1990) suggests that both policy and curriculum/teaching issues must be considered. Policy considerations include the following:

- Issuing policy statements concerning race, ethnicity, religion, and gender that cover broad school and district philosophy, as well as adhering to hiring practices and the treatment of bias-motivated incidents.
- Maintaining racial and cultural diversity among members of the administration, faculty, and staff.
- Providing services for victims of bias-motivated violence.
- Reporting and monitoring trends in racial attitudes.
- Establishing committees on human relations that include students, faculty, and staff.

Vernay suggests the following curriculum and teaching considerations:

- Use the arts to encourage critical thinking about social issues.
- Check textbooks and other resources for bias.
- Reflect the cultural diversity of the school in teaching strategies.
- Affirm racial and cultural differences with regular and special activities, not only during a special time, such as Black History Month, Women's History Month, Chinese New Year, and so on, but throughout the school year.

Finally, teachers should use a variety of teaching methods and provide opportunities for students to work cooperatively as well as individually. Supplement lectures with audiovisual materials; use discussion, simulation, role-playing, and active, hands-on experiences. Give students choices in how to complete an assignment—a paper, an art project, an oral report. (For additional ideas, see Cano, Jones, & Chism, 1991; Kepler, Royse, & Kepler, 1996).

As teachers, we need to examine our own ethnocentrism. A concept particularly useful for teachers is **mindfulness**—the state of "alert and lively awareness" (Langer, 1989, p. 140). Teachers should cultivate this sense of awareness and avoid what Langer refers to as *mindlessness*—a state of reduced attention. Langer outlines three characteristics of mindfulness. The first is the creation of new categories. According to Langer, we need to create more, not fewer, categories. If we have a category "foreigner" and we treat all people in this category the same, we begin to treat the category in which we place a person (in this case, "foreigner") as his identity. If, however, we make more distinctions within this category (create new categories), we stop treating the person as a category.

In addition to new categories, mindfulness involves openness to new information and awareness of more than one perspective. These two characteristics of mindfulness are related to the idea that we need to focus on the process of communication, not the outcome. Langer explains

> An outcome orientation in social situations can induce mindlessness. If we think we know how to handle a situation, we don't feel a need to pay attention. If we respond to the situation as very familiar (as a result, for example, of over-learning), we notice only minimal cues necessary to carry out the proper scenarios. If, on the other hand, the situation is strange, we might be so preoccupied with the thought of failure ("What if I make a fool of

myself?"), that we miss nuances of our own and others' behavior. In this sense, we are mindless with respect to the immediate situation, although we may be thinking quite actively about outcome-related issues. (p. 34)

Thus, focusing on the process of communication (i.e., how we communicate) forces us to be mindful of our behavior in the situations in which we find ourselves. If teachers are mindful, they will be able to communicate with each student as an individual rather than as a category.

In terms of classroom interaction, teachers can promote nonstereotyped interaction among students by integrating teams, lines, seating arrangements, and instructional groups. They can assign classroom tasks on a nonstereotypical basis. For example, girls can help carry chairs and boys can be class secretaries. One of the most extensive lists of behaviors for nonsexist teaching is presented by Hall and Sandler (1982). Their ideas relate to racism and ethnicity as well. They suggest that communication behaviors, such as using language that does not reinforce limited or stereotyped views of race, gender, and ethnicity, and giving all students an equal amount of time to respond after asking questions, can begin to communicate the expectations that all students are equally competent intellectually.

Language can also be a problem in educational materials and educational interaction. As several researchers suggest, the generic grammatical structure (using *he* instead of *he and she*) "cannot fail to suggest to young readers that females are a substandard . . . form of being" (Burr, Dunn, & Farquhar, 1972, p. 843). Richmond and Gorham (1988), in their study of current generic-referent usage among 1,529 public school children in grades 3 through 12, report that, in general, masculine generic usage is still prevalent. Webb (1986) provides pedagogical strategies for persuading students to use nonsexist language in class-related communication. Teachers should not only act as models by using nonsexist language but also use teaching strategies that encourage their students to do the same.

Reading Objectives and Discussion Prompts

10.5 Strategies for Change

What do you know?
What strategies does the text mention that could lead to change in the classroom?

What do you think?
Do you think these could work in your own classroom?

In Sum

In light of the research reviewed in this chapter, we need to be very cognizant of the "isms" in our classrooms. For example, after three decades of researching gender-related issues, Sadker (2000) suggests that the " 'glass wall' continues to keep women from the most lucrative careers and keeps men from entering traditionally female jobs. Men continue to dominate the high pay, high status college majors" (p. 6). Fleming (2000) agrees. Although women seem to be improving in overall proficiency and achievement, are participating more in sports, and are choosing professional career paths, bias still exists in the classroom. This bias is reflected in lower expectations, gender stereotypes, and male-focused student-teacher interaction patterns. Sadker (2000) indicates that although bias is less problematic today, "its influence is no less virulent" (p. 80). The same is true of racism and ethnicity. A recent *New York Times* study suggests that although the majority of Americans believe racism and its effects have declined in the United States, real progress has only begun and any amount of racism is problematic and destructive.

When schools ignore sexism, racism, homophobia, ethnic and cultural diversity, ableism, and violent interactions among students, tacit approval is given to such behaviors. "Environments where students do not feel accepted are not environments where effective learning can take place" (AAUW, 1992, p. 74).

Key Terms

Gender Bias
Sexism
Sexual Harassment
Ethnocentrism
Iindividualism/Collectivism
Power distance
Uncertainty avoidance
Masculinity/Femininity

Cognitive Patterns (Analytical
   and Relational style)
Stereotypes
Prejudice
Discrimination
Classism
Ableism
Learning Disabilities

Inclusion
At-Risk Students
Gifted Students
Feminist Perspective
Equity Pedagogy
Mindfulness

Appendix A

Systematic Observation

> Teaching is more than acquiring a repertoire of teaching techniques. . . . This does not negate the importance of helping potential teachers acquire a repertoire of teaching skills. This is obviously necessary—but not sufficient. Teachers must learn to discern the state of a classroom or pupil at a given point during an educational interchange. They must select the teaching behavior or patterns which are the most likely to be effective. This is the essence of teaching. (Semmel, 1978, p. 27)

Educational reports and educational literature are contemplating the quality of American education. To say that we live in a time of increasing emphasis on teacher assessment is to state the obvious. In no other era has the emphasis on assessment been greater.

The purposes of teacher assessment are four; these are shown in Table A.1 (Costa, Garmston, & Lambert, 1988, p.). Two of these purposes focus on the teacher—improving teacher performance and informing personnel decisions about teachers. The other two focus on the educational institution—improving the institution's performance and informing institutional decisions.

In this appendix, we are primarily concerned with the teacher focus. In this regard, assessment can be either formative or summative. The purpose of formative teacher assessment is to help form or modify the teacher's future instructional behaviors. The purpose of summative assessment concerns decisions based on the teacher's past behavior (tenure, termination, merit pay decisions, etc.).

The issues of teacher assessment are complex. For example, what type of assessment (systematic observation, pencil-paper tests, portfolios, etc.) should be used? Who should be responsible for the assessment? What should be the minimum standard for performance? Will that be the same for all teaching levels and teaching areas? Should the standards be state or national? What should be assessed? Should the findings of educational research be incorporated into assessment policies? Who should control the allocation of funds necessary for assessment? What are the legal issues inherent in assessment?

The focus of this chapter is not on trying to answer these questions about assessment. To do so is beyond the scope of this text. Rather, our focus is on ways to assess teacher communication competencies.

TABLE A.1   Four Purposes of Teacher Assessment

		Individual	Organization
G A T H E R I N G	D A T A	*Improve Teacher Performance* • Develop formative information about teaching performance. • Assess hiring criteria and job specifications. • Develop formative information about teacher characteristics and capacities. • Identify supervision goals. • Identify supervision approaches. • Model decision-making processes.	*Improve Organizational Performance* • Gather data about the effective ness of the staff development system. • Gather data about the congruence between hypothetical and actual curriculum. • Measure student access to and variety of teaching methodologies. • Identify organizational goals and action plans. • Assess school climate/trust level.
M A K I N G	D E C I S I O N S	*Inform Personnel Decisions* • Produce summative information related to evaluation criteria. • Grant tenure. • Award promotions, advance ments to leadership roles. • Administer disciplinary actions. • Dismiss teachers.	*Inform Organizational Decisions* • Design staff development program for subject matter of teachers. • Inform teachers well in advance of any systemwide changes in instructional methodologies or policies. • Allocate budget resources for staff development, supervision, evaluation. • Align curriculum.

Of the twenty subfunctions of a comprehensive evaluation system, only one is for the sole purpose of dismissing teachers. However, many districts may be tempted to allow that motive to overwhelm other design considerations.

WHY COMMUNICATION?

Certainly assessment can focus on numerous classroom and educational variables. However, remember that we began this text with the idea that communication is the crux of education. Elements of communication particularly important to effective teaching have been isolated, and we have discussed them throughout this text. Specific skills have been identified by the Speech Communication Association (Cooper, 1988a). Researchers have written about communication competencies important for teachers (see, for example, McCaleb, 1987). In general, these authors have noted the validity of using observational and behavioral measures to identify the strengths and weaknesses of teachers as communicators and have stressed the value to be gained from systematic and multifaceted evaluations.

WHY SYSTEMATIC OBSERVATION? AN OVERVIEW

Systematic observation systems are classificatory systems used to record

> relevant aspects of classroom behaviors as (or within a negligible time after) they occur, with a minimum of quantification intervening between the observation of a behavior and the recording of it. Typically behaviors are recorded in the form of tallies, checks, or other marks which code them into predefined categories and yield information about which behaviors occurred, or how they occurred, during the period of observation. (Medley & Mitsel, 1963, p. 253)

Systematic observation is an effective way to assess teacher competency. Through the use of systematic observation, you can analyze your communication in the classroom, your response style, types and levels of questions you ask, ways you reinforce student communication, and the general pattern of communication in your classroom. Using the information you receive from the use of various appropriate observation instruments, you can alter your communication if you need to. Systematic observation can answer three basic questions:

1. Is this how I want to teach?
2. Is it the best method of instruction for the goals and objectives of the course?
3. If this is not how I want to teach, how far am I from my goal?

In this chapter we examine types of systems available and spend considerable time on two systems. First, however, we discuss what systematic observation can do for you and your students.

What's in It for Me?

Teachers are often reluctant to use systematic observation for three reasons:

1. They are unaware of the benefits of using systematic observation techniques.
2. Learning to use a systematic observation technique can be time consuming.
3. The observation instruments do not relate specifically to the evaluation instruments an administrator uses in evaluating a teacher's instructional strategies.

However, numerous studies indicate that teacher use of systematic observation instruments can make positive changes in teacher behavior. For example, teachers become more flexible, more accepting, less critical, and more sensitive to pupil attitudes, and they must actively encourage student-initiated comments after using systematic observation. In addition, the use of systematic observation by teachers has been linked to increased student learning.

Systematic observation is one method by which we can increase our effectiveness. True, systematic observation is time-consuming (but then, no one ever said teaching doesn't take time) and may not relate specifically to the evaluation instruments our administrators use to evaluate our teaching. Nevertheless, the use of systematic observation can provide insight into our teaching and help us determine what changes we need to make to be more effective. The more effective we are, the more that effectiveness will be reflected in our classrooms, regardless of the instrument the administrator chooses to use to evaluate our teaching.

What's Available?

Basically there are two types of observation instruments—expert prepared and teacher prepared. Expert-prepared instruments are prepared by professionals in the field of observation. Teacher-prepared instruments are prepared by teachers for use in their own classrooms.

EXPERT-PREPARED SYSTEMS

A Verbal Observation System—Flanders

One of the best known and most often used expert-prepared systems is the one developed by Amidon and Flanders (1967). The system divides classroom communication into three major categories: teacher talk, student talk, and noncodable. Each of these major categories is divided into smaller categories. The entire system is presented next.

Teacher Talk: Indirect Influence

1. *Accepts Feeling.* Accepts and clarifies the feeling tone of the student in a nonthreatening manner. Feelings may be positive or negative. Predicting or recalling feelings is included.
2. *Praises or Encourages.* Praises or encourages student action or behavior. Jokes that release tension—but not at the expense of another individual, nodding head, or saying "Um hm?" or "Go on"—are included.
3. *Accepts or Uses Ideas of Students.* Clarifying, building on, or developing ideas suggested by a student. As teacher brings more of own ideas into play, shift to category 5.
4. *Asks Questions.* Asking a question about content or procedure with the intent that a student answer.

Teacher Talk: Direct Influence

5. *Lecturing.* Giving facts or opinions about content or procedures; expressing own ideas, asking rhetorical questions.
6. *Giving Directions.* Directions, commands, or orders with which a student is expected to comply.
7. *Criticizing or Justifying Authority.* Statements intended to change student behavior from unacceptable to acceptable pattern; bawling someone out; stating why the teacher is taking particular action; extreme self-reference.

Student Talk

8. *Student Talk—Response.* Talk by student in response to teacher. Teacher initiates the contact or solicits student statement.
9. *Student Talk—Initiation.* Talk by students that they initiate. If teacher's "calling on" student is only to indicate who may talk next, observer must decide whether student wanted to talk. If so, use this category.

Noncodable

10. *Silence or Confusion.* Pauses, short periods of silence, and periods of confusion in which communication cannot be understood by the observer.

	Knowledge	Comprehension	Application	Analysis	Synthesis	Evaluation
Teacher Questions						
Student Questions						

FIGURE A.1   Teacher-Prepared Form for Data Collection on Level of Questions Asked.

	3	6	9	12	15
Single Word Sentence					
Humor					
Movement Toward Student					
Gesture Toward Student					
Enthusiastic Vocal Tone					

FIGURE A.2   Teacher-Prepared Form for Data Collection on Type and Frequency of Positive Reinforcement by Teacher.

To use the instrument, the observer (another teacher, for example) sits in the back of the classroom and adjusts to the classroom (about 10 to 15 minutes). The observer then records behavior according to one of the categories every 3 seconds or as often as behavior changes. The numbers of the categories are recorded in sequence on a sheet like the ones shown in Figures A.1 and A.2. The observer should record for 10 to 15 minutes. A complete explanation of the Flanders system is found in Appendix B.

A Nonverbal Observation System—Grant and Hennings

Flanders's system focuses on verbal communication in the classroom. However, the use of a teacher's nonverbal communication seems particularly important to the classroom situation. It is imperative that your nonverbal behavior enhance instruction. If students are confused because of contradictions between verbal and nonverbal aspects of the classroom, the classroom climate, and thus learning, can be affected.

Grant and Hennings (1971) developed an instrument that focuses on nonverbal teacher behavior. The instrument divides nonverbal communication into four areas:

1. *Conducting*—motions that enable teacher to control student participation and obtain attending behavior.
2. *Acting*—motions that amplify and clarify meanings.
3. *Wielding*—motions in which teacher interacts with objects, materials, or parts of the room.
4. *Personal motions*—motions not related to instruction.

In addition to examining nonverbal communication, the instrument gives you an idea of how your nonverbal communication relates to your verbal communication. A complete explanation and inventory is included in Appendix B.

TEACHER-PREPARED SYSTEMS

Often teachers have a specific behavior they want to examine—such as level and sequence of questions asked, types of reinforcement, or specific nonverbal behaviors such as movement or gesture. Regardless of the specific behavior(s) the teacher wishes to observe, several steps must be followed when developing an observation tool. Gerald Bailey (1981) suggests the following steps:

1. Identify the behaviors that will be observed.
2. Examine a number of expert-prepared instruments to get an idea of the design of observation instruments. The expert-prepared observation forms will assist in determining (1) the type of form to be designed; (2) techniques for identifying behavior; and (3) methods for interpreting and analyzing collected information.
3. Construct the observation form to illustrate one or more of these facets: (1) identification of a specific behavior; (2) the frequency of a behavior; and (3) the sequence of behaviors. Design the directions and format for actual data collection.
4. Audiotape or videotape a classroom session; analyze data in terms of how well the classroom interaction was collected.
5. Revise the observation form on the basis of the findings, record another classroom session, and use this recording to collect data on the revised form. (p. 59)

Suppose you want to know the level of questions you ask in your classroom and the level of questions your students ask. You might devise a form similar to the one in Figure A.1. An observer would simply check the appropriate column each time you or your students asked a question. You could also videotape or audiotape a class period and then tally the results yourself.

Perhaps you are interested in the types and frequency of positive reinforcement you use in the classroom. A form such as the one in Figure A.2 could be used. The observer would place a check after each behavior when it occurred in the designated 3-minute interval.

Perhaps you are interested in a more global view of the classroom, rather than any specific behavior. If this is the case, you might adapt for your purposes an observation instrument such as that developed by anthropologist Dell Hymes (1972). Hymes suggests the SPEAKING system:

Situation.   Setting and scene in which the communication takes place

Participants.   People involved—their roles and relationship

Ends.   Goals and outcome of the communication

Acts.   Message content, form, sequence

Key.   Tone of the communication

Instrumentality.   Channel or medium of the communication

Norms.   Guidelines for or standards of interaction

Genre.   Categories such as lecture, sermon, commercial, and so on

Consider the following example:

The *situation* is a high school math class. The participants are the students (eleven males and fourteen females age 16 to 17, and one teacher, Ms. Chan). The goal (*end*) of the lesson is for students to be able to solve algebraic equations.

The *acts* are what the teacher and the students say and do. You would not try to write down every single word or nonverbal cue. You are trying to "get the gist." You probably would want to jot down some notes and then write these in a more formal way soon after the lesson was completed. Remember, you're looking for the general content of what Ms. Chan says about algebraic equations, the students' responses and questions to Ms. Chan and their classmates, and the subsequent responses. In other words, what is the general message content and the sequence? For example, is a teacher question generally followed by a student response or a rephrasing of the question by the teacher? Do student responses ever "spark" further student questions or reactions or does the teacher always answer the questions?

The *key* to the lesson is primarily serious because the teacher wants the students to learn algebraic equations. However, mixed with this serious tone might well be humor. *Instrumentality* considers the medium or channel of the communication. For example, is the communication primarily oral or do students spend a great deal of time writing their answers?

What are the *norms* of this classroom? Do students always raise their hands when they wish to speak? Is the teacher the only giver of information in the classroom? Where does the teacher stand or sit? Is the classroom arranged in a traditional straight row arrangement? Do the students call the teacher by first name or title and last name?

Finally, the *genre* of this particular speech situation should be considered. Is the lesson a lecture? A discussion? A combination of both?

Teacher-made observation systems are not without their shortcomings. The process of constructing them is time-consuming. The bias of the creator is difficult to avoid. As a result, reliability and validity are difficult to determine. However, these limitations may be less important than the advantage of using an instrument tailor-made for observing the behaviors on which the teacher wishes to focus. Two teacher-prepared observation systems, the *Teacher Behaviors Inventory* and the *Teacher Communication Rating Scale,* are included in Appendix B.

In Sum

We have presented you with a brief discussion of teacher assessment and an overview of systematic observation and how it can help you analyze your teaching. A variety of instruments exist. Choose the one most appropriate to your needs or develop your own. However, remember that no observation system tells you whether you are a "good" teacher. It merely describes your behavior. What you do with that information is up to you.

Appendix B

Instruments for Systematic Observation

FLANDERS

As discussed in Appendix A, Amidon and Flanders (1967) developed one of the best and most used systematic observation systems. The authors of this instrument present ground rules to aid the user in categorizing behaviors correctly. These are outlined as follows:

1. When not certain in which of two or more categories a statement belongs, choose the category that is numerically farthest from category 5.
2. If the primary tone of the teacher's behavior has been consistently direct or consistently indirect, do not shift into the opposite classification unless a clear indication of shift is given by the teacher.
3. The effect of a statement on the pupils, and not the teacher's intent, is the crucial criterion for categorizing a statement.
4. If more than one category occurs during the 3-second interval, then all categories used in that interval are recorded; therefore, record each change in category. If no change occurs within 3 seconds, repeat that category.
5. Directions are statements that result (or are expected to result) in observable behavior on the part of children.
6. When the teacher calls on a child by name, the observer ordinarily records a 4.
7. If there is a discernible period of silence (at least 3 seconds), record one 10 for every 3 seconds of silence, laughter, board work, and so on.
8. When the teacher repeats a student answer, and the answer is a correct answer, this is recorded as a 2.
9. When the teacher repeats a student idea and communicates only that the idea will be considered or accepted as something to be discussed, a 3 is used.
10. If a student begins talking after another student (without the teacher's talking), a 10 is inserted between the 9s or 8s to indicate a change of student.

Tally Sheet

1. ___	26. ___	51. ___	76. ___	101. ___
2. ___	27. ___	52. ___	77. ___	102. ___
3. ___	28. ___	53. ___	78. ___	103. ___
4. ___	29. ___	54. ___	79. ___	104. ___
5. ___	30. ___	55. ___	80. ___	105. ___
6. ___	31. ___	56. ___	81. ___	106. ___
7. ___	32. ___	57. ___	82. ___	107. ___

8. ____	33. ____	58. ____	83. ____	108. ____
9. ____	34. ____	59. ____	84. ____	109. ____
10. ____	35. ____	60. ____	85. ____	110. ____
11. ____	36. ____	61. ____	86. ____	111. ____
12. ____	37. ____	62. ____	87. ____	112. ____
13. ____	38. ____	63. ____	88. ____	113. ____
14. ____	39. ____	64. ____	89. ____	114. ____
15. ____	40. ____	65. ____	90. ____	115. ____
16. ____	41. ____	66. ____	91. ____	116. ____
17. ____	42. ____	67. ____	92. ____	117. ____
18. ____	43. ____	68. ____	93. ____	118. ____
19. ____	44. ____	69. ____	94. ____	119. ____
20. ____	45. ____	70. ____	95. ____	120. ____
21. ____	46. ____	71. ____	96. ____	121. ____
22. ____	47. ____	72. ____	97. ____	122. ____
23. ____	48. ____	73. ____	98. ____	123. ____
24. ____	49. ____	74. ____	99. ____	124. ____
25. ____	50. ____	75. ____	100. ____	125. ____

11. Statements, such as "Uh huh, yes, yeah, all right, okay," which occur between two 9s are recorded as a 2 (encouragement).
12. A teacher joke, not made at the expense of the children, is a 2.
13. Rhetorical questions are not really questions but are merely part of lecturing techniques and should be categorized as a 5.
14. A narrow question is a signal to expect an 8.
15. An 8 is recorded when several students respond in unison to a narrow question.

The numbers from the coding sheet can then be recorded on a 10×10 matrix such as that in Figure B.1.

The tallies in Figure B.1 are paired, and then recorded on the matrix. The first number in the pair designates the appropriate horizontal row; the second number in the pair designates the appropriate column. For example, assume the first six categories in your observation were

1. 10
2. 5
3. 5
4. 4
5. 8
6. 4

The first pair (10, 5) would be tallied in row 10, column 5 of the matrix. Pair two (5, 5) would be in row 5, column 5 and so forth. These six tallies would appear as shown in Figure B.2.

Once the tallies in Figure B.2 are entered on the matrix, the sequence, the amount, and the pattern of verbal communication in the classroom can be analyzed. The steps in this analysis are as follows:

1. Check the matrix total in order to estimate the elapsed coding time. Number of tallies multiplied by 3 equals seconds; divided by 60 equals minutes.

Work Matrix

	1	2	3	4	5	6	7	8	9	10	
1											
2											
3											
4											
5											
6											
7											
8											
9											
10											Matrix Total
TOTAL											
%											

FIGURE B.1 Flanders Work Matrix

Work Matrix

	1	2	3	4	5	6	7	8	9	10	
1											
2											
3											
4								I			
5				I	I						
6											
7											
8				I							
9											
10					I						Matrix Total
TOTAL											
%											

FIGURE B.2 Flanders Work Matrix

212

2. Check the percent of teacher talk, pupil talk, and silence or confusion, and use this information in combination with ... (average of about 68 percent teacher talk, 20 percent pupil talk, and 11 or 12 percent silence or confusion).

3. ... [Examine] the balance of teacher response and initiation in contrast with pupil initiation.
   a. Indirect-to-direct ratios; useful for matrices with more than 1,000 tallies
      1. I/D ratio: 1 + 2 + 3 divided by 6 + 7.
      2. I/D ratio: 1 + 2 + 3 + 4 divided by 5 + 6 + 7.
   b. TRR (teacher response ratio): teacher tendency to react to ideas and feelings of pupils. 1 + 2 + 3 times 100 divided by 1 + 2 + 3 + 6 + 7. Average is about 42.
   c. TQR (teacher question ratio): teacher tendency to use questions when dealing with content. Category 4 times 100 divided by 4 + 5. Average is 26.
   d. PIR (pupil initiation ratio): proportion of pupil talk judged initiation. Category 9 times 100 divided by 8 + 9. Average is close to 34.

4. Check the initial reaction of the teacher to the termination of pupil talk.
   a. TRR89 (instantaneous teacher response ratio): teacher tendency to praise or integrate pupil ideas or feelings when student terminates. Add cell frequencies in rows 8 and 9, columns 1, 2, and 3 times 100 divided by tallies in rows 8 and 9, columns 1, 2, 3, 6, and 7. Average is about 60.
   b. TQR89 (instantaneous teacher questions ratio): teacher tendency to respond to pupil talk with questions compared to lecture. Add cells (8 − 4) + (9 − 4) times 100 divided by (8 − 4) + (8 − 5) + (9 − 5). Average is about 44.

5. Check the proportions of tallies to be found in the "content cross" and "steady state cells" in order to estimate the rapidity of exchange, tendency toward sustained talk, and content emphasis.
   a. CCR (content cross ratio): concerns categories most concerned with content. Calculate the percent of all tallies that lie within the columns and rows of 4 and 5. Average is close to 55 percent.
   b. SSR (steady state ratio): tendency of teacher and pupil talk to stay in same category. Percentage of all tallies in 10 steady state cells (1 − 1), (2 − 2), and so on. Average is around 50.
   c. PSSR (pupil steady state ratio): tendency of pupils to stay in same category. Frequencies in (8 − 8) + (9 − 9) cells times 100 divided by all pupil talk tallies. Average is around 35 or 40.

GRANT AND HENNINGS

As discussed in Appendix A, the Grant and Hennings (1971) system focuses on nonverbal teaching behavior. The inventory is presented next. Although it is stated in terms of self-analysis, it could be used by another teacher to observe you. It might be useful for you to complete the inventory and then have another teacher observe you, completing the inventory "on the scene" as you teach. You could then compare your view with the observer's.

Part I

What kinds of motions tend to predominate in my nonverbal teaching style?

A. **Conducting.** How do I control participation, focus attention, and obtain attending behavior?

	Very Typical	Typical	Atypical
1. *To indicate who the participant is, I:*			
smile at the participant	_____	_____	_____
focus my eyes on the participant	_____	_____	_____
orient my body in the direction of the participant	_____	_____	_____
nod at the chosen participant	_____	_____	_____

	Very Typical	Typical	Atypical
point at the participant with finger, hand, stick, chalk, microphone, book	_____	_____	_____
walk toward the participant	_____	_____	_____
hand the pointer, chalk, book, microphone to the participant	_____	_____	_____
touch the participant	_____	_____	_____
other: _____	_____	_____	_____

2. *To rate a student's participation, I:*			
use facial expressions: smiling, frowning, grinning, wrinkling my brow, raising my eyebrows	_____	_____	_____
shake my head	_____	_____	_____
shrug my shoulders	_____	_____	_____
clap my hands	_____	_____	_____
make the OK sign with my fingers, forming an "O" by touching thumb to forefinger	_____	_____	_____
put my hands to my face	_____	_____	_____
hold my head	_____	_____	_____
scratch my head	_____	_____	_____
write the correct response on the board or on a chart	_____	_____	_____
pat the student on back	_____	_____	_____
move my hand from respondent to another student who has hand up to respond	_____	_____	_____
other: _____	_____	_____	_____

3. *To respond to a student's participation, I:*			
use facial expressions	_____	_____	_____
shake or nod head	_____	_____	_____
walk toward or away from the participant	_____	_____	_____
point or wave hand	_____	_____	_____
write something on the board	_____	_____	_____
other: _____	_____	_____	_____

4. *To regulate the speed of classroom
    interaction, I:*
beckon to student to continue
wave at student to stop
select motions of different speeds
other: _____

	Very Typical	Typical	Atypical

5. *To focus student attention on a
    significant point in the lesson, I:*
write the significant point on the
    board
underline a word or words written
    on the board
point to each word written on
    the board
write over each word written on
    the board, perhaps with colored
    chalk
point to a related chart, bulletin
    board display, or picture
point to a location on map or globe
point to the actual object
hold up the actual object
point to a person being discussed
point to a picture or statement
    projected by an audiovisual device
put words or letters into a
    pocket chart
attach word cards or pictures to
    the chalkboard using magnets
    or masking tape
hold up word card or picture
add the key ingredient to a
    demonstration I am doing
other: _____

6. *To get the attention of the total class
    or portion of the class, I:*
close the door to indicate the
    lesson is beginning
flick the lights
tap a desk bell
pull down a chart or map
pick up a textbook or lesson
    plan book or record book
walk to the front and center
    of the room

	Very Typical	Typical	Atypical
survey the class, making eye contact	_____	_____	_____
stand at attention	_____	_____	_____
hold up my hand	_____	_____	_____
play a note on the piano	_____	_____	_____
arrange my chair or stool and sit down	_____	_____	_____
tap fingers or pencil on desk	_____	_____	_____
other: _____	_____	_____	_____

7. *To get the attention of a misbehaving student or group of students, I:*

orient my body toward and focus my eyes on the inattentive student(s)	_____	_____	_____
frown or raise eyebrows at misbehaving student(s)	_____	_____	_____
shake my head at the misbehaving student(s)	_____	_____	_____
snap fingers in direction of misbehaving student(s)	_____	_____	_____
clap hands	_____	_____	_____
walk toward the misbehaving student(s)	_____	_____	_____
touch misbehaving student(s)	_____	_____	_____
sit down near misbehaving student(s)	_____	_____	_____
touch object misbehaving student is touching	_____	_____	_____
other: _____	_____	_____	_____

B. Acting. How do I use bodily motion to clarify and amplify meanings?

1. *To emphasize meanings, I:*

use motion of my head	_____	_____	_____
use facial expressions	_____	_____	_____
use motions of my feet	_____	_____	_____
use motions of my entire body	_____	_____	_____

2. *To illustrate a concept, an object, or a process, I:*

use motions of my hands	_____	_____	_____
use motions of my head	_____	_____	_____
use facial expressions	_____	_____	_____
use motions of my feet	_____	_____	_____
other: _____	_____	_____	_____

3. *To illustrate even more completely, I use role-playing motions to:*

pretend I am an object	_____	_____	_____
imitate an animal	_____	_____	_____
pretend I am a particular character	_____	_____	_____

pretend I am a puppet character
other: _____

C. **Wielding.** In what ways do I manipulate objects, materials, or other parts of the environment when students are not expected to focus on my motions? What kinds of materials do I tend to manipulate?

	Very Typical	Typical	Atypical

1. *I tend to manipulate:*
chalk and chalkboard
books or workbooks
audiovisual equipment
paper, pens, or pencils
flow pens and charting paper
pictures or cards
materials related specifically to the
    teaching of my discipline
other: _____

2. *During the lesson, I focus my eyes on:*
written materials
my lesson plans
the teacher's manual
the students' books
reference books
material recorded on chalkboard
numerals of the clock
other: _____

3. *Teacher-oriented wieldings I delegate
    to students are:*
distribution and collection of material
setting up equipment
putting material on board or
    bulletin board
reading questions that other
    students answer
other: _____

4. *I manipulate or wield materials:*
before students come into the room
while students come into the room
while students are performing
    some other task
just before using the material
during the actual use of the material
other: _____

D. **Personal Motions.** How do I use motions that are more of a personal nature than they are instructional?

	Very Typical	Typical	Atypical
1. *Motions I make that are related to my clothing are:*			
adjusting my tie or bow	_____	_____	_____
adjusting my collar	_____	_____	_____
straightening jacket	_____	_____	_____
pulling down sweater or skirt	_____	_____	_____
tucking in blouse, sweater, or shirt	_____	_____	_____
other: _____	_____	_____	_____
2. *Motions I make in the classroom that are aspects of my own personality are:*			
pushing back hair	_____	_____	_____
pulling on beads, necklace, locket, and so on	_____	_____	_____
adjusting glasses	_____	_____	_____
placing hands in pockets	_____	_____	_____
jiggling coins in pocket	_____	_____	_____
twiddling with ring	_____	_____	_____
curling hair around finger	_____	_____	_____
scratching head, nose, neck, leg	_____	_____	_____
other: _____	_____	_____	_____
3. *My physical motions that might be called mannerisms because I repeatedly make them are:*	_____	_____	_____

Part II

How does my nonverbal activity relate to my verbal activity?

1. To communicate meaning, I use nonverbal motion without any verbal accompaniment.	_____	_____	_____
2. I use nonverbal motion in my classroom to support my verbal remarks.	_____	_____	_____
3. I use nonverbal motion in my classroom to support other nonverbal activity.	_____	_____	_____
4. I use verbal remarks without nonverbal accompaniment.	_____	_____	_____

Part III

How do I carry on classroom activity? I generally:

	Very Typical	Typical	Atypical
sit at the teacher's desk	_____	_____	_____
sit on the teacher's desk	_____	_____	_____

sit on a stool	___	___	___
sit on a student's chair	___	___	___
sit on the floor	___	___	___
lean on the chalkboard	___	___	___
lean on a desk	___	___	___
stand at the front of the room	___	___	___
stand at the side or rear of the room	___	___	___
move up and down the aisles	___	___	___
move from group to group	___	___	___
move from child to child	___	___	___
move across the front of room	___	___	___
move from desk to chalkboard	___	___	___
move around the outside edge of the room	___	___	___
sit at a table with the students	___	___	___
other: _____	___	___	___

Part IV

What are the general characteristics of my nonverbal classroom behavior?

A. **Acuity Level.** Consider the number of nonverbal clues you tend to generate in a classroom. Are you very active, active, not too active? Plot yourself on the following activity continuum:

very active   active   not too active

├─────────────────────────────┼─────────────────────────────┤

B. **Speed of Motion.** Consider the nonverbal motions you make in the classroom. Do you tend to move rapidly? Do you tend to move rather slowly? Plot yourself on the following activity continuum:

rapid   medium   slow

├─────────────────────────────┼─────────────────────────────┤

C. **Size of Motion.** Consider the nonverbal motions you make. Do you tend to make such large motions as gestures of the hand? Or do you tend to make such small motions as a nod or smile? Plot yourself on the following size continuum:

large   medium   small

├─────────────────────────────┼─────────────────────────────┤

D. **Personal Motions.** Consider the personal motions you use in a classroom. Do you use many personal motions? Do you use a minimal number of personal motions? Plot yourself on the following continuum:

many personal motions   few personal motions

├─────────────────────────────┼─────────────────────────────┤

E. **Verbal and Nonverbal Orientation.** Consider the nonverbal activity and the verbal activity that you carry on in the classroom. Do you have a nonverbal orientation in your teaching? Do you have a verbal orientation? Plot yourself on the following verbal and nonverbal continuum:

verbal   verbal/nonverbal   nonverbal

```
├──────────────────────────────┼──────────────────────────────┤
```

F. **Clarity of Communication.** Consider these questions:

Is my bodily stance communicating what I want it to communicate? Is my manner of sitting communicating what I want to communicate?

Is my manner of walking communicating what I want it to communicate?

Is my gesturing communicating what I want to communicate?

Are my facial expressions communicating what I want to communicate?

In terms of these questions plot yourself on the following clarity of communication continuum:

motion communicates   motion does not communicate

what is intended   what is intended

```
├──────────────────────────────┼──────────────────────────────┤
```

TEACHER BEHAVIORS INVENTORY

Instructions to Student

In this inventory you are asked to assess your instructor's specific classroom behaviors. Your instructor has requested this information for purposes of instructional analysis and improvement. Please try to be both thoughtful and candid in your responses so as to maximize the value of feedback.

Your judgments should reflect that type of teaching you think is best for this particular course and your particular learning style. Try to assess each behavior independently rather than letting your overall impression of the instructor determine each individual rating.

Each section of the inventory begins with a definition of the category of teaching to be assessed in that section. For each specific teaching behavior, please indicate your judgment as to whether your instructor should increase, decrease, or make no change in the frequency with which he exhibits the behavior in question. Please use the following rating scale in making your judgments:

1 = almost never

2 = rarely

3 = sometimes

4 = often

5 = almost always

Clarity: method to explain or clarify concepts and principles

Gives several examples of each concept	1	2	3	4	5
Uses concrete everyday examples to explain concepts and principles	1	2	3	4	5
Fails to define new or unfamiliar terms	1	2	3	4	5
Repeats difficult ideas several times	1	2	3	4	5
Stresses most important points by pausing, speaking slowly, raising voice, and so on	1	2	3	4	5
Uses graphs or diagrams to facilitate explanation	1	2	3	4	5
Points out practical applications of concepts	1	2	3	4	5
Answers students' questions thoroughly	1	2	3	4	5
Suggests ways of memorizing complicated ideas	1	2	3	4	5
Writes key terms on blackboard or overhead screen	1	2	3	4	5
Explains subject matter in familiar colloquial language	1	2	3	4	5

Enthusiasm: use of behavior to solicit student attention and interest

Speaks in a dramatic or expressive way	1	2	3	4	5
Moves about while lecturing	1	2	3	4	5
Gestures with hands or arms	1	2	3	4	5
Exhibits facial gestures or expressions	1	2	3	4	5
Avoids eye contact with students	1	2	3	4	5
Walks up aisles beside students	1	2	3	4	5
Gestures with head or body	1	2	3	4	5
Tells jokes or humorous anecdotes	1	2	3	4	5
Reads lecture verbatim from prepared notes or text	1	2	3	4	5
Smiles or laughs while teaching	1	2	3	4	5
Shows distracting mannerisms	1	2	3	4	5

Interaction: techniques used to foster students' class participation

Encourages students' questions and comments during lectures	1	2	3	4	5
Criticizes students when they make errors	1	2	3	4	5
Praises students for good ideas	1	2	3	4	5
Asks questions of individual students	1	2	3	4	5
Asks questions of class as a whole	1	2	3	4	5
Incorporates students' ideas into lecture	1	2	3	4	5
Presents challenging, thought-provoking ideas	1	2	3	4	5
Uses a variety of media and activities in class	1	2	3	4	5
Asks rhetorical questions	1	2	3	4	5

Organization: ways of organizing or structuring subject matter

Uses headings and subheadings to organize lectures	1	2	3	4	5
Puts outline of lecture on blackboard or overhead screen	1	2	3	4	5

Clearly indicates transition from one topic to the next	1	2	3	4	5
Gives preliminary overview of lecture at beginning of class	1	2	3	4	5
Explains how each topic fits into the course as a whole	1	2	3	4	5
Begins class with a review of topics covered last time	1	2	3	4	5
Periodically summarizes points previously made	1	2	3	4	5

Pacing: rate of information presentation, efficient use of time

Dwells excessively on obvious points	1	2	3	4	5
Digresses from major theme of lecture	1	2	3	4	5
Covers very little material in class sessions	1	2	3	4	5
Asks if students understand before proceeding to next topic	1	2	3	4	5
Sticks to the point in answering students' questions	1	2	3	4	5

Disclosure: explicitness concerning course requirements and grading criteria

Advises students on how to prepare for tests or exams	1	2	3	4	5
Provides sample exam questions	1	2	3	4	5
Tells students exactly what is expected of them on tests, essays, or assignments	1	2	3	4	5
States objectives of each lecture	1	2	3	4	5
Reminds students of test dates or assignment deadlines	1	2	3	4	5
States objectives of course as a whole	1	2	3	4	5

Speech: characteristics of voice relevant to classroom teaching

Stutters, mumbles, or slurs words	1	2	3	4	5
Speaks at appropriate volume	1	2	3	4	5
Speaks clearly	1	2	3	4	5
Speaks at appropriate pace	1	2	3	4	5
Says "um" or "ah"	1	2	3	4	5
Voice lacks proper modulation (speaks in monotone)	1	2	3	4	5

Rapport: quality of interpersonal relations between teacher and students

Addresses individual students by name	1	2	3	4	5
Announces availability for consultation outside of class	1	2	3	4	5
Offers to help students with problems	1	2	3	4	5
Shows tolerance of other points of view	1	2	3	4	5
Talks with students before or after class	1	2	3	4	5

TEACHER COMMUNICATION RATING SCALE

Teacher name _____   Date _____

School _____   Evaluator _____

Grade Level _____   Student Teacher? _____

Certified? _____

This evaluation form follows the Speech Communication Association's newly developed description of teacher communication competencies. It can be used as a basis for observation in evaluating the classroom communication skills of student teachers to determine the presence or absence of these communication skills.

It is suggested that the following criteria for rating each item be followed for consistency in using this instrument.

Let a #1 rating mean . . . Behavior did not appear in this observation.

Let a #2 rating mean . . . Opportunities for behavior were present, but student did not demonstrate the behavior at the appropriate time.

Let a #3 rating mean . . . Behavior demonstrated occasionally.

Let a #4 rating mean . . . Behavior demonstrated consistently with average effectiveness.

Let a #5 rating mean . . . Behavior demonstrated consistently with obvious skill.

Column #6—Confidence of judgment. In observing a teacher for a short period of time, not all behaviors may be judged with equal confidence. Column #6 asks the rater to give a confidence level for the judgment of the indicated skill.

Rating of 1 indicates low confidence in judgment. There were low levels of the observed behaviors.

Rating of 2 indicates average confidence in judgment.

Rating of 3 indicates high confidence in judgment.

Ratings do not need to be made in the order presented here. In some instances, the rating for a behavior may be done during the observation. In other instances, the rating may need to be done at the completion of the observation to ensure an adequate sample.

I. Informative Messages
  A. Sending
    1. Structures informative messages effectively by using devices such as initial partitions, transitions, internal summaries, and concluding summaries.

    _____   _____   _____   _____   _____   _____
    1-NR   2   3   4   5   6-CJ

    2. Amplifies information effectively through the use of verbal and audiovisual supporting materials.

    _____   _____   _____   _____   _____   _____
    1-NR   2   3   4   5   6-CJ

3. Asks effective questions to assess student understanding of information given in lectures.

_____   _____   _____   _____   _____   _____
1-NR   2   3   4   5   6-CJ

4. Presents information in an animated and interesting way.

_____   _____   _____   _____   _____   _____
1-NR   2   3   4   5   6-CJ

B. Receiving
1. Is able to identify main point of student comment.

_____   _____   _____   _____   _____   _____
1-NR   2   3   4   5   6-CJ

2. Can identify structural patterns or problems of informative messages.

_____   _____   _____   _____   _____   _____
1-NR   2   3   4   5   6-CJ

3. Can evaluate the adequacy of verbal supporting materials.

_____   _____   _____   _____   _____   _____
1-NR   2   3   4   5   6-CJ

4. Can formulate questions that probe for the informative content of messages.

_____   _____   _____   _____   _____   _____
1-NR   2   3   4   5   6-CJ

5. Can distinguish messages that are delivered in an animated manner and those that are not.

_____   _____   _____   _____   _____   _____
1-NR   2   3   4   5   6-CJ

II. Affective Messages. Teacher should demonstrate competence in sending and receiving affective messages (i.e., messages that express or respond to feelings).
A. Sending
1. Expresses positive and negative feelings about self to students.

_____   _____   _____   _____   _____   _____
1-NR   2   3   4   5   6-CJ

2. Expresses positive and negative feelings about students to students.

_____   _____   _____   _____   _____   _____
1-NR   2   3   4   5   6-CJ

3. Expresses opinions about classroom content, events, and real-world occurrences.

_____   _____   _____   _____   _____   _____
1-NR   2   3   4   5   6-CJ

4. Demonstrates interpersonal openness, warmth, and positive regard for students.

1-NR   2   3   4   5   6-CJ

5. Demonstrates energy and enthusiasm when relating to students.

1-NR   2   3   4   5   6-CJ

B. Receiving
  1. Recognizes verbal and nonverbal cues concerning student feelings.

1-NR   2   3   4   5   6-CJ

  2. Invites students to express feelings.

1-NR   2   3   4   5   6-CJ

  3. Is nonjudgmental in responding to student feelings.

1-NR   2   3   4   5   6-CJ

  4. Asks open-ended questions in response to student expressions of feelings.

1-NR   2   3   4   5   6-CJ

  5. If necessary, offers advice tactfully.

1-NR   2   3   4   5   6-CJ

III. Imaginative Messages. Teacher should demonstrate competence in sending and receiving imaginative messages (i.e., messages that speculate, theorize, or include fantasy).
  A. Sending
    1. Uses vivid descriptive language.

1-NR   2   3   4   5   6-CJ

    2. Uses expressive vocal and physical behavior when creating or re-creating examples, stories, or messages from exemplars.

1-NR   2   3   4   5   6-CJ

B. Receiving
    1. Responds to imaginative messages enthusiastically.

    1-NR   2   3   4   5   6-CJ

    2. Is nondirective when encouraging student creativity.

    1-NR   2   3   4   5   6-CJ

IV. Ritualistic Messages. Teacher should demonstrate competence in sending and receiving ritualistic messages (i.e., messages that serve to maintain and facilitate social interaction).
    A. Sending
    1. Demonstrates appropriate behavior in performing everyday speech acts such as greeting, turn-taking, and leave-taking.

    1-NR   2   3   4   5   6-CJ

    2. Models appropriate social amenities in ordinary classroom interaction.

    1-NR   2   3   4   5   6-CJ

    3. Demonstrates competence when participating in or role-playing interviews, conversations, problem-solving groups, legislative groups, and public ceremonies.

    1-NR   2   3   4   5   6-CJ

    B. Receiving
    1. Recognizes when students perform everyday speech acts appropriately.

    1-NR   2   3   4   5   6-CJ

    2. Recognizes appropriate and inappropriate performances of social amenities.

    1-NR   2   3   4   5   6-CJ

    3. Recognizes competence and incompetence when students participate in interviews, conversations, problem-solving groups, legislative groups, and public ceremonies.

    1-NR   2   3   4   5   6-CJ

V. Persuasive Messages. Teacher should demonstrate competence in sending and receiving persuasive messages (i.e., messages that seek to convince).

A. Sending

1. Can differentiate between fact and opinion.

    1-NR   2   3   4   5   6-CJ

2. Can recognize audience factors that may encourage or constrain acceptance of ideas.

    1-NR   2   3   4   5   6-CJ

3. Offers sound reasons and evidence in support of ideas.

    1-NR   2   3   4   5   6-CJ

4. Recognizes underlying assumptions in own arguments.

    1-NR   2   3   4   5   6-CJ

5. Demonstrates a preference for reason-giving over power moves when interacting with students.

    1-NR   2   3   4   5   6-CJ

B. Receiving

1. Recognizes own bias in responding to ideas.

    1-NR   2   3   4   5   6-CJ

2. Questions the adequacy of reasons and evidence given.

    1-NR   2   3   4   5   6-CJ

3. Evaluates evidence and reasons presented.

    1-NR   2   3   4   5   6-CJ

4. Recognizes underlying assumptions in arguments of others.

    1-NR   2   3   4   5   6-CJ

References

Aitken, J. E., & Neer, M. R. (1993). College student question-asking: The relationship of classroom communication apprehension and motivation. *Southern States Communication Journal, 59*, 73–81.

Allen, M., & Bourhis, J. (1996). The relationship of communication apprehension to communication behavior: A meta-analysis. *Communication Quarterly, 44*, 214–226.

Allen, M., & Preiss, R. (1990). Using meta-analysis to evaluate curriculum: An examination of selected college textbooks. *Communication Education, 39*, 103–116.

Allen, R., Brown, K., & Sprague, J. (1991). *Communication in the secondary school: A pedagogy.* Scottsdale, AZ: Gorsuch Scarisbrick.

Allen, R., & Reuter, T. (1990). *Teaching assistant strategies: An introduction to college teaching.* Dubuque, IA: Kendall/Hunt.

Allinder, R. M. (1994). The relationship between efficacy and the instructional practices of special education teachers and consultants. *Teacher Education and Special Education, 17*, 86–95.

American Association of University Women (AAUW). (1991). *Shortchanging girls, shortchanging America.* Washington, DC: Greenberg-Lake Analysis Group.

American Association of University Women (AAUW). (1992). *How schools shortchange girls.* Washington, DC: AAUW Educational Foundation and National Education Association.

American Association of University Women (AAUW). (1993). *Hostile hallways: The AAUW survey on sexual harassment in America's Schools.* Washington, DC: AAUW.

American Association of University Women (AAUW). (1998). *Gender gaps: Where schools still fail children.* Washington, DC: AAUW Education Foundation and National Education Association.

Amidon, E., & Hunter, E. (1966). *Improving teaching.* New York: Holt, Rinehart & Winston.

Amidon, E. J., & Flanders, N. A. (1967). *The role of the teacher in the classroom: A manual for understanding and improving teacher classroom behavior.* Minneapolis, MN: Association for Productive Teaching.

Amstutz, J. (1987, November). In defense of telling stories. *Teaching Forum.*

Andersen, J. (1979). The relationship between teacher immediacy and teaching effectiveness. In D. Nimmo (Ed.), *Communication yearbook 3* (pp. 543–561). New Brunswick, NJ: Transaction Books.

Andersen, J. (1986). Instructor nonverbal communication: Listening to our silent messages. In J. M. Civikly (Ed.), *Communicating in college classrooms* (pp. 39–47). San Francisco: Jossey-Bass.

Andersen, J., & Powell, R. (1994). Cultural and classroom communication. In L. Samovar & R. Porter (Eds.), *Intercultural communication: A reader* (pp. 322–334). Belmont, CA: Wadsworth.

Andersen, J. F., & Nussbaum, J. (1990). Interaction skill in instructional settings. In J. A. Daly, G. W. Friedrich, & A. Vangelisti

(Eds.), *Teaching communication: Theory, research, and methods* (pp. 301–316). Hillsdale, NJ: Erlbaum.

Andersen, K. E. (1990). Ethical issues in teaching. In J. Daly, G. Friedrich, & A. Vangelisti (Eds.), *Teaching communication: Theory, research, and methods* (pp. 459–470). Hillsdale, NJ: Erlbaum.

Andersen, P., & Andersen, J. (1982). Nonverbal intimacy in instruction. In L. Barker (Ed.), *Communication in the classroom* (pp. 99–105). Englewood Cliffs, NJ: Prentice Hall.

Anderson, I. (1989). Classroom instruction. In M. Reynolds (Ed.), Knowledge *base for the beginning teacher* (pp. 101–116). New York: Pergamon.

Anderson, J. A. (1988). Cognitive studies and multicultural populations. *Journal of Teacher Education, 39*(1), 2–9.

Anderson, J., & Powell, R. (1988). Cultural influences on educational processes. In L. Samovar & L. Porter (Eds.), *Intercultural communication: A reader.* (pp. 207–214). Belmont, CA: Wadsworth.

Anderson, K., & Miller, E. (1997). Gender and student evaluations of teaching. *PS: Political Sciences and Politics, 30*(2), 216–219.

Angell, M., Boyd, M., Hunt, S., Lippert, L., Moore, M., & Kolloff, P. (2004). Partnership power: Developing preservice and inservice modules on teaching and teaching diverse learners. In S. D. Lenski & W. L. Black (Eds.), *Transforming teacher education through partnerships* (pp. 434–448). Lewiston, NY: The Edwin Mellen Press.

Arlow, P., & Froschel, M. (1976). Women in the high school curriculum: A review of U.S. history and English literature texts. In C. Ahlum, J. Fralley, & F. Howe (Eds.), *High school feminist studies* (pp. 11–28). Old Westbury, NY: Feminist Press.

Arnold, A. J. (1983, March). What's new? *Learning, 12,* 10.

Asselin, G., & Mastron, R. (2001). *Au contraire!: Figuring out the French.* Yarmouth, ME: Intercultural Press.

Astin, A. W. (1984). Student involvement: A developmental theory for higher education. *Journal of College Student Personnel, 25,* 297–308.

Atkins-Sayre, W., Hopkins, S., Mohundro, S., & Sayre, W. (1998, November). *Rewards and liabilities of presentation software as an ancillary tool: Prison or paradise?* Paper presented at the National Communication Association, New York. (ERIC Document Reproduction Service No. ED 430 260)

Au, K. H. (1993). *Literacy instruction in multicultural settings.* New York: Harcourt.

Audi, R. (1994, September–October). On the ethics of teaching and the ideals of learning. *Academe, 80*(5), 26–36.

Auster, C., & MacRone, M. (1994). The classroom as a negotiated social setting: An empirical study of the effects of faculty members' behavior on students' participation. *Teaching Sociology, 22,* 289–300.

Aylor, B. (2003). The impact of sex, gender, and cognitive complexity on the perceived importance of teacher communication skills. *Communication Studies, 54*(4), 496–509.

Ayres, J., & Hopf, T. (1993). *Coping with speech anxiety.* Norwood, NJ: Ablex.

Ayres, J., Hopf, T., & Ayres, D. (1994). An examination of whether imaging ability enhances the effectiveness of an intervention designed to reduce speech anxiety. *Communication Education, 43,* 252–258.

Bachen, C., McLaughlin, M., & Garcia, S. (1999). Assessing the role of gender in college students' evaluations of faculty. *Communication Education, 48,* 193–210.

Badini, A., & Rosenthal, R. (1989). Visual cues, student sex, material taught, and the magnitude of teacher expectancy effects. *Communication Education, 38,* 162–166.

Bailey, G. (1981). *Teacher self-assessment: A means for improving instruction.* Washington, DC: National Education Association.

Balli, S. J., & Diggs, L. L. (1996). Educational technology research section. *Educational Technology, 36*(1), 56–61.

Bandura, A. (1997). *Self-efficacy: The exercise of control.* New York: Freeman.

Banks, J. (1998). Multicultural education: Development, dimensions, and challenges. In M. Bennett (Ed.), *Basic concepts of intercultural communication* (pp. 69–84). Yarmouth, ME: Intercultural Press.

Banks, J. A. (1988). *Multiethnic education: Theory and practice.* Boston: Allyn & Bacon.

Baringer, D., & McCroskey, J. C. (2000). Immediacy in the classroom: Student immediacy. *Communication Education, 49,* 178–186.

Barker, L. L. (1971). *Listening behavior.* Englewood Cliffs, NJ: Prentice Hall.

Barker, L. L. (Ed.). (1981). *Communication in the classroom.* Englewood Cliffs, NJ: Prentice Hall.

Barna, L. (1988). Stumbling blocks in intercultural communication. In L. Samovar & R. Porter (Eds.), *Intercultural communication: A reader* (pp. 322–330). Belmont, CA: Wadsworth.

Barnlund, D. (1975). *The public and private self in Japan and the United States.* Tokyo: Simul Press.

Barraclough, R. A., & Stewart, R. A. (1992). Power and control: Social science perspectives. In V. P. Richmond & J. C. McCroskey (Eds.), *Power in the classroom: Communication, control, and concern* (pp. 1–18). Hillsdale, NJ: Erlbaum.

Barton, L. (1984). What are boys like in books these days? *Learning, 13,* 130–131.

Basow, S. A. (1992). *Gender: Stereotypes and roles* (3rd ed.). Pacific Grove, CA: Brooks/Cole.

Bassett, R., & Smythe, M. J. (1979). *Communication and instruction.* New York: Harper & Row.

Bate, B. (1988). *Communication between the sexes.* New York: Harper & Row.

Beagan, B. (2005). Everyday classism in medical school: Experiencing marginality and resistance. *Medical Education, 39*(8), 77.

Beane, A. L. (2000). *The bully-free classroom: Over 100 tips and strategies for teacher K–8.* Murray, KY: Free Spirit Publishing.

Beatty, M. (1988, January). Situational and pre-dispositional correlates of public speaking anxiety. *Communication Education, 37,* 28–39.

Beatty, M. J., & Behnke, R. R. (1980). Teacher credibility as a function of verbal content and paralinguistic cues. *Communication Quarterly, 28,* 55–59.

Beatty, M. J., & Zahn, C. J. (1990). Are student ratings of communication instructors due to "easy" grading practices?: An analysis of teacher credibility and student-reported performance levels. *Communication Education, 39,* 275–292.

Beebe, S. (1980). *The role of nonverbal communication in education: Research and theoretical perspectives.* Paper presented at the meeting of the Speech Communication Association, New York.

Beebe, S. A., & Butland, M. J. (1993, November). *Implicit communication and learning: Explaining affinity-seeking behaviors in the classroom.* Paper presented at the Speech Communication Association Convention, Miami, FL.

Beilke, J. R., & Yasel, N. (1999). The chilly climate for students with disabilities in higher education. *College Student Journal, 33*(3), 364–371.

Berger, C. (1977). The covering law perspective as a theoretical basis for the study of human communication. *Communication Quarterly, 25,* 7–18.

Berger, E., & Goldberger, L. (1979). Field dependence and short-term memory. *Perceptual and Motor Skills, 49,* 87–96.

Berger, P. L., & Luckman, T. (1966). *The social construction of reality.* New York: Doubleday.

Berliner, D. C. (1968). *The effects of testlike events and note-taking on learning from lecture instruction.* Unpublished doctoral dissertation, Stanford University, Stanford, CA.

Berliner, D. C., & Fisher, C. W. (1985). *Perspectives on instructional time*. New York: Longman.

Berlo, D. (1960). *The process of communication*. New York: Holt, Rinehart & Winston.

Berman, P., McLaughlin, M., Bass, G., Pauly, E., & Zellman, G. (1977). *Federal programs supporting educational change*. Vol. VII: *Factors affecting implementation and continuation* (Report No. R-1589/7HEW). Santa Monica, CA: RAND. (ERIC Document Reproduction Service No. 140-432)

Berthoff, A. (1981). *The making of meaning: Metaphors, models, and maxims for writing teachers*. Montclair, NJ: Boynton/Cook.

Birdwhistell, R. L. (1970). *Kinesics and context*. Philadelphia: University of Pennsylvania Press.

Bloom, B. S., Englehart, M., Furst, E., Hill, W., & Krathwohl, D. (1956). *Taxonomy of educational objectives: Cognitive domain*. New York: David McKay.

Bochner, A. (1985). Perspective on inquiry: Representation, conversation and reflection. In M. Knapp & G. Miller (Eds.), *Handbook of interpersonal communication* (pp. 27–58). Beverly Hills, CA: Sage.

Bohlken, B. (1991). A hearing aid: Improving classroom listening skills. *The Teaching Professor, 7*, 6–7.

Bolls, P., & Tan, A. (1996). Communication anxiety and teacher communication competence among native American and Caucasian students. *Communication Research Reports, 13*, 205–213.

Bond, M. H. (1991). *Beyond the Chinese face: Insights from psychology*. United Kingdom: Oxford University Press.

Booth-Butterfield, M. (1986, October). Stifle or stimulate? The effects of communication task structure on apprehensive and non-apprehensive students. *Communication Education, 35*, 337–348.

Booth-Butterfield, S. (1988, July). Instructional interventions for reducing situational anxiety and avoidance. *Communication Education, 37*, 214–224.

Borisoff, D. (1990). *Community in a multicultural society: Issues and strategies for the 21st century*. Paper presented at the meeting of the Speech Communication Association of Puerto Rico, San Juan.

Borton, W. (1991). *Empowering teacher and students in a restructuring school: A teacher efficacy interaction model and the effect on reading outcomes*. Paper presented at the American Educational Research Association, Chicago.

Bosacki, S., Innerd, W., & Towson, S. (1997). Field independence-dependence and self-esteem in preadolescents: Does gender make a difference? *Journal of Youth and Adolescence, 26*, 691–703.

Bosworth, K., & Hamilton, S. (Eds.). (1994). *Collaborative learning: Underlying processes and effective techniques. New Directions for Teaching and Learning* (vol. 59). San Francisco: Jossey-Bass.

Bourhis, J., & Allen, M. (1992). Meta-analysis of the relationship between communication apprehension and cognitive performance. *Communication Education, 41*, 68–76.

Bowman, B. (1989, October). Educating language-minority children: Challenges and opportunities. *Phi Delta Kappan, 71*, 118–120.

Bozik, B. (1989). Teaching students to listen. *Teacher Talk, 7, 2*, 7.

Braithwaite, D., & Eckstein, C. (2003). How people with disabilities communicatively manage assistance: Helping as instrumental support. *Journal of Applied Communication Research, 31*, 1–26.

Braithwaite, D. O. (1990). From majority to minority: An analysis of cultural change from able bodied to disabled. *International Journal of Intercultural Relations, 14*, 465–483.

Braithwaite, D. O. (1991). Just how much did that wheelchair cost? Management of privacy boundaries by persons with disabilities. *Western Journal of Speech Communication, 55*, 254–274.

Braithwaite, D. O. (1996). "I am a person first": Different perspectives on the communication of persons with disabilities. In E. B. Ray (Ed.), *Communication and disenfranchisement: Social health issues and implications* (pp. 257–272). Mahwah, NJ: Erlbaum.

Braithwaite, D. O., & Braithwaite, C. A. (2000). Understanding communication of persons with disabilities as cultural communication. In L. A. Samovar & R. E. Porter (Eds.), *Intercultural communication* (pp. 136–145). Belmont, CA: Wadsworth.

Branon, J. M. (1972). Negative human interaction. *Journal of Counseling Psychology, 19*(1), 81–89.

Braun, C. (1976). Teacher expectation: Sociopsychological dynamics. *Review of Educational Research, 46,* 206.

Bray, J. H., & Howard, G. S. (1980). Interaction of teacher and student sex and sex role orientations and student evaluations of college instruction. *Contemporary Educational Psychology, 5,* 241–248.

Brislin, R. (1993). *Understanding culture's influence on behavior.* San Diego: Harcourt.

Brodsky, S. M. (1991). Behavioral instructional and departmental strategies for retention of college students in science, engineering, or technology programs: How to become an even more effective teacher or departmental administrator. *CASE 15*(91). Albany: New York State Education Department.

Brophy, J. (1987, October). Synthesis of research on strategies for motivating students to learn. *Educational Leadership, 45,* 4–13.

Brophy, J., & Good, T. (1974). *Teacher-student relationships: Causes and consequences.* New York: Holt, Rinehart & Winston.

Brophy, J., & Good, T. (1986). Teacher behavior and student achievement. In M. C. Wittock (Ed.), *Handbook of research on teaching.* New York: Macmillan.

Brophy, J. E. (1983). Classroom organization and management. *Elementary School Journal, 83,* 265–286.

Brophy, J. E. (1987). Synthesis of research on strategies for motivating students to learn. *Educational Leadership, 45*(2), 40–48.

Brown, C., & Keller, P. (1979). *Monologue to dialogue.* Englewood Cliffs, NJ: Prentice Hall.

Brown, H. (2006). *Principles of language learning and teaching* (5th ed.). White Plains, NY: Pearson ESL.

Brownell, J. (2009). *Listening: Attitudes, principles, and skills* (4th ed.). White Plains, NY: Pearson Education.

Bruffee, K. (1984). Collaborative learning and the conversation of mankind. *College English, 46,* 634–640.

Bruffee, K. (1997). *A short course in writing* (4th ed.). New York: Longman.

Bruffee, K. (1998). *Collaborative learning: Higher education, interdependence, and the authority of knowledge* (2nd ed.). Baltimore: Johns Hopkins University Press.

Bryant, J., Comisky, P., & Zillman, D. (1979). Teachers' humor in the college classroom. *Communication Education, 28,* 110–118.

Buber, M. (2005). *I and thou* (R. Smith, Trans.). London: Continuum International Publishing.

Buck, S., & Tiene, D. (1989). The impact of physical attractiveness, gender, and teaching philosophy on evaluations. *Journal of Educational Research, 82,* 172–177.

Burleson, B. R., & Samter, W. (1990). Effects of cognitive complexity on the perceived importance of communication skills in friends. *Communication Quarterly, 42,* 259–273.

Burleson, B. R., & Waltman, M. S. (1993, May). *Assessing the validity of message behavior check lists: Some conceptual and empirical requirements.* Paper presented at the annual meeting of the International Communication Association, Washington, DC.

Burley, W. W., Hall, B. W., Villeme, M. G., & Brockmeier, L. L. (1991, April). *A path analysis of the mediating role of efficacy in first-year teachers' experiences, reactions, and plans.* Paper presented at the Annual Meeting of the American Educational Research Association, Chicago.

Burr, E., Dunn, S., & Farquhar, N. (1972). Women and the language of inequality. *Social Education, 36*, 841–845.

Burroughs, N., Kearney, P., & Plax, T. (1989). Compliance-resistance in the college classroom. *Communication Education, 38*, 214–229.

Buttner, E. H. (2004). How do we "dis" students?: A model of (dis)respectful business instructor behavior. *Journal of Management Education, 28*(3), 319–334.

Calloway-Thomas, C., Cooper, P., & Simonds, C. J. (2007). *Intercultural communication: A text with readings.* Boston: Allyn & Bacon.

Campbell, J., & Hepler, H. (Eds.). (1970). *Dimensions in communication: Readings.* Belmont, CA: Wadsworth.

Campbell, K. (1991). Hearing women's voices. *Communication Education, 40*, 33–48.

Cano, J., Jones, C., & Chism, N. (1991). TA teaching of an increasingly diverse undergraduate population. In J. Nyquist, R. Abbott, D. Wulff, & J. Sprague (Eds.), *Preparing the professorate of tomorrow to teach* (pp. 87–94). Dubuque, IA: Kendall Hunt.

Carlson, M. (1989). Guidelines for a gender-based curriculum in English, grades 7–12. *English Journal, 36*, 30–33.

Carnahan, S. (1994). Preventing school failure and dropout. In R. Simeonsson (Ed.), *Risk, resilience and prevention: Promoting the well-being of all children* (pp. 103–123). Baltimore, MD: Paul H. Brooks.

Carr, D. (1986). *Time, narrative, and history.* Bloomington: University of Indiana Press.

Carter, K., & Spitzack, C. (Eds.). (1989). *Doing research on women's communication: Perspectives on theory and method.* Norwood, NJ: Ablex.

Cashin, W. (1995, January). *Answering and asking questions.* IDEA paper no. 31, Center for Faculty Evaluation and Development. Kansas State University, Manhattan.

Cawyer, C., Bystrom, D., Miller, J., Simonds, C., O'Brien, M., & Storey-Martin, J. (1994). Community gender equity: Representation and portrayal of women and men in introductory communication textbooks. *Communication Education, 45*, 325–331.

Cawyer, C. S. (1994). *A cross-disciplinary assessment of teacher communications behaviors in the classroom.* Unpublished doctoral dissertation, University of Oklahoma, Norman.

Cayanus, J., & Martin, M. (2004). An instructor self-disclosure scale. *Communication Research Reports, 21*(3), 252–263.

Cazden, C. B. (1988). *Classroom discourse: The language of teaching and learning.* Portsmouth, NH: Heinemann Educational Books. (ERIC Document Reproduction Service No. ED 288 206)

Cegala, D. J. (1981). Interaction involvement: A cognitive dimension of communicative competence. *Communication Education, 30*, 109–121.

Centra, J., & Gaubatz, N. (2000). Is there gender bias in student evaluations of teaching? *Journal of Higher Education, 71*, 17.

Chesebro, J. L., & McCroskey, J. C. (2001). The relationship of teacher clarity and immediacy with student state receiver apprehension, affect, and cognitive learning. *Communication Education, 50*, 59–68.

Chesebro, J., McCroskey, J., Atwater, D., Behrenfuss, R., Cawelt, G., Gaudino, J., & Hodges, H. (1992). Communication apprehension and self-perceived communication competence of at-risk students. *Communication Education, 41*, 345–360.

Chethik, N. (1994, August 28). Boys, too, short-changed in classroom. *Cleveland Plain Dealer*, p. 5.

Chickering, A. W., & Gamson, G. F. (1987). Seven principles for good practices in undergraduate education. *AAHE Bulletin, 39*(7), 3–7.

Chisholm, I. (1994). Preparing teachers for multicultural classrooms. *Journal of Educational Issues of Language Minority Students, 14*, 43–67.

Chism, N., Cano, J., & Pruitt, A. (1989). Teaching in a diverse environment: Knowledge and skills needed by TAs. In J. Nyquist, R. Abbott, & D. Wulff (Eds.), *Teaching assistant training in the 1990s: New directions for teaching and learning* (pp. 23–35). San Franciso: Jossey-Bass.

Chmielewski, T. L., Dansereau, D. F., & Moreland, J. L. (1998). Using common region in node-link displays: The roles of field dependence/independence. *Journal of Experimental Education, 66*, 197–207.

Chou, P. P. (1979). *An empirical study of Chinese communicative competence in an American cultural setting.* Unpublished master's thesis, Texas Tech University, Lubbock.

Christensen, C. R., Hansen, A. J., & Barnes, L. B. (1994). *Teaching and the case method.* Boston: Harvard Business School.

Christophel, D. (1990). The relationship among teacher immediacy behaviors, student motivation, and learning. *Communication Education, 39*, 323–340.

Christophel, D. (1996). Russian communication orientations: A cross-cultural examination. *Communication Research Reports, 13*(1), 43–51.

Christophel, D., & Gorham, J. (1995). A test-retest analysis of student motivation, teacher immediacy, and perceived sources of motivation and demotivation in college classes. *Communication Education, 44*, 293–306.

Civikly, J. (1982). Self-concept, significant others, and classroom communication. In L. Barker (Ed.), *Communication in the classroom.* Englewood Cliffs, NJ: Prentice Hall.

Civikly, J. M. (1992). Clarity: Teachers and students making sense of instruction. *Communication Education, 41*, 138–152.

Civikly, J. M. (1995). *Classroom communication: Principles and practice.* New York: McGraw Hill.

Cohen, E. (1987). *Design group work: Strategies for the heterogeneous classroom.* New York: Teachers College Press.

Cohen, J. (1998). *Disability etiquette.* Jackson Heights, NY: EPVA.

Coladarci, T. (1992). Teachers' sense of efficacy and commitment to teaching. *Journal of Experimental Education, 60*, 323–337.

Cole, R. (Ed.). (1995). *Educating everybody's children: Diverse teaching strategies for diverse learners.* Alexandria, VA: ASCD.

Coleman, L., & DePaulo, B. (1991). Uncovering the human spirit: Moving beyond disability and "missed" communications. In N. Coupland, H. Giles, & J. M. Wiemann (Eds.), *Miscommunication and problematic talk* (pp. 61–84). Newbury Park, CA: Sage.

Coles, R. (1989). *The call of stories: Teaching and the moral imagination.* Boston: Houghton Mifflin.

Collier, M. J., & Powell, R. (1990). Ethnicity instructional communication and classroom systems. *Communication Quarterly, 4*, 334–349.

Collins, C. (1993). Teacher skills with classroom discussion: Impact on student mastery of subject matter, self-concept, and oral expression skills. *Roeper Review, 43*(1), 45–53.

Collins, R., & Cooper, P. (2005). *The power of story: Teaching through storytelling* (2nd ed.). Boston: Allyn & Bacon.

Comadena, M. E., Hunt, S. K., & Simonds, C. J. (2007). The effects of teaching clarity, nonverbal immediacy, and caring on student motivation, affective- and cognitive learning: A research note. *Communication Research Reports, 24* (3), 241–248.

Comadena, M. E., & Prusank, D. T. (1988). Communication apprehension and academic achievement among elementary and middle school students. *Communication Education, 37*, 270–277.

Combs, A. W. (1965). *The professional education of teachers.* Boston: Allyn & Bacon.

Condon, J. (1986). The ethnocentric classroom. In J. M. Civikly (Ed.), *Communicating in college classrooms* (pp. 11–20). San Francisco: Jossey-Bass.

Condravy, J., Skirboll, E., & Taylor, R. (1998). Faculty perceptions of classroom gender dynamics. *Women and Language, 21,* 18–27.

Constantinople, A., Cornelius, R., & Gray, J. (1998). The chilly climate: Fact or artifact? *Journal of Higher Education, 59,* 527–550.

Cooper, B. (1956). *Pam.* [Unpublished personal collection.]

Cooper, B. (1960). *The spaces in between.* [Unpublished personal collection.]

Cooper, B. (1965). *I was sure to follow.* [Unpublished personal collection.]

Cooper, E., & Allen, M. (1998). A meta-analytic examination of the impact of student race on classroom interaction. *Communication Research Reports, 15,* 151–161.

Cooper, H. (1985). Models of teacher expectation communication. In J. Dusek (Ed.), *Teacher expectancies* (pp. 135–158). Hillsdale, NJ: Erlbaum.

Cooper, H., & Good, T. (1983). *Pygmalion grows up: Studies in the expectation communication process.* New York: Longman.

Cooper, H., & Tom, D. (1984). Teacher expectation research: A review with implications for classroom instruction. *Elementary School Journal, 85,* 77–89.

Cooper, P. (1987). Sex role stereotypes of stepparents in children's literature. In L. P. Stewart & S. Ting-Toomey (Eds.), *Communication gender, and sex roles in diverse interaction contexts* (pp. 61–82). Norwood, NJ: Ablex.

Cooper, P. (1988a). *Communication competencies for teachers.* Annandale, VA: Speech Communication Association.

Cooper, P. (1988b). *Teacher effectiveness as a function of communicator style.* Annandale, VA: Speech Communication Association.

Cooper, P. (1989). Children's literature: The extent of sexism. In C. Lont & S. Friedley (Eds.), *Beyond boundaries: Sex and gender diversity in education* (pp. 233–250). Fairfax, VA: George Mason University Press.

Cooper, P. (1993). Women and power in the Caldecott and Newbery winners, 1980–90. In C. Berryman-Fink, D. Ballard-Reisch, & L. Newman (Eds.), *Communication and sex-role socialization* (pp. 7–27). New York: Garland.

Cooper, P. (1994). The image of stepmothers in children's literature 1980–1991. In L. Turner & H. Sterk (Eds.), *Differences that make a difference.* Westport, CT: Bergin & Gravey.

Cooper, P. (2000). *Image of stepmothers in children's literature, 1980–2000.* Paper presented at the Organization for the Study of Communication, Language and Gender Conference, Milwaukee, WI.

Cooper, P. (2004). Narrative as a way of knowing. *Journal of Communication Studies, 22*(1), 56–60. (Note: This is a journal published in Sunderpur, India by the National Council of Development Communication.)

Cooper, P., & Galvin, K. (1983). *Improving classroom communication.* Washington, DC: Dingle Associates.

Cooper, P. J., Stewart, L. P., & Gudykunst, W. B. (1982). Relationship with instructor and other variables influencing student evaluations of instruction. *Communication Quarterly, 30,* 308–315.

Cornett, C. (1983). *What you should know about teaching and learning styles.* Bloomington, IN: Phi Delta Kappa Educational Foundation.

Costa, A., Garmston, R., & Lambert, L. (1988). Evaluation of teaching: The cognitive development view. In S. Stanley & W. J. Popham (Eds.), *Teacher evaluation: Six prescriptions for success* (p. 148). Alexandria, VA: ASCD.

Covert, A. (1978). *Communication: People speak, instructor's manual.* New York: McGraw-Hill.

Crawford, M., & MacLeod, M. (1990). Gender in the college classroom: An assessment of the "chilly climate" for women. *Sex Roles, 23,* 101–122.

Cruickshank, D. R. (1985). Applying research on teacher clarity. *Journal of Teacher Education, 36,* 44–48.

Cullum, A. (1971). *The geranium on the window sill just died but teacher you went right on.* New York: Harlin Quist.

Cullum, A. (1978). *Blackboard, blackboard on the wall who is the fairest one of all?* New York: Harlin Quist.

Curwin, R., & Mendler, A. (1999). *Discipline with dignity.* Alexandria, VA: ASCD.

Cushner, K., & Brislin, R. (1996). *Intercultural interactions: A practical guide* (2nd ed.). Thousand Oaks, CA: Sage.

Cyber Dialogue. (1999). *The American Internet User Survey* (online). Available at www.cyberdialogue.com/free_data/index.html

Czubaj, C. A. (1996). Maintaining teacher motivation. *Education, 116,* 372–378.

Daly, J. A., & Friedrich, G. (1981). The development of communication apprehension: A retrospective analysis of contributory correlates. *Communication Quarterly, 29,* 243–255.

Daly, J. A., & Kreiser, P. O. (1993). Affinity in the classroom. In V. P. Richmond & J. C. McCroskey (Eds.), *Power in the classroom: Communication, control, and concern* (pp. 121–143). Hillsdale, NJ: Erlbaum.

Darling, A. (1989). Signaling non-comprehensions in the classroom: Toward a descriptive typology. *Communication Education, 38,* 34–40.

Darling, A. (1990). Instructional models. In J. Daly, G. Friedrich, & A. Vangelisti (Eds.), *Teaching communication: Theory, research, and methods* (pp. 267–278). Hillsdale, NJ: Erlbaum.

Darling, A., & Civikly, J. (1987). The effect of teacher humor on student perceptions of classroom communicative climate. *Journal of Classroom Interaction, 22,* 24–30.

Davidson, C., & Ambrose, S. (1995). *The new professor's handbook.* Boston: Anker Publishing.

Davis, B. G. (2004). *Tools for teaching* (2nd ed.). Chichester, UK: Wiley.

Dean, K. (2002, March 23). Lility: Geek music to girls' ears. *Wired News.* Downloaded from www.wired.com/new/print/0.1294.51249.00htm

Decker, S. (1969). *An empty spoon.* New York: Harper & Row.

Deemer, D. (1986). Structuring controversy in the classroom. In S. F. Schomberg (Ed.), *Strategies for active teaching and learning in university classrooms.* Minneapolis: Office of Educational Development Programs, University of Minnesota.

Deethardt, J. E. (1974). The use of questions in the speech-communication classroom. *Speech Teacher, 23,* 15–20.

DeFleur, M. L., Kearney, P., & Plax, T. G. (2004). *Fundamentals of human communication* (3rd ed.). Fort Worth, TX: Harcourt.

DeVito, J. A. (1986). Teaching as relational development. In J. M. Civikly (Ed.), *Communicating in college classrooms* (pp. 51–59). San Francisco: Jossey-Bass.

Dillon, J. T. (1988). The remedial status of student questioning. *Journal of Curriculum Studies, 20,* 197–210.

Dillon, J. T. (1990). *The practice of questioning.* London: Routledge.

Dillon, J. T. (2004). *Questioning and teaching.* Bristol: Resource Publishing.

Dobransky, N., & Frymier, A. B. (2004). Developing teacher-student relationships through out of class communication. *Communication Quarterly, 52*(3), 211–223.

Dodd, C. H. (1997). *Dynamics of intercultural communication* (5th ed.). Madison, WI: Brown & Benchmark.

Dolin, D. J. (1995). *Ain't misbehavin: A study of teacher misbehaviors, related communication behaviors, and student resistance.* Unpublished doctoral dissertation, West Virginia University, Morgantown.

Donlan, D. (1972). The negative image of women in children's literature. *Elementary English, 49,* 604–611.

Dorman, M. (1998). Using e-mail to enhance instruction. *Journal of School Health, 68*(6), 260–261.

Dougherty, R., Bowen, C., Berger, T., Rees, W., Mellon, E., & Pulliam, E. (1995). Cooperative learning and enhanced communication: Effects on student performance, retention, and attitudes in general chemistry. *Journal of Chemical Education, 72,* 793–797.

Dougherty, W., & Engel, R. (1987). An 80s look for sex equality in Caldecott winners and honor books. *The Reading Teacher, 40,* 394–398.

Downing, J., & Garmon, C. (2001). Teaching students in the basic course how to use presentation software. *Communication Education, 50*(3), 218–229.

Downs, V. C., Javidi, M., & Nussbaum, J. F. (1988). An analysis of teachers' verbal communication within the college classroom: Use of humor, self-disclosure, and narratives. *Communication Education, 37,* 127–141.

Duke, C. (1971). Questions teachers ask: By-pass or through-ways? *The Clearing House, 45,* 468–472.

Dunn, R., Beaudry, J., & Klavas, A. (1989). A survey of research on learning styles. *Educational Leadership, 50,* 58.

Dunn, R., Dunn, K., & Price, G. (1979). Identifying individual learning styles. In O. Kiernan (Ed.), *Student learning styles: Diagnosing and prescribing programs.* Reston, VA: National Association of Secondary School Principals.

Ekman, P., & Friesen, W. V. (1969). The repertoire of nonverbal behavior: Categories, origins, usage, and coding. *Semiotica, 1,* 49–98.

Eleser, C., Longman, D., & Steib, P. (1996, October). A dozen responses to incorrect answers. *The Teaching Professor, 10,* 1.

Elliott, S., Scott, M. D., Jensen, A. D., & McDonough, M. (1981). Perceptions of reticence: A cross-cultural investigation. In D. Nimmo (Ed.), *Communication yearbook* (vol. 5, pp. 591–602). New Brunswick, NJ: Transaction Books.

Ellis, K. (1995). Apprehension, self-perceived competency, and teacher immediacy in the laboratory-supported public speaking course: Trends and relationships. *Communication Education, 44,* 64–78.

Elsen, A. (1969). The pleasures of teaching. In *The study of education at Stanford: Report to the university, VIII, teaching, research, and the faculty* (pp. 78–87). Stanford, CA: Stanford University.

Engen, D. (2002). The communication imagination and its cultivation. *Communication Quarterly, 50*(1), 41–57.

Ennis, R. (1985). Goals for a critical thinking curriculum. In A. Costa (Ed.), *Developing minds: A resource book for teaching thinking* (p. 54). Alexandria, VA: Association for Supervision and Curriculum Development.

Epperson, S. E. (1988, September 16). Studies link subtle sex bias in schools with women's behavior in the work-place. *Wall Street Journal,* p. 27.

Ericson, P., & Gardner, J. (1992). Two longitudinal studies of communication apprehension and its effects on college students' success. *Communication Quarterly, 40,* 127–137.

Evertson, C. M. (1987). Creating conditions for learning: From research to practice. *Theory into Practice, 26,* 44–50.

Evertson, C. M., & Emmer, E. T. (1982). Effective management at the beginning of the school year in junior high classes. *Journal of Educational Psychology, 74*(4), 485–498.

Evertson, C. M., & Harris, A. H. (1992, April). What we know about managing classrooms. *Educational Leadership,* 74–78.

Fagot, B. I. (1984). Teacher and peer reactions to boys' and girls' play styles. *Sex Roles, 11,* 691–702.

Fassinger, P. (1995). Understanding classroom interaction: Students' and professors' contributions to students' silence. *Journal of Higher Education, 66*(1), 82–97.

Fassinger, P. (1996). Professors and students perceptions of why students participate in class. *Teaching Sociology, 24,* 25–33.

Fayer, J. M., Gorham, J., & McCroskey, J. C. (1993). Teacher immediacy and student learning: A comparison between U.S. mainland and Puerto Rican classrooms. In J. Fayer (Ed.), *Puerto Rican communication studies* (pp. 111–126). Puerto Rico: Fundacion Arquelogica, Anthropologica, Historica de Puerto Rico.

Feiner, S., & Morgan, B. (1987). Women and minorities in introductory economics textbooks: 1974 to 1984. *Journal of Economic Education, 18,* 376–392.

Feiner, S., & Roberts, B. (1990). Hidden by the invisible hand: Neoclassical economic theory and the textbook treatment of race and gender. *Gender and Society, 4,* 159–181.

Feitler, F. C. (1971, September). Teacher's desk. Reprinted in K. Goodoll, Time line. *Psychology Today, 6,* 12.

Feldhusen, J. (1989, March). Synthesis of research on gifted youth. *Educational Leadership, 46,* 6–11.

Ferree, M. M., & Hall, E. J. (1990). Visual images of American society: Gender and race in introductory sociology textbooks. *Gender and Society, 4,* 500–533.

Fisch, L. (1992, November). *The teaching professor.* Madison, WI: Magna Publications.

Fisher, B. A. (1970). Decision emergence: Phases in group decision making. *Speech Monographs, 37,* 53–66.

Fisher, W. R. (1984). Narration as a human paradigm. *Communication Monographs, 51,* 1–22.

Fisher, W. R. (1987). *Human communication as narration: Toward a philosophy of reason, value, and action.* Columbia: University of South Carolina Press.

Fisher, W. R. (1989). Narration, knowledge, and the possibility of wisdom. In R. Goodman & W. R. Fisher (Eds.), *Rethinking knowledge: Reflections across the disciplines* (pp. 169–192). Albany: State University of New York Press.

Fitch-Hauser, M., Barker, D., & Hughes, A. (1992). Receiver apprehension and listening apprehension: A linear or curvilinear relationship? *Southern Communication Journal, 57,* 62–77.

Fleming, P. M. (2000). Three decades of education progress (and continuing barriers) for women and girls. *Equity and Excellence in Education, 33,* 74–79.

Fouts, J., & Myers, R. (1992). Classroom environments and middle school students' views of science. *Journal of Educational Research, 85,* 356–361.

Frankel, C. (1965). *The neglected aspect of foreign affairs.* Washington, DC: Brookings Institution.

Freeman, C. (2004). *Trends in the educational equity of girls and women: 2004.* National Center for Education Statistics. Washington, DC: U.S. Department of Education.

French, R. P., & Raven, B. (1959). The bases for social power. In D. Cartwright (Ed.), *Studies in social power* (pp. 150–167). Ann Arbor, MI: Institute for Social Research.

French, R. P., & Raven, B. (1960). The bases of social power. In D. Cartwright & A. Zander (Eds.), *Group dynamics* (pp. 607–623). Evanston, IL: Row, Peterson.

French-Lazovik, G. (1974). Predictability of students' evaluations of college teachers from component ratings. *Journal of Educational Psychology, 66,* 373–385.

Frey, P., Leonard, D., & Beatty, W. (1975). Student ratings of instruction: Validation research. *American Educational Research Journal, 12,* 435–447.

Friedrich, G., & Cooper, P. (1999). First day. In J. Daly, G. Friedrich, & A. Vangelisti (Eds.), *Teaching communication: Theory, research, and methods* (pp. 287–296). Hillsdale, NJ: Erlbaum.

Friedrich, G. W. (1982). Communication in the classroom: Original essays. In L. L. Barker (Ed.), *Teacher as only native.* Englewood Cliffs, NJ: Prentice Hall.

Friedrich, G. W. (1987). Instructional communication research. *Journal of Thought, 22,* 4–10.

Frost, G. E. (1974). *Bless my growing.* Minneapolis, MN: Augsburg Publishing.

Fry, P. G. (1994). Equity: A vision for multicultural education. *Equity and Excellence, 25,* 139–144.

Frymier, A., & Wanzer, M. (2003). Examining differences in perceptions of students' communication with professors: A comparison of students with and without disabilities. *Communication Quarterly, 51*(1), 1–26.

Frymier, A. B. (1994a). A model of immediacy in the classroom. *Communication Quarterly, 42*(2), 133–144.

Frymier, A. B. (1994b). The use of affinity-seeking in producing liking and learning in the classroom. *Journal of Applied Communication Research, 22,* 87–105.

Frymier, A. B., & Houser, M. L. (2000). The teacher-student relationship as an interpersonal relationship. *Communication Education, 49*(3), 207–219.

Frymier, A., & Shulman, G. (1995). What's in it for me? Increasing content relevance to enhance students' motivation. *Communication Education, 44,* 40–50.

Frymier, A., & Thompson, C. (1992). Perceived teacher affinity-seeking in relation to perceived teacher credibility. *Communication Education, 41,* 388–399.

Fuchs, L. S., Fuchs, D., & Bishop, N. (1992). Instructional adaptation for students at risk. *Journal of Educational Research, 86,* 70–84.

Fulghum, R. (1988). *All I really need to know I learned in kindergarten.* New York: Villard Books.

Fusani, D. S. (1994). Extra-class communication: Frequency, immediacy, self-disclosure, and satisfaction in student-faculty interaction outside the classroom. *Journal of Applied Communication Research, 22,* 232–255.

Gabriel, S. L., & Smithson, I. (Eds.). (1990). *Gender in the classroom: Power and pedagogy.* Urbana: University of Illinois Press.

Gage, N. L., & Berliner, D. C. (1975). *Educational Psychology: Study Guide.* Boston: Houghton Mifflin.

Gall, M. (1970). The use of questions in teaching. *Review of Educational Research, 40,* 707–721.

Gall, M. (1984). Synthesis of research on teachers' questioning. *Educational Leadership, 42,* 40–47.

Gall, M., & Rhody, T. (1987). Review of research on questioning techniques. In W. Wilen (Ed.), *Questions, questioning techniques, and effective teaching* (pp. 23–48). Washington, DC: NEA.

Galvin, K. (1988). *Listening by doing.* Lincolnwood, IL: National Textbook.

Gamble, T. K., & Gamble, M. (2001). *Communication works* (6th ed.). New York: McGraw-Hill.

Gambrell, L. (1983). The occurrence of think-time during reading comprehension. *Journal of Educational Research, 77,* 77–80.

Garside, C. (1996). Look who's talking: A comparison of lecture and group discussion teaching strategies in developing critical thinking skills. *Communication Education, 45,* 212–227.

Garwood, S. (1983, March). *Learning, 11,* 8.

Gay, G. (1978). Viewing the pluralistic classroom as a cultural microcosm. *Educational Research Quarterly, 2,* 49–55.

Gendrin, D., & Rucker, M. (2002). The impact of gender on teacher immediacy and student learning in the HBCU classroom. *Communication Research Reports, 19*(3), 291–299.

Gerritz, K. (1983, February). Dear Ms. McCrea, about that conference next week. *Learning, 11*, 46.

Gibaldi, J. (2003). *MLA handbook for writers of research papers* (6th ed.). New York: Ballantine Books.

Gibb, J. (1961). Defensive communication. *Journal of Communication, 11*, 142–148.

Gibson, J. (1982, June 2). Do looks help children make the grade? *Family Weekly*, 9.

Gill, M. (1994). Accent and stereotypes: Their effect on perceptions of teachers and lecture comprehension. *Journal of Applied Communication, 22*, 348–361.

Glasser, W. (1969). *Schools without failure.* New York: Harper & Row.

Glickman, C., & Tamashiro, R. (1982). A comparison of first-year, fifth-year, and former teachers on efficacy, ego development, and problem solving. *Psychology in Schools, 19*, 197–219.

Gloeckner, B. (1983). *An investigation into the effectiveness of a preservice teacher clarity training unit in two different experimental settings.* Unpublished doctoral dissertation, Ohio State University, Columbus.

Gold, D., Crombie, G., & Noble, S. (1987). Relations between teachers' judgments of girls' and boys' compliance and intellectual competence. *Sex Roles, 16*, 351–358.

Golish, T. D., & Olson, L. N. (2000). Students' use of power in the classroom: An investigation of student power, teacher power, and teacher immediacy. *Communication Quarterly, 48*(3), 293–310.

Gollnick, D. M., & Chinn, P. C. (1994). *Multicultural education in a pluralistic society.* New York: Merrill.

Golub, J. (1988). *Focus on collaborative learning.* Urbana, IL: National Council of Teachers of English.

Good, T., & Brophy, J. (2007). *Looking in classrooms* (10th ed.). Boston: Allyn & Bacon.

Gordon, T. (1974). *T. E. T.: Teacher effectiveness training.* New York: David McKay.

Gorham, J. (1988). The relationship between verbal teacher immediacy behavior and student learning. *Communication Education, 37*, 40–53.

Gorham, J., & Christophel, D. (1990, January). The relationship of teachers' use of humor in the classroom to immediacy and student learning. *Communication Education, 39*, 46–62.

Gorham, J., & Christophel, D. M. (1992). Students' perceptions of teacher behaviors as motivating and demotivating factors in college classes. *Communication Quarterly, 40*, 237–252.

Gorham, J., Kelley, D. H., & McCroskey, J. C. (1989). The affinity-seeking of classroom teachers: A second perspective. *Communication Quarterly, 37*, 16–26.

Gorham, J., & Zakahi, W. (1990). A comparison of teacher and student perceptions of immediacy and learning: Monitoring process and product. *Communication Education, 39*, 454–368.

Goza, B. (1993). Graffiti needs assessment: Involving students in the first class session. *Journal of Management Education, 17*, 99–106.

Graham, E. E., West R., & Schaller, K. A. (1992). The association between the relational teaching approach teacher job satisfaction. *Communication Reports, 5*, 11–22.

Grant, B., & Hennings, D. (1971). *The teacher moves.* New York: Columbia University.

Grauerholz, E., & Pescosolido, B. (1989). Gender presentation in children's literature: 1900–1984. *Gender and Society, 3*, 113–125.

Gray, P. (1998). Leading classroom activities. In L. W. Hugenberg & B. S. Moyer (Eds.), *Teaching ideas for the basic communication course,* (Vol. 1, pp. 3–20). Dubuque, IA: Kendall/ Hunt.

Gray, P. L. (2007). Leading classroom activities. In Hugenburg, L. W., Morreale, S., Worley, D. W., Hugenberg, B., & Worley, D. A. (Eds.), *Best practices in the basic communication course: A training manual for instructors* (pp. 81–90). Dubuque, IA: Kendall-Hunt Publishing Company.

Greene, J. (1983) Teaching and learning: A linguistic perspective. *Elementary School Journal, 33,* 353–391.

Greene, E., & Simms, L. (1982, May 26). What would happen if there were no stories in the world? *Chicago Journal.*

Guild, P. (1994). The culture/learning style connection. *Educational Leadership, 51,* 16–21.

Gullicks, K., Pearson, J., Child, J., & Schwab, D. (2005). Diversity and power in public speaking textbooks. *Communication Quarterly, 53*(2), 247–258.

Guskey, T. R., & Passaro, P. D. (1994). Teacher efficacy: A study of construct dimensions. *American Educational Research Journal, 31,* 627–643.

Hall, E. T. (1992). *Beyond culture.* New York: Smith Peter.

Hall, R., & Sandler, B. (1982). *The classroom climate. A chilly one for women?* Washington, DC: Association of American Colleges Project on the Status and Education of Women.

Hall, R. M., & Sandler, B. R. (1984). *Out of the classroom: A chilly campus climate for women.* Washington, DC: Association of American Colleges Project on the Status and Education of Women.

Haney, W. V. (1967). *Communication and organizational behavior: Text and cases.* Homewood, IL: Richard D. Irwin.

Hanson, T. (1999). Gender sensitivity and diversity in selected basic public speaking texts. *Women and Language, 22*(2), 13–20.

Harari, H., & McDavid, J. (1983, March). *Learning, 11,* 8.

Hargett, J. (1999). Students' perceptions of male and female instructors' level of immediacy and teacher credibility. *Women and Language, 22*(2), 46.

Harris, J. A. (2002). Listening in the global marketplace. *EarPiece: Magazine of the International Listening Association, 1*(1), 24–27.

Hart, R. P. (1973). *Lecturing as communication: Problems and potentialities.* West Lafayette, IN: Purdue Research Foundation.

Hart, R., & Williams, D. (1995). Able-bodied instructors and students with physical disabilities: A relationship handicapped by communication. *Communication Education, 44,* 140–154.

Harwood, N. (1992). Writing women into textbooks. *Feminist Teacher, 6*(3), 16–17, 31.

Hawkins, K., & Stewart, R. (1991). Effects of communication apprehension on perceptions of leadership and intragroup attraction in small task-oriented groups. *Southern Communication Journal, 57,* 1–10.

Hehir, T. (2002). Eliminating ableism in education. *Harvard Educational Review, 72*(1), 15–27.

Heilbrun, C. (1989). *Writing a woman's life.* New York: W. W. Norton.

Heinz, K. (1987). An examination of sex and occupational role presentations of female characters in children's picture books. *Women's Studies in Communication, 11,* 67–78.

Hendrix, K. (1998). Student perceptions of the influence of race on professor credibility. *Journal of Black Studies, 28,* 738–764.

Henry, O. (1982). *The gift of the magi.* Neugebauer Press USA. Distributed by Natick, MA: Alphabet.

Herek, G. M. (1990). The context of anti-gay violence: Notes on cultural and psychological heterosexism. *Journal of Interpersonal Violence, 5,* 316–333.

Herek, G. M. (2000). The psychology of sexual prejudice. *Current Directions in Psychological Science, 9,* 19–22.

Higgins, P. C. (1992). *Making disability: Exploring the social transformation of human variation.* Springfield, IL: Charles C Thomas.

Hilliard, A. G. (1989). Teachers and cultural styles in a pluralistic society. *NEA Today.* Washington, DC: National Education Association.

Hines, C. V., Cruickshank, D. R., & Kennedy, J. J. (1985). Teacher clarity and its relationship to student achievement and satisfaction. *American Educational Research Journal, 22,* 87–89.

Hofstede, G. (2005). *Cultural differences in teaching and learning* (7th Ed.). Verperweg, Netherlands: Institute for Research on Intercultural Cooperation.

Hofstede, G. (1991). *Culture and organizations: Software of the mind.* London: McGraw-Hill.

Hogben, M., & Waterman, C. (1997). Are all of your students represented in their textbooks? A content analysis of coverage of diversity issues in introductory psychology textbooks. *Teaching Psychology, 24,* 95–100.

Holladay, S. J. (1984). *Student and teacher perception of teacher self-disclosure.* Unpublished master's thesis. University of Oklahoma, Norman.

Hollins, E. R., King, J. E., & Hayman, W. C. (Eds.). (1994). *Teaching diverse populations: Formulating a knowledge base.* Albany: State University of New York Press.

Hunt, S., Angell, M., Boyd, M., Lippert, L., & Moore, M. (2005). *Communication, diversity, and teacher education: Meeting the needs of all learners.* Manuscript submitted for publication.

Hunt, S. K., & Lippert, L. (1999). Instructor training for implementing technology and media in the speech communication classroom. *Journal of the Illinois Speech and Theatre Association, (DL),* 65–72.

Hurd, T., & Brabeck, M. (1997). Presentation of women and Gilligan's ethic of care in college textbooks: 1970–1990. An examination of bias. *Teaching of Psychology, 24,* 159–167.

Hurt, H. T., Scott, M. D., & McCroskey, J. C. (1978). *Communication in the classroom.* Reading, MA: Addison-Wesley.

Hutchinson, L., & Beadle, M. (1992). Professors' communication styles: How they influence male and female seminar participation. *Teaching and Teacher Education, 8*(4), 405–418.

Hyman, R. (1987). Discussion strategies and tactics. In W. Wilen (Ed.), *Questions, questioning techniques, and effective teaching* (pp. 138–139). Washington, DC: National Educational Association.

Hymes, D. (1972). Models of the interaction of language and social life. In J. Gumperz & D. Hymes (Eds.), *Directions in sociolinguistics: The ethnography of communication* (pp. 419–429). New York: Holt, Rinehart & Winston.

Ibarra, H., & Lineback, K. (2005, January). What's your story? *Harvard Business Review,* Reprint R0501F, available from www.hbr.org.

Imants, J., & Van Zoelen, A. (1995). Teachers' sickness absence in primary schools, school climate, and teachers' sense of efficacy. *School Organization, 15,* 77–86.

Infante, D. A. (1995). Teaching students to understand and control verbal aggression. *Communication Education, 44,* 51–63.

Jaasma, M. A., & Koper, R. J. (1999). The relationship of student-faculty out-of-class communication to instructor immediacy and trust and to student motivation. *Communication Education, 48*(1), 41–47.

Jamieson, D. W., & Thomas, K. (1974). Power and conflict in the student-teacher relationship. *Journal of Applied Behavioral Science, 10,* 321–336.

Jaques, D. (2000). *Learning in groups* (3rd ed.). London: Kogan Page.

Javidi, M., Downs, V., & Nussbaum, J. (1988). A comparative analysis of dramatic style behaviors at higher and secondary educational levels. *Communication Education, 37,* 278–288.

Javidi, M., & Long, L. (1989). Teachers' use of humor, self-disclosure, and narrative activity as a function of experience. *Communication Research Reports, 1,* 47–52.

Johannesen, R. L. (2001). *Ethics in human communication* (5th ed.). Prospect Heights, IL: Waveland Press.

Johnson, D., & Johnson, E. (2002). *Joining together: Group theory and group skills* (8th ed.). Boston: Allyn & Bacon.

Johnson, D. W., & Johnson, R. (1985). Classroom conflict: Controversy versus debate in learning groups. *American Educational Research Journal, 22,* 237–256.

Johnson, R., & Johnson, D. (1985, July/August). Student-student interaction: Ignored but powerful. *Journal of Teacher Education, 36,* 22–26.

Johnson, S. D., & Miller, A. N. (2002). A cross-cultural study of immediacy, credibility, and learning in the U.S. and Kenya. *Communication Education, 51,* 280–292.

Jonassen, D., & Grabowski, B. (1993). *Handbook of individual differences, learning and instruction.* Hillsdale, NJ: Lawrence Erlbaum Associates.

Jones, M. (1989). Gender issues in teacher education. *Journal of Teacher Education, 40,* 33–44.

Jordan, F. F., McGreal, E. A., & Wheeless, V. E. (1990). Student perceptions of teacher sex-role orientation and use of power strategies and teacher sex as determinants of student attitudes toward learning. *Communication Quarterly, 38,* 43–53.

Joss, M. W. (1999). *Looking good in presentations* (3rd ed.). Scottsdale, AZ: Coriolis.

Joyce, B., Weil, M., & Calhoun, E. (2003). *Models of teaching* (8th ed.). Boston: Allyn & Bacon.

Karabenick, S., & Sharma, R. (1994). Perceived teacher support of student questioning in the college classroom: Its relation to student characteristics and role in classroom questioning process. *Journal of Educational Psychology, 86,* 90–103.

Karp, D. A., & Yoels, E. W. C. (1976) The college classroom: Some observations on the meanings of student participation. *Sociology and Social Research, 60,* 421–439.

Katzman, L. I. (2001). *The effects of high-stakes testing on students with disabilities: What do we know?* Unpublished qualifying paper. Harvard Graduate School of Education, Cambridge, MA.

Kearney, P., & Plax, T. G. (1987). Situational and individual determinants of teacher's reported use of behavior alteration techniques. *Human Communication Research, 14,* 145–166.

Kearney, P., Plax, T. G., & Burroughs, N. F. (1991). An attributional analysis of college students' resistance decisions. *Communication Education, 40,* 325–342.

Kearney, P., Plax, T. G., Richmond, V. P., & McCroskey, J. C. (1984). Power in the classroom III: Teacher communication techniques and messages. *Communication Education, 34,* 19–28.

Kearney, P., Plax, T., Richmond, V., & McCroskey, J. (1985). Power in the classroom IV: Teacher communication techniques as alternatives to discipline. In R. Bostrom (Ed.), *Communication yearbook 8* (pp. 8–47). Beverly Hills, CA: Sage.

Kearney, P., Plax, T., Smith, V., & Sorensen, G. (1988). Effects of teacher immediacy and strategy type on college student resistance. *Communication Education, 37,* 54–67.

Keefe, J. (1982). Assessing student learning styles: An overview. In J. Keefe (Ed.), *Student learning styles and brain behavior.* Reston, VA: National Association of Secondary Principals.

Kelley, D. H., & Gorham, J. (1988). Effects of immediacy on recall of information. *Communication Education, 17,* 198–207.

Kelley, H. (1950). The warm-cold variable in first impressions of persons. *Journal of Personality, 18,* 433.

Kendon, A. (1967). Some functions of gaze-direction in social interaction. *Acat Psychologica, 26,* 22–63.

Kendrick, W. L. (1987). *Receiver clarifying in response to problems of understanding.* Unpublished doctoral dissertation, University of Washington, Seattle.

Kendrick, W. L., & Darling, A. L. (1990). Problems of understanding in classrooms: Students' use of clarifying tactics. *Communication Education, 39,* 15–39.

Kepler, P., Royse, B., & Kepler, J. (1996). *Windows to the world.* Glenview, IL: Good Year Books.

Kiewra, K. A., & Frank, B. M. (1988). Encoding and external-storage effects of personal lecture notes, skeletal notes, and detailed notes for field-independent and field-dependent learners. *Journal of Educational Research, 81,* 143–148.

Kinch, J. (1963). A formalized theory in self-concept. *American Journal of Sociology, 68,* 481–486.

Kindaichi, H. (1975). *Hihonjin no gengohyogen.* Tokyo, Japan: Kodansha.

King, E. W. (1994). *Educating young children in a diverse society.* Boston: Allyn & Bacon.

Kirkwood, W. (2000). Stories that bring peace to the mind: Communication and the education of feeling. *Southern Communication Journal, 66*(1), 16–26.

Klein, S. (1971). Student influence on teacher behavior. *American Educational Research Journal, 8,* 403–421.

Kleinfeld, J. (1994). Learning styles and culture. In W. J. Lonner & R. S. Malpass (Eds.), *Psychology and culture* (pp. 151–156). Boston: Allyn & Bacon.

Klopf, D. W. (1984). Cross-cultural apprehension research. A summary of Pacific basin studies. In J. A. Daly & J. C. McCroskey (Eds.), *Avoiding communication: Shyness, reticence and communication apprehension* (pp. 157–169). Beverly Hills, CA: Sage.

Klopf, D. W. (1991). Japanese communication practices: Recent comparative research. *Communication Quarterly, 39,* 130–143.

Knapp, J. L., Martin, M. M., & Myers, S. A. (2003). *Out-of-class communication: The development and testing of a measure.* Paper submitted for publication.

Knapp, M., & Hall, J. (2005). *Nonverbal communication in human interaction* (6th ed.). Belmont, CA: Thompson Wadsworth.

Knapp, M., & Vangelisti, A. (2008). *Interpersonal communication and human relationships* (6th ed.). Boston: Allyn & Bacon.

Knobloch, N. A. (2003, September). College teachers "making a difference"—A research review. *NACTA Journal,* 47–53.

Koblinsky, S. G., & Sugawara, A. I. (1984). Nonsexist curricula, sex of teacher, and children's sex role learning. *Sex Roles, 10,* 357–367.

Koester, J., & Lusting, M. (1991). Communicating curricula in the multicultural university. *Communication Education, 40,* 250–254.

Koff, E., Rierdan, J., & Stubbs, M. (1990). Gender, body image, and self-concept in early adolescence. *Journal of Early Adolescence, 10,* 37–55.

Kolb, A., & Kolb, D. A. (2001). *Experiential learning theory bibliography 1971–2001.* Boston: McBer and Co.

Kolbe, R., & LaVoie, J. C. (1981). Sex-role stereotyping in preschool children's picture books. *Social Psychology Quarterly, 44,* 369–374.

Koneya, M. (1976). Location and interaction in row and column seating arrangements. *Environment and Behavior, 8,* 265–282.

Kounin, J. S. (1977). *Discipline and group management in classrooms.* Melbourne, FL: Krieger Publishing.

KPBS (Producer). (1994). *Frontline: School colors.* San Diego: KPBS.

Kramarae, C., Schulz, M., & O'Barr, W. (Eds.). (1984). *Language and power.* Beverly Hills, CA: Sage.

Kramer, M., & Berman, J. (2001). Making sense of a university's culture: An examination of undergraduate students' stories. *Southern Communication Journal, 66*(4), 297–311.

Krasnow, J. H. (1992). *The social competency program of the reach out to schools project: Project report no. 3.* Wellesley College, MA: Stone Center for Development Services.

Kreidler, W. J. (1984, January). How well do you resolve … conflict? *Instructor, 93,* 30–34.

Krupnick, C. G. (1985, May). Women and men in the classroom: Inequality and its remedies. *On Teaching and Learning: The Journal of the Harvard-Danforth Center for Teaching and Learning,* 18–25.

Kunda, Z., & Sherman-Williams, B. (1993). Stereotypes and the construal of the individuating information. *Personality and Social Psychology Bulletin, 19,* 12–17.

Kurfill, J. (1988). Critical thinking: Theory, research, practice and possibilities. *ASHE-ERIC Higher Education Report, 2.*

Kurtz, E., & Ketcham, K. (1992). *The spirituality of imperfection: Storytelling and the journey to wholeness.* New York: Bantam.

Langer, E. (1989). *Mindfulness.* Reading, MA: Addison-Wesley.

Lapakko, D. (1997). Three cheers for language: A closer examination of a widely cited study of nonverbal communication. *Communication Education, 46,* 63–67.

Lawrenz, F. P., & Welch, W. W. (1983). Student perceptions of science classes taught by males and females. *Journal of Research in Science Teaching, 20,* 655–662.

Leach, M. (1990). Toward writing feminist scholarship into history education. *Educational Theory, 40,* 453–461.

Leatherman, C. (1994, June 15). The minefield of diversity. *Chronicle of Higher Education,* A15.

Lee, C., & Galati, F. (1977). *Oral interpretation* (5th ed.). Boston: Houghton Mifflin.

Lee, C. R., Levine, T. R., & Cambra, R. (1997). Resisting compliance in the multicultural classroom. *Communication Education, 46,* 29–43.

Lehr, J., & Harris, H. (1988). *At-risk, low-achieving students in the classroom.* Washington, DC: National Education Association.

Leonardi, P. (2002). Cultural transference in perceptions and uses of communication technology: A qualitative study. *Qualitative Research Reports in Communication,* 53–62.

Lerner, R., Delaney, M., Hess, L., Javonovic, L. J., & VonEye, A. (1990). Early adolescent physical attractiveness and academic competence. *Journal of Early Adolescence, 10,* 4–20.

Lerner, R., Lerner, J., Hess, L., Schwab, J., Javonovic, J., Talwan, R., & Kucher, J. (1991). Physical attractiveness and psychosocial functioning among early adolescents. *Journal of Early Adolescence, 11,* 300–320.

Lieberman, D. (1994). Ethnocognitivism, problem solving and hemisphericity. In L. Samovar & R. Porter (Eds.), *Intercultural communication: A reader* (7th ed., pp. 178–193). Belmont, CA: Wadsworth.

Lim, B. (1996). Student's expectations of professors. *The Teaching Professor, 10*(4), 3–4.

Littell, J., & Littell, J. (1972). *The language of man* (vol. 1). Evanston, IL: McDougal Littell.

Littlejohn, S. W. (1989). *Theories of human communication* (3rd ed.). Belmont, CA: Wadsworth.

Love, A., & Roderick, J. (1971). Teacher nonverbal communication: The development and field testing of an awareness unit. *Theory into Practice, 10,* 295–299.

Lu, S. (1997). Culture and compliance gaining in the classroom: A preliminary investigation of Chinese college teachers' use of behavior alteration techniques. *Communication Education, 46,* 9–28.

Lutzker, M. (1995). *Multiculturalism in the college curriculum: A handbook of strategies and resources for faculty.* Westport, CT: Greenwood.

Macke, A. S., & Richardson, L. W. (1980). *Sex-typed teaching styles of university professors and student reactions.* Columbus: Ohio State University Research Foundation.

Mahlios, M. C. (1981). Effects of teacher-student cognitive style on patterns of dyadic classroom interaction. *Journal of Experimental Education, 49,* 147–157.

Malandro, L. A., & Barker, L. (1983). *Nonverbal communication*. Reading, MA: Addison.

Marshall, H., & Weinstein, R. (1984). Classroom factors affecting students' self evaluations: An interactional model. *Review of Educational Research, 54,* 301–325.

Martin, M., Behnke, R., & King, P. (1992). The communication of public speaking anxiety: Perceptions of Asian and American speakers. *Communication Quarterly, 3,* 279–288.

Martin, M. M., Myers, S. A., & Mottet, T. P. (2002). Students' motives for communicating with their instructors. In J. L. Chesebro & J. C. McCroskey (Eds.), *Communication of teachers* (pp. 36–36). Boston: Allyn & Bacon.

Martin, M. M., Myers, S. A., & Mottet, T. P. (2002). Students' motives for communicating with their instructors and affective and cognitive learning. *Psychological Reports, 87,* 830–834.

Martin-White, C., & Staton-Spicer, A. (1987). Instructional communication in the elementary gifted classroom. *Communication Education, 36,* 259–271.

Marzanno, R., Brant, R., Hughes, C., Jones, B., Presseisen, S., Rankin, S., & Shuor, C. (1988). *Dimensions of thinking: A framework for curriculum and instruction*. Alexandria, VA: Association for Supervision and Curriculum Development.

Maslow, A. H. (1954). *Motivation and personality*. New York: Harper & Row.

Maslow, A. H., & Mintz, N. L. (1956). Effects of esthetic surroundings: Initial effects of three esthetic conditions upon perceiving "energy" and "well-being" in faces. *Journal of Psychology, 41,* 254–257.

Mayer, R. (1968). *Developing an attitude toward learning*. Palo Alto, CA: Fearon.

Mazer, J., Murphy, R., & Simonds, C. (2009). The effects of teacher self-disclosure via Facebook on teacher credibility. *Learning, Media, and Technology, 34* (2), 175–183.

Mazer, J. P., Hunt, S. K., & Simonds, C. J. (2007). Incorporating critical thinking instructional strategies in the basic communication course. In Hugenburg, L. W., Morreale, S., Worley, D. W., Hugenberg, B., & Worley, D. A. (Eds.), *Best practices in the basic communication course: A training manual for instructors* (pp. 81–90). Dubuque, IA: Kendall-Hunt Publishing Company.

Mazer, J., Murphy, R., & Simonds, C. (2007). I'll See You On "Facebook": The Effects of Computer-Mediated Teacher Self-Disclosure on Student Motivation, Affective Learning, and Classroom Climate. *Communication Education, 56,* 1–17.

McCaleb, J. L. (Ed.). (1987). *How do teachers communicate? A review and critique of assessment practices. Teacher Education Monograph No. 7.* Washington, DC: ERIC Clearinghouse on Teacher Education.

McCroskey, J. C., Andersen, J., Richmond, V., & Wheeless, L. (1981, April). Communication apprehension of elementary and secondary students and teachers. *Communication Education, 30,* 122–132.

McCroskey, J. C., & Dunham, R. E. (1974). Ethos: A confounding element in communication research. *Speech Monographs, 33,* 456–463.

McCroskey, J. C., Fayer, J., Richmond, V., Sulliven, A., & Barraclough, R. (1996). A multi-cultural examination of the relationship between nonverbal immediacy and affective learning. *Communication Quarterly, 44,* 297–307.

McCroskey, J. C., Holdridge, W., & Toomb, J. K. (1974). An instrument for measuring source credibility of basic speech communication instructors. *Speech Teacher, 23,* 30.

McCroskey, J. C., & McCroskey, L. L. (1986). The affinity-seeking of classroom teachers. *Communication Research Reports, 3,* 158–167.

McCroskey, J. C., & McVetta, R. W. (1978, March). Classroom seating arrangements: Instructional communication theory versus student preferences. *Communication Education, 27,* 101–102.

McCroskey, J. C., & Richmond, V. P. (1983). Power in the classroom I: Teacher and student perceptions. *Communication Education, 32,* 176–184.

McCroskey, J. C., & Richmond, V. P. (1990). Willingness to communicate: Differing cultural perspectives. *Southern Communication Journal, 56*, 72–77.

McCroskey, J. C., & Richmond, V. P. (1991). *Quiet children and the classroom teacher.* Urbana, IL: ERIC Clearinghouse on Reading and Communication Skills.

McCroskey, J. C., & Richmond, V. P. (1992). Increasing teacher influence through immediacy. In V. P. Richmond & J. C. McCroskey (Eds.), *Power in the classroom: Communication, control, and concern* (pp. 101–119). Hillsdale, NJ: Erlbaum.

McCroskey, J. C., Richmond, V. P., Plax, T. G., & Kearney, P. (1985). Power in the classroom V: Behavior alteration techniques, communication training, and learning. *Communication Education, 34*, 214–226.

McCroskey, J. C., Richmond, V. P., Sulliven, A., Fayer, J., & Barraclough, R. (1995). A cross-cultural and multi-behavioral analysis of the relationship between nonverbal immediacy and teacher evaluation. *Communication Education, 44*, 281–306.

McCroskey, J. C., Sallinen, A., Fayer, J. M., Richmond, V. P., & Barraclough, R. A. (1996). Nonverbal immediacy and cognitive learning: A cross-cultural investigation. *Communication Education, 54*, 200–211.

McCroskey, J. C., & Teven, J. (1999). Goodwill: A reexamination of the construct and its measurement. *Communication Monographs, 66*, 90–103.

McCroskey, J. C., Valencic, K. M., & Richmond, V. P. (2004). Toward a general model of instructional communication. *Communication Quarterly, 52*, 197–210.

McCroskey, J. C., & Wheeless, L. R. (1976). *Introduction to human communication.* Boston: Allyn & Bacon.

McGuire, J. (1988). Sounds and sensibilities: Storytelling as an educational process. *Children's Literature Association Quarterly, 13*, 11–15.

McKeachie, W. (1986). *Teaching tips: A guidebook for the beginning teacher* (8th ed.). Lexington, MA: D. C. Heath.

McLaughlin, M., Erickson, K., & Ellison, M. (1980, January). A scale for the measurement of teachers' affective communication. *Communication Education, 29*, 21–32.

Meade, G. H. (1934). *Mind, self, and society.* C. W. Morris (Ed.). University of Chicago Press.

Medley, D., & Mitsel, H. (1963). Measuring classroom behavior by systematic observation. In N. W. Gage (Ed.), *Handbook of research on teaching* (p. 253). Chicago: Rand McNally.

Mehan, H. (1979). *The competent student. Sociolinguistic working paper number 61.* Austin, TX: Southwest Educational Development Lab. (ERIC Document Reproduction Service No. ED 250 934)

Menzel, K. E., & Carrell, L. J. (1999). The impact of gender and immediacy on willingness to talk and perceived learning. *Communication Education, 48*, 31–40.

Merton, R., Reader, G., & Kendall, P. (1957). *The student physician.* Cambridge, MA: Harvard University Press.

Meyer, K. R., Hunt, S. K., Comadena, M. E., Simonds, C. J., Simonds, B. K., & Baldwin, J. R. (2008). Assessing classroom management training for basic course instructors. *Basic Communication Course Annual, 20*, 35–71.

Meyer, K. R., Simonds, C. J., Simonds, B. K., Baldwin, J. R., Hunt, S. K., & Comadena, M. E. (2007). Designing classroom management training for basic course instructors. *Basic Communication Course Annual, 19*, 1–36.

Meyers, S. (1995). Student perceptions of teacher affinity-seeking and classroom climate. *Communication Research Reports, 12*, 192–199.

Midgley, C., Feldlaufer, H., & Eccles, J. (1989). Change in teacher efficacy and student self-and task-related beliefs in mathematics during the transition to junior high school. *Journal of Educational Psychology, 81*, 247–258.

Miskel, C., McDonald, D., & Bloom, S. (1983). Structural and expectancy linkages within schools and organizational effectiveness. *Educational Administration Quarterly, 19*(1), 49–82.

Mliner, J. (1977). *Sex stereotypes in mathematics and science textbooks for elementary and junior high schools: Report of sex bias in the public schools.* New York: National Organization for Women.

Montagu, M. F. A. (1971). *Teaching: The human significance of the skin.* New York: Columbia Press.

Morganett, L. (1995). Ten tips for improving teacher-student relationships. *Social Education, 59,* 27–28.

Morreale, S., & Andersen, K. (1999). Intense discussion at summer conference yields draft of NCA credo for communication ethics. *Spectra.* National Communication Association.

Morreale, S., & Jones, A. (Eds.). (1997). *Racial and ethnic diversity in the twenty-first century: A communication perspective.* Annandale, VA: National Communication Association.

Morris, T. L., Gorham, J., Cohen, S. H., & Huffman, D. (1996). Fashion in the classroom: Effects of attire on student perceptions of instructors in college classes. *Communication Education, 45,* 135–148.

Mottet, T. P. (2000). Interactive television instructors' perception of students' nonverbal responsiveness and their influence on distance teaching. *Communication Education, 49,* 146–164.

Mottet, T. P., & Beebe, S. A. (2005). Foundations of instructional communication. In T. P. Mottet, V. P. Richmond, & J. C. McCroskey (Eds.), *Handbook of instructional communication: Rhetorical and relational perspectives* (ch. 1). Boston: Allyn & Bacon.

Mottet, T. P., Beebe, S. A., Raffeld, P. C., & Medlock, A. L. (2004). The effects of student verbal and nonverbal responsiveness on teacher self-efficacy and job satisfaction. *Communication Education, 53,* 150–164.

Mottet, T. P., Beebe, S. A., Raffeld, P. C., & Paulsel, M. (2004). The effects of student verbal and nonverbal responsiveness on teachers' liking of students and willingness to comply with student requests. *Communication Quarterly, 52*(1), 27–38.

Mottet, T. P., Martin, M. M., & Myers, S. A. (2004). Relationships among perceived instructor verbal approach and avoidance strategies and students' motives for communicating with their instructors. *Communication Education, 53,* 116–122.

Mottet, T. P., & Richmond, V. P. (2000). Student nonverbal communication and its influence on teachers and teaching. In J. L. Chesebro & J. C. McCroskey (Eds.), *Communication of teachers* (pp. 47–61) Boston: Allyn & Bacon.

Murray, H. G. (1985). Classroom teaching behaviors related to college teaching effectiveness. In J. G. Donals & A. M. Sullivan (Eds.), *Using research to improve teaching* (pp. 21–34). San Francisco: Jossey-Bass.

Myers, S. (1998). Students' self-disclosure in college classrooms. *Psychological Reports, 83,* 1067–1970.

Myers, S. A. (2001). Perceived instructor credibility and verbal aggressiveness in the classroom. *Communication Research Reports, 18,* 354–364.

Myers, S. A. (2003). Strategies to prevent and reduce conflict in college classrooms. *College Teaching, 51*(3), 94–98.

Myers, S. A. (2004). The relationship between perceived instructor credibility and student in-class and out-of-class communication. *Communication Reports, 17,* 129–137.

Myers, S. A., & Bryant, L. E. (2002). Perceived understanding, interaction involvement and college student outcomes. *Communication Research Reports, 19,* 146–155.

Myers, S. A., & Martin, M. M. (2005). Understanding the source: Teacher credibility and aggressive communication traits. In T. P. Mottet, V. P. Richmond, & J. C. McCroskey (Eds.), *Handbook of instructional communication: Rhetorical and relational perspectives* (ch. 4). Boston: Allyn & Bacon.

Myers, S. A., Martin, M. M., & Knapp, J. L. (2003). *The relationship between instructors' interpersonal behaviors and out-of-class communication involving instructors and students*. Paper submitted for publication.

Myers, S. A., Martin, M. M., & Mottet, T. P. (2002). The relationship between students' communication motives and information seeking. *Communication Research Reports, 19,* 352–361.

Myers, S. A., Martin, M. M., & Mottet, T. P. (2002). Students' motives for communicating with instructors: Considering instructor socio-communication style, student socio-communicative orientation, and student gender. *Communication Education, 51,* 121–133.

Myers, S. A., Mottet, T. P., & Martin, M. M. (2000). The relationship between student communication motives and perceived instructor communication style. *Communication Research Reports, 17,* 161–170.

Nadler, L., & Nadler, M. (1990). Perceptions of sex differences in classroom communication. *Women's Studies in Communication, 13,* 46–65.

Nadler, M. K., & Nadler, L. B. (2000). Out-of-class communication between faculty and students: A faculty perspective. *Communication Studies, 51,* 176–188.

Nadler, M. K., & Nadler, L. B. (2001). The roles of sex, empathy, and credibility in out-of-class communication between faculty and students. *Women's Studies in Communication, 24,* 241–261.

Nakane, C. (1970). *Japanese society*. London: Werdenfeld & Nicholson.

National Coalition for Women and Girls in Education (NCWGE). (2002). *Title IX at 30: Report card on gender equity*. Washington, DC: NCWGE.

National Longitudinal Transition Study of Special Education Students. (2004). *What makes a difference? Influences of postschool outcomes of youth with disabilities*. Washington, DC: U.S. Department of Education.

Neer, M. (1987). The development of an instrument to measure classroom apprehension. *Communication Education, 36,* 154–166.

Neer, M. (1990). Reducing situational anxiety and avoidance behavior associated with classroom apprehension. *Southern Communication Journal, 56,* 49–61.

Neer, M. (1992). Reducing situational anxiety and avoidance behavior associated with classroom apprehension. *Southern Communication Journal, 57,* 49–62.

Neer, M., & Kircher, W. F. (1989). Apprehensives' perception of classroom factors influencing their participation. *Communication Research Reports, 6,* 70–77.

Nell, V. (1988). *Lost in a book: The psychology of reading for pleasure*. New Haven, CT: Yale University Press.

Neuliep, J. (1991). An examination of the content of high school teachers' humor in the classroom and the development of an inductively derived taxonomy of classroom humor. *Communication Education, 40,* 341–355.

Neuliep, J. (1995). A comparison of teacher immediacy in African-American and Euro-American college classrooms. *Communication Education, 44,* 267–277.

Neuliep, J., & McCroskey, J. (1998). *Ethnocentrism trait measurement: Intercultural communication research instruments*. International and Intercultural Communication Conference, School of Communication, University of Miami.

Nicklin, J. L. (1991). Teacher-education programs face pressure to provide multicultural training. *Chronicle of Higher Education,* A16.

Nilsen, A. P. (1987). Three decades of sexism in school science materials. *School Library Journal, 33,* 117–122.

Nishida, H. (1985). Japanese intercultural communication competence and cross cultural adjustment. *International Journal of Intercultural Relations, 9,* 247–269.

Norton, R. W. (1977). Teacher effectiveness as a function of communicator style. In B. D. Ruben (Ed.), *Communication yearbook 1* (pp. 525–555). New Brunswick, NJ: Transaction.

Norton, R. W. (1978). Foundation of a communicator style construct. *Human Communication Research 4*, 99.

Norton, R. W. (1983). *Communicator style: Theory, applications, and measures.* Beverly Hills, CA: Sage.

Nussbaum, J., & Prusank, D. (1989). The interface between human development and instructional communication. *Communication Education, 38*, 334–344.

Nussbaum, J., & Scott, M. (1979). The relationship among communicator style, perceived self-disclosure, and classroom learning. In D. Nimmo (Ed.), *Communication yearbook 3* (pp. 561–584). New Brunswick, NJ: Transaction.

Nussbaum, J., & Scott, M. (1980). Student learning as relational outcome of teacher-student interaction. In D. Nimmo (Ed.), *Communication yearbook 4* (pp. 533–552). New Brunswick, NJ: Transaction.

Nyquist, J., & Wulff, D. (1990). Selected active learning strategies. In J. Daly, G. Friedrich, & A. Vangelisti (Eds.), *Teaching communication: Theory, research, and methods* (pp. 337–362). Hillsdale, NJ: Erlbaum.

Ogden, C. K., & Richards, I. A. (1927). *The meaning of meaning.* New York: Harcourt.

Olaniran, B. A., & Roach, K. D. (1994). Communication apprehension in Nigerian culture. *Communication Quarterly, 42*, 379–389.

Olaniran, B., & Stewart, R. (1996). Instructional practices and classroom community apprehension: A cultural explanation. *Communication Reports, 9*, 193–203.

O'Mara, J., Allen, J., Long, K., & Judd, B. (1996). Communication apprehension, nonverbal immediacy, and negative expectations for learning. *Communication Research Reports, 13*, 109–128.

Orem, R. A. (1991). Preparing adult educators for cultural change. *Adult Learning, 9*, 8–10.

Orenstein, P. (1994). *School girls.* New York: Doubleday.

O'Sullivan, P. B., Hunts, S. K., & Lippert, S. R. (2004). Mediated immediacy: A language of affiliation in a technological age. *Journal of Language and Social Psychology, 23*, 464–490.

Page, R. (1992). Feelings of physical unattractiveness and hopelessness among high school students. *High School Journal, 75*, 150–156.

Pahnos, M. L., & Butt, K. L. (1992). Ethnocentrism—A universal pride in one's ethnic background: Its impact on teaching and learning. *Education, 112*, 113, 118–120.

Palmer, P. (1998). *The courage to teach: Exploring the inner landscape of a teacher's life.* San Francisco: Jossey-Bass.

Parsons, C. (1997, January 28). Uniform success in schools. *Chicago Tribune,* Metro Chicago, 1–5.

Patterson, M. (1999). *Storytelling: The art form of painting pictures with your tongue.* Available at www.hollowtop.com/storytelling.html

Paul, R. W. (1986). *Program for the fourth international conference on critical thinking and educational reform.* Rohnert Park, CA: Sonoma State University Center for Critical Thinking and Moral Critique.

Pearson, J. C., & West, R. (1991). An initial investigation of the effects of gender on student questions in the classroom: Developing a descriptive base. *Communication Education, 41*, 167–180.

Pemberton, G. (1988). *On teaching the minority student: Problems and strategies.* Brunswick, ME: Bowdoin College.

Peterson, K. (1994, September 7). Teens' tales from the classroom. *USA Today,* 1D–2D.

Peterson, S., & Lach, M. (1990). Gender stereotypes in children's books: Their prevalence and influence on cognitive and affective development. *Gender and Education, 2*, 185–197.

Plax, T., & Kearney, P. (1992). Teacher power in the classroom: Defining and advancing a program of research. In V. P. Richmond & J. C. McCroskey (Eds.), *Power in the classroom: Communication, control, and concern* (pp. 67–84). Hillsdale, NJ: Erlbaum.

Plax, T. G., Kearney, P., McCroskey, J. C., & Richmond, V. P. (1986). Power in the classroom VI: Verbal control strategies, nonverbal immediacy and affective learning. *Communication Education, 35,* 43–55.

Postman, N., & Weingartner, G. (1971). *Teaching as a subversive activity.* New York: Dell.

Potter, W., & Emanuel, R. (1990). Student's preferences for communication styles and their relationship to achievement. *Communication Education, 39,* 234–249.

Powell, B. (1990). *Conflict resolution, communication, and problem solving.* Part IV of the *Biloxi, Mississippi, family English literacy curriculum.* Biloxi: Mississippi Board of Education.

Powell, J. (1990). *Why am I afraid to tell you who I am?* Allen, TX: Thomas More.

Prather, H. (1970). *Notes to myself.* New York: Bantam Books.

Proctor, R., Douglas, A., Garera-Izquierdo, T., & Wartman, S. (1994). Approach, avoidance, and apprehension: Talking with high California students about getting help. *Communication Education, 43,* 312–321.

Purcell, P., & Stewart, L. (1990). Dick and Jane in 1989. *Sex Roles, 22,* 177–185.

Qin, Z., Johnson, D., & Johnson, R. (1995). Cooperative versus competitive efforts and problem solving. *Review of Educational Research, 65,* 129–143.

Rattenborg, A., Simonds, C., & Hunt, S. (2005). Preparing to participate: An exploration of student engagement through student work and instructor's observations. *Basic Communication Course Annual, 17,* 94–133.

Rauscher, L., & McClintock, J. (1996). Ableism curriculum design. In M. Adams, L. A. Bell, P. Griffen (Eds.), *Teaching for diversity and social justice* (pp. 198–231), New York: Routledge.

Redfield, D., & Rousseau, A. (1981). A meta-analysis of experimental research on teacher questioning behavior. *Review of Educational Research, 51,* 237–246.

Reed, J. H., & Hallock, D. E. (1996, January). Encouraging ethical behavior in class. *The Teaching Professor, 10*(1), 1.

Reiff, J. (1996). Multiple intelligences: Different ways of learning. Retrieved December 20, 2003, from www.udel.edu/bateman/acei/multint9.htm

Remen, R. N. (1996). *Kitchen table wisdom: Stories that heal.* New York: Putnam.

Resnick, L., & Klopfer, L. (1988). *Toward the thinking curriculum: Current cognitive research.* Annandale, VA: Association for Supervision and Curriculum Development.

Reynolds, D., Hunt, S., Simonds, C., & Cutbirth, C. (2004). Written speech feedback in the basic communication course: Are instructors too polite to students? *Basic Communication Course Annual, 16,* 36–71.

Richardson, J., & Turner, A. (2000). A large-scale 'local' evaluation of students' learning experiences using virtual learning environments. *Educational Technology and Society, 3,* 108–125.

Richman, J., & Bowman, G. (1997). School failure: An eco-interactional-developmental perspective. In M. Fraser (Ed.), *Risk and resiliency in childhood: An ecological perspective* (pp. 95–116). Washington, DC: National Association of Social Workers.

Richman, J., Rosenfeld, L., & Bowen, G. (1998). Social support for adolescents at risk of school failure. *Social Work, 43,* 309–323.

Richmond, V. P. (1990). Communication in the classroom: Power and motivation. *Communication Education, 39,* 181–195.

Richmond, V. P., & Andriate, G. S. (1984, April). *Communication apprehension: Cross-cultural perspectives.* Paper presented at the annual meeting of the Eastern Communication Association, Philadelphia, PA.

Richmond, V. P., & Gorham, J. (1988). Language patterns and gender role orientation among students in grades 3–12. *Communication Education, 37,* 142–149.

Richmond, V. P., Gorham, J. S., & McCroskey, J. C. (1986). The relationship between selected immediacy behaviors and cognitive learning. In M. L. McLaughlin (Ed.), *Communication yearbook 10.* Beverly Hills, CA: Sage.

Richmond, V. P., Lane, D., & McCroskey, J. C. (2005). Teacher immediacy and the teacher-student relationship. In T. P. Mottet, V. P. Richmond, & J. C. McCroskey (Eds.), *Handbook of instructional communication: Rhetorical and relational perspectives* (ch. 8). Boston: Allyn & Bacon.

Richmond, V. P., & McCroskey, J. C. (1984). Power in the classroom II: Power and learning. *Communication Education, 33,* 125–136.

Richmond, V. P., & McCroskey, J. C. (1997). *Communication apprehension, avoidance, and effectiveness* (5th ed.). Scottsdale, AZ: Gorsuch Scarisbrick.

Richmond, V. P., McCroskey, J. C., Kearney, P., & Plax, T. (1987). Power in the classroom VII: Linking behavior alteration techniques to cognitive learning. *Communication Education, 36,* 1–12.

Richmond, V. P., McCroskey, J. C., & Payne, S. (2007). *Nonverbal behavior in interpersonal relations* (6th ed.). Englewood Cliffs, NJ: Prentice Hall.

Richmond, V. P., & Roach, K. D. (1992). Power in the classroom: Seminal studies. In V. P. Richmond & J. C. McCroskey (Eds.), *Power in the classroom: Communication, control, and concern* (pp. 1–18). Hillsdale, NJ: Erlbaum.

Rickards, J. P., Fajen, B. R., Sullivan, J. F., & Gillespie, G. (1997). Signaling, notetaking, and field independence-dependence in text comprehension and recall. *Journal of Educational Psychology, 89,* 508–517.

Riding, R., & Cheema, I. (1991). Cognitive styles—an overview and integration. *Educational Psychology, 11,* 193–215.

Rierdan, J., Koff, E., & Stubbs, M. (1988). Gender, depression and body image in early adolescence. *Journal of Early Adolescence, 8,* 109–117.

Rierdan, J., Koff, E., & Stubbs, M. (1989). A longitudinal analysis of body image as a predictor of the onset and persistence of adolescent girls' depression. *Journal of Early Adolescence, 9,* 454–466.

Roach, K., & Byrne, P. R. (2001). A cross-cultural comparison of instructor communication in American and German classrooms. *Communication Education, 50,* 1–14.

Roach, K., Cornett-Devito, M., & Devito, R. (2005). A cross-cultural comparison of instructor communication in American and French classrooms. *Communication Education, 53*(1), 87–107.

Roach, K. D. (1991). Graduate teaching assistants' use of behavior alteration techniques in the university classroom. *Communication Quarterly, 39,* 178–188.

Roe, B., Ross, E., & Bums, P. (2009). *Student teaching and field experiences handbook* (7th ed.). Columbus, OH: Merrill.

Rogers, C. (1962, Fall). The interpersonal relationship: The core of guidance. *Harvard Education Review, 32,* 46.

Rogers, E., & Steinfatt, T. (2009). *Intercultural communication* (7th ed.). Project Heights, IL: Waveland Press.

Rogge, E. (1959). Evaluating the ethics of a speaker in a democracy. *Quarterly Journal of Speech, 45,* 419–425.

Rose, J., & Medway, F. (1981). Measurement of teachers' belief in their control over student outcomes. *Journal of Educational Research, 74,* 185–190.

Rosenfeld, L. (1973). *Human interaction in the small group setting.* Columbus, OH: Merrill.

Rosenfeld, L. (1983). Communication climate and coping mechanisms in the college classroom. *Communication Education, 32,* 170–176.

Rosenfeld, L., Grant, C., & McCroskey, J. (1995). Communication apprehension and self-perceived communication competence of academically gifted students. *Communication Education, 44,* 79–86.

Rosenfeld, L. B., & Jarrard, M. W. (1985). The effects of perceived sexism in female and male college professors on students' descriptions of classroom climate. *Communication Education, 34,* 205–213.

Rosenfeld, L., & Richman, J. (1999). Supportive communication and school outcomes, Part II: Academically "at-risk" low income high school students. *Communication Education, 48,* 294–307.

Rosenfeld, L., Richman, J., & Bowen, G. (1998). Supportive communication and school outcomes for academically "at-risk" and other low income middle school students. *Communication Education, 47,* 311–325.

Rosenthal, R., & Jacobson, L. (1968). *Pygmalion in the classroom.* New York: Holt, Rinehart & Winston.

Roth, M. (1987). Teaching modern art history from a feminist perspective: Challenging conventions, my own and others. *Women's Studies Quarterly, 15,* 21–24.

Rothman, H., & Cosden, M. (1995). The relationship between self-perception of a learning disability and achievement, self-concept, and social support. *Learning Disability Quarterly, 18*(3), 203–213.

Rothwell, J. D. (2003). *In mixed company: Small group communication* (5th ed.). Belmont, CA: Wadsworth.

Rowe, M. (1986, January–February). Wait time: Slowing down may be a way of speeding up! *Journal of Teacher Education, 36,* 43–48.

Rowe, M. (1987). Using wait time to stimulate inquiry. In W. Wilen (Ed.), *Questions, questioning techniques, and effective teaching* (pp. 95–106). Washington, DC: NEA.

Rubin, D. (1998). Help! My professor (or doctor or boss) doesn't talk English!

In J. Martin, T. Nakayama, & L. Flores (Eds.), *Readings in cultural contexts* (pp. 149–160). Mountain View, CA: Mayfield.

Rubin, R. B., & Feezel, J. D. (1986). Elements of teacher communication competence. *Communication Education, 35,* 254–268.

Russ, T., Simonds, C., & Hunt, S. (2002). Coming out in the classroom . . . An occupational hazard? The influence of sexual orientation on teacher credibility and perceived student learning. *Communication Education, 51*(3), (in press).

Sadker, D. (2000). Gender equity: Still knocking at the classroom door. *Equity and Excellence, 33,* 80–83.

Sadker, M., & Sadker, D. (1981). The development and field trial of a nonsexist teacher education curriculum. *High School Journal, 64,* 331–336.

Sadker, M., & Sadker, D. (1994). *Failing at fairness: How our schools cheat girls.* New York: Simon & Schuster.

Salinas, J. P. (2002). The effectiveness of minority teachers on minority student success. In *Proceedings of the National Association of African American Studies & National Associations of Hispanic and Latino Studies: 2000 Literature Monograph Series, 24.*

Sammons, M. C. (1995, May). Students assess computer-aided classroom presentation. *T.H.E.: Technological Horizons in Education, 22,* 74–92.

Samovar, L., & Porter, R. (2008). *Intercultural communication: A reader* (12th ed.). Belmont, CA: Wadsworth.

Samovar, L. A., & Porter, R. E. (2009). *Communication between cultures* (7th ed.). Belmont, CA: Wadsworth.

Sanders, J. A., & Wiseman, R. L. (1990). The effects of verbal and nonverbal immediacy on perceived cognitive, affective, and behavioral learning in the multicultural classroom. *Communication Education, 39,* 341–353.

Sandler, B. (1991). Women faculty at work in the classroom, or Why it still hurts to be a woman in labor. *Communication Education, 40*, 6–15.

Sandler, B., & Hall, R. (1986). *The campus climate revisited: Chilly for women faculty, administrators, and graduate students.* Washington, DC: Project on the Status and Education of Women, Association of American Colleges.

Schlesinger, A. M. (1992). *The disuniting of America: Reflections on a multicultural society.* New York: Norton.

Schlossen, L., & Algozzine, B. (1980, Spring). Sex, behavior, and teacher expectancies. *Journal of Experimental Education, 48*, 78–92.

Schmier, L. (1995). *Random thoughts: The humanity of teaching.* Madison, WI: Magna.

Schneider, M. J., & Jordan, W. (1981). Perception of the communicative performance of Americans and Chinese in intercultural contact: A literature review. *Intercultural Relations, 5*, 175–191.

Schrodt, P. (2003). Students' appraisals of instructors as a function of students' perceptions of instructors' aggressive communication. *Communication Education, 52*, 106–121.

Schumaker, D. (1986, April). What are thinking skills? *Instructor, 37.*

Sedlacek, W., Helm, E., & Prieto, D. (1997). *The relationship between attitudes toward diversity and overall satisfaction of university students by race.* (ERIC Document Reproduction Service, No. ED 411 752)

Semmel, M. I. (1978, March–April). Systematic observation. *Journal of Teacher Education, 29*, 27.

Shade, B., & New, C. (1993). Cultural influences on learning: Teaching implications. In J. Banks & C. Banks (Eds.), *Multicultural education: Issues and perspectives* (2nd ed., pp. 315–327). Boston: Allyn & Bacon.

Sharon, S., & Sharon, Y. (1965). *Small group teaching.* Englewood Cliffs, NJ: Educational Technologies Publications.

Shulman, L. (1987). The wisdom of the practitioner. In D. Berliner & B. Rosenshine (Eds.), *Talk to teachers* (p. 382). New York: Random House.

Sills, C. (1988). Interactive learning in the composition classroom. In J. Golub (Ed.), *Focus on collaborative learning* (p. 21). Urbana, IL: National Council of Teachers of English.

Simonds, B. K., Lippert, L. R., Hunt, S. K., Angell, M. E., & Moore, M. K. (2008). Communication and diversity: Innovations in teacher education. *Communication Teacher, 22*, 56–65.

Simonds, B. K., Meyer, K. R., Quinlan, M. M., & Hunt, S. K. (2006). Effects of instructor speech rate on student affective learning, recall, and perceptions of nonverbal immediacy, credibility, and clarity. *Communication Research Reports, 23*, 187–197.

Simonds, C. J. (1995). *Have I made myself clear: The effects of teacher clarity on challenge behavior in the college classroom.* Unpublished doctoral dissertation. University of Oklahoma, Norman.

Simonds, C. J. (1997a). Classroom understanding: Expanding the notion of teacher clarity. *Communication Research Reports, 14*(3), 279–290.

Simonds, C. J. (1997b). Challenge behavior in the college classroom. *Communication Research Reports, 14*(4), 481–492.

Simonds, C. (2001). Reflecting on the relationship between instructional communication theory and teaching practices. *Communication Studies, 52*(4), 260–265.

Simonds, C., & Cooper, P. (2001). Communication and gender in the classroom. In D. Borisoff & L. Arliss (Eds.), *Women and men communicating* (2nd ed., pp. 232–253). Fort Worth, TX: Harcourt.

Simonds, C., Meyer, K., Hunt, S., & Simonds, B. (2009). Speech evaluation assessment: An analysis of written speech feedback on instructor evaluation forms in the basic communication course. *Basic Communication Course Annual, 21*, 65–90.

Sinatra, R. (1986). *Visual literacy connections to thinking, reading and writing.* Springfield, IL: Charles C Thomas.

Skow, L. M., & Stephan, L. (2000). Intercultural communication in the university classroom. In L. A. Samovar & R. E. Porter (Eds.), *Intercultural communication: A reader* (9th ed., pp. 355–370). Belmont, CA: Wadsworth.

Slavin, R. (1986). *Using student team learning.* Baltimore: Johns Hopkins University Press.

Slavin, R., & Madden, W. (1989, February). What works for students at risk: A research synthesis. *Educational Leadership, 47,* 3–9.

Smagorinsky, P., & Fly, P. (1993). The social environment of the classroom: A Vygotskian perspective on small group process. *Communication Education, 42,* 159–171.

Smith, G. (2001, July 20). Backtalk: The brother in the wheelchair. *Essence,* 162.

Sommer, R. (1969). *Personal space: The behavioral basis of design.* Englewood Cliffs, NJ: Prentice Hall.

Sommer, R., & Olsen, H. (1980). The soft classroom. *Environment and Behavior, 12,* 3–16.

Sommers, C. H. (2000). *The war against boys.* New York: Simon & Schuster.

Sorensen, G. (1989a). The relationship among teachers' self-disclosive statements, students' perceptions, and affective learning. *Communication Education, 38,* 259–276.

Sorensen, G. (1989b). Teaching teachers from East to West: A look at common myths. *Communication Education, 38,* 331–332.

Sorensen, G., Plax, T. G., & Kearney, P. (1989). The strategy selection-construction controversy: A coding scheme for analyzing teacher compliance-gaining message constructions. *Communication Education, 38,* 102–118.

Spender, D. (1989). *Invisible women: The schooling scandal.* London: Women's Press.

Sprague, J. (1992). Expanding the research agenda for instructional communication: Raising some unasked questions. *Communication Education, 41,* 1–25.

Staton, A. (1990). *Communication and student socialization.* Norwood, NJ: Ablex.

Staton, A., & Darling, A. (1986). Communication in the socialization of preservice teachers. *Communication Education, 35,* 215–230.

Staton, A., & Hunt, S. (1992). Teacher socialization: Review and conceptualization. *Communication Education, 41,* 110–137.

Stefani, L. (1997). The influence of culture on classroom communication. In L. Samovar & R. Porter (Eds.), *Intercultural communication: A reader* (8th ed., pp. 349–364). Belmont, CA: Wadsworth.

Steil, L. (1980). *Your personal listening profile.* Minneapolis, MN: Sperry Corporation.

Steinbeck, J. (1962). *Travels with Charley: In search of America.* New York: Viking.

Stepp, P. (2001). Sexual harassment in communication extra-curricular activities: Intercollegiate debate and individual events. *Communication Education, 50,* 34–51.

Sternglass, M. (1997, March). *Effects of race, class, and gender on writing: Report from a longitudinal study.* Paper presented at the meeting of the Conference on College Composition and Communication, Phoenix, AZ.

Stewart, J. (1999, April 7). Go figure: A closer look at equal pay. *Chicago Tribune,* sec. 8, 1.

Stewart, L., Cooper, P., & Stewart, A. (2003). *Communication and Gender.* Boston: Allyn & Bacon.

Stewart, J., & Thomas, M. (1990). Dialogue listening: Sculpting mutual meanings. In J. Stewart (Ed.), *Bridges not walls* (pp. 192–210). New York: McGraw-Hill.

Stitt, J., Simonds, C., & Hunt, S. (2003). Evaluation fidelity: An examination of criterion-based assessment and rater training in the speech communication classroom, *Communication Studies, 54* (3), 341–353.

Stone, P. (1996). Ghettoized and marginalized: The coverage of racial and ethnic groups in introductory sociology texts. *Teaching Sociology, 24,* 356–363.

Stuart, W., & Rosenfeld, L. (1994). Student perceptions of teacher humor and classroom climate. *Communication Research Reports, 11,* 87–97.

Sumner, W. (1906/1940). *Folkways.* Boston: Ginn.

Suzuki, T. (1973). *Kotoba to bunka (Language and culture).* Tokyo: Iwanami Shoten.

Swinton, M., & Bassett, R. (1981, April). Teachers' perceptions of competencies needed for effective speech communication and drama instruction. *Communication Education, 30,* 140–151.

Tantleff-Dunn, S., Dunn, M. E., & Gokee, J. L. (2002). Understanding faculty-student conflict: Student perceptions of precipitating events and faculty responses. *Teaching of Psychology, 29*(3), 197–202.

Tetenbaum, T. J., & Pearson, J. (1989). The voices in children's literature: The impact of gender on the moral decisions of storybook characters. *Sex Roles, 20,* 381–395.

Teven, J. J. (2001). The relationships among teacher characteristics and perceived learning. *Communication Education, 50,* 159–169.

Teven, J., & Comadena, M. (1996). The effects of office aesthetic quality on students' perceptions of teacher credibility and communicator style. *Communication Research Reports, 13,* 101–108.

Teven, J., & McCroskey, J. (1996). The relationship of perceived teacher caring with student learning and teacher evaluation. *Communication Education, 46,* 1–9.

Teven, J. J., & Hanson, T. L. (2004). The impact of teacher immediacy and perceived caring on teacher competence and trustworthiness. *Communication Quarterly, 52*(1), 39–53.

Thomas, C. E. (1994). *An analysis of teacher socio-communicative style as a predictor of classroom communication behaviors, student liking, motivation and learning.* Unpublished doctoral dissertation, West Virginia University, Morgantown.

Thomas, C. E., Richmond, V. P., & McCroskey, J. C. (1994). The association between immediacy and socio-communicative style. *Communication Research Reports, 11,* 107–114.

Thompson, B. (2008). Characteristics of parent-teacher email communication. *Communication Education, 57*(2), 201–223.

Thompson, J. J. (1973). *Beyond words: Nonverbal communication.* New York: Citation Press.

Thweatt, K., & McCroskey, J. (1996). Teacher nonimmediacy and misbehavior: Unintentional negative communication. *Communication Research Reports, 13,* 198–204.

Thweatt, K. S., & McCroskey, J. C. (1998). The impact of teacher immediacy and misbehavior on teacher credibility. *Communication Education, 47*(4), 351–356.

Tiberius, R. G. (1990). *Small group teaching: A trouble-shooting guide.* Toronto: Ontario Institute for Studies in Education Press.

Tinto, V. (1993). *Building learning communities for new college students: A summary of research findings of the collaborative learning project.* University Park, PA: National Center on Post Secondary Teaching, Learning, & Assessment.

Titsworth, B. S. (2001). The effects of teacher immediacy, use of organizational lecture cues and students' note taking on cognitive learning. *Communication Education, 50,* 283–297.

Todd-Mancillas, W. (1982). Classroom environment and nonverbal behavior. In L. Barker (Ed.), *Communication in the classroom* (pp. 77–97). Englewood Cliffs, NJ: Prentice Hall.

Totusek, T. (1978, November). *The relationship between classroom seating preference and student personality characteristics.* Paper presented at the meeting of the Speech Communication Association Convention, Minneapolis, MN.

Totusek, P., & Staton-Spicer, A. Q. (1982). Classroom speaking preference as a function of student personality. *Journal of Experimental Education, 50,* 159–163.

Tran, M. T., Young, R. K., & DiLella, J. D. (1994). Multicultural education courses and the student teacher: Eliminating stereotypical attitudes in our ethnically diverse classroom. *Journal of Teacher Education, 45,* 183–189.

Turner, V. (1980). Social dramas and stories about them. *Critical Inquiry, 7,* 141–168.

Twain, M. (1923). *The adventures of Huckleberry Finn.* New York: Harper & Row.

U.S. Department of Education, National Center for Education Statistics (2000). *Educational Equity of Girls and Women* (NCES 2000-030), by Y. Bae, S. Choy, C. Geddes, J. Sable, & T. Snyder. Washington, DC: U.S. Government Printing Office.

Van Note Chism, N., Cano, J., & Pruitt, A. (1989). Teaching in a diverse environment: Knowledge and skills needed by TAs. In J. Nyquist, R. Abbott, & D. Wulff (Eds.), *Teaching assistant training in the 1990s, new directions for teaching and learning* (no. 39; pp. 23–35). San Francisco: Jossey-Bass.

Vaughan-Roberson, C., Tompkins, G., Hitchcock, M., & Oldham, M. (1989). Sexism in basal readers: An analysis of male main characters. *Journal of Research in Childhood Education, 4*(1), 62–68.

Vermunt, J. D., & Verloop, N. (2000). Dissonance in students' regulation of learning processes. *European Journal of Psychologie of Education, 15,* 75–87.

Vernay, M. (1990). *Curriculum and instruction to reduce racial conflict.* New York: ERIC Clearinghouse on Urban Education, Document ED0-UD-89-7.

Vonnegut, K. (1992). Listening for women's voices: Revisioning courses in American public address. *Communication Education, 41,* 26–39.

Wagner, M., Blackorby, J., Cameto, R., & Newman, L. (1993). What makes a difference? Influences on postschool outcomes of youth with disabilities. *The third comprehensive report from the National Longitudinal Transition Study of Special Education Students.* Menlo Park, CA: SRI International.

Waldeck, J. H., Kearney, P., & Plax, T. G. (2001). Teacher e-mail message strategies and students' willingness to communicate online. *Journal of Applied Communication Research, 29*(1), 54–70.

Walker, E. J., & McKeachie, W. J. (1967). *Some thoughts about teaching the beginning course in psychology.* Belmont, CA: Brooks/Cole.

Wallach, J., & Metcalf, G. (1995). *Working with Americans: A practical guide for Asians on how to succeed with U.S. managers.* New York: McGraw-Hill.

Walsh, P. (1986). *Tales out of school.* New York: Viking.

Waltman, M. (1995). An assessment of the discriminant validity of the checklist of behavior alteration techniques: A test of the item desirability bias in prospective and experienced teachers' likelihood-of-use ratings. *Journal of Applied Communication Research, 23,* 201–211.

Wamback, C., & Brothen, T. (1997). Teacher self-disclosure and student classroom participation revisited. *Teaching of Psychology, 24,* 262–263.

Wanzer, M. B., & Frymier, A. B. (1999). The relationship between student perceptions in instructor humor and student's reports of learning. *Communication Education, 48,* 48–62.

Watson, A., & Monroe, E. (1990). Academic achievement: A study of relationships of IQ, communication apprehension, and teacher perception. *Communication Reports, 3,* 28–36.

Watson, K. W., Monroe, E. E., & Atterstrom, A. (1989). Comparison of communication apprehension across cultures: American and Swedish children. *Communication Quarterly, 37,* 67–76.

Weaver, J., & Kintley, M. (1995). Listening styles and empathy. *Southern Communication Journal, 60,* 131–140.

Weaver, R. L., II. (1974). The use of exercises and games. *Speech Teacher, 23,* 302–311.

Webb, L. (1986). Eliminating sexist language in the classroom. *Women's Studies in Communication, 9*, 21–29.

Weiller, K., & Higgs, C. (1989). Female learned helplessness in sport: An analysis of children's literature. *Journal of Physical Education, Recreation, and Dance, 60*(6), 65–67.

Weiner, H. (1986). Collaborative learning in the classroom: A guide to evaluation. *College English, 48*, 55–61.

Weitzman, L. J., Eifler, D., Hokada, E., & Ross, C. (1972). Sex role socialization in picture books for preschool children. *American Journal of Sociology, 77*, 1125–1150.

Weitzman, L. J., & Rizzo, D. (1975). Sex bias in textbooks. *Today's Education, 64*(1), 49–52.

Welch, L. (1991). College students need nurturing too. *The Teaching Professor, 5*, 7.

Wenburg, J., & Wilmot, W. (1981). *The personal communication process.* Melbourne, FL: Krieger Publishing.

West, R. (1994). Teacher-student communication: A descriptive typology of students' interpersonal experiences with teachers. *Communication Research Reports, 7*, 109–118.

West, R., & Pearson, J. C. (1994). Antecedent and consequent conditions of student questioning: An analysis of classroom discourse across the university. *Communication Education, 43*, 299–311.

Wheeless, L. R. (1974). The relationship of attitude and credibility to comprehension and selective exposure. *Western Speech Communication, 38*, 88–97.

Wheeless, L. R. (1975). The relationship of four elements to immediate recall and student-instructor interaction. *Western Speech Communication, 39*, 131–140.

Wheeless, V. E., & Potorti, P. (1987). *Student assessment of teacher masculinity and femininity: A test of the sex role congruency hypothesis on student learning.* Paper presented at the Tenth Annual Communication, Language and Gender Conference, Milwaukee, WI.

Whitworth, R. (1988). Collaborative learning and other disasters. In J. Golub (Ed.), *Focus on collaborative learning* (p. 13). Urbana, IL: National Council of Teachers of English.

Whitworth, R., & Cochran, C. (1996). Evaluation of integrated versus unitary treatments for reducing public speaking anxiety. *Communication Education, 45*, 306–314.

Wilen, W. (1987). Effective questions and questioning: A classroom application. In W. Wilen (Ed.), *Questions, questioning techniques, and effective teaching* (pp. 153–172). Washington, DC: National Education Association.

Wilen, W., & Clegg, A. (1986). Effective questions and questioning: A research review. *Theory and Research in Social Education, 21*, 153–161.

Williams, V. G., & Winkworth, J. M. (1974, July). The faculty looks at student behavior. *Journal of College Student Personnel, 15*(4), 305–310.

Wilmot, W. W. (1976). *The influence of personal conflict styles of teachers on student attitudes toward conflict.* Paper presented at the annual meeting of the International Communication Association, Portland, OR.

Witkin, H. A. (1976). Cognitive style in academic performance and in teacher-student relations. In S. Messick (Ed.), *Individuality in learning* (pp. 38–72). San Francisco: Jossey-Bass.

Witkin, H. A., Dyk, R. B., Faterson, H. F., & Karp, S. A. (1962). *Psychological differentiation studies of development.* New York: John Wiley and Sons, Inc.

Witkin, H. A., Moore, C. A., Oltman, P. K., Goodenough, D. R., Friedman, F., Owen, D. R., & Raskin E. (1977). Role of field dependent and field independent cognitive styles in academic evolution: A longitudinal study. *Journal of Educational Psychology, 69*, 197–211.

Wolvin, A., & Coakley, C. (1991). A survey of the status of listening training in some fortune 500 corporations. *Communication Education, 40*, 152–164.

Wood, B. (1977). *Communication competencies: Grade 7–12*. Urbana, IL: ERIC/SCA.

Wood, D., & Wood, H. (1987). Questioning and student initiative. In J. Dillon (Ed.), *Questioning and discussion: A multidisciplinary study*. Norwood, NJ: Ablex.

Wood, J. (1989). *Feminist pedagogy in interpersonal communication courses*. Paper presented at the Speech Communication Association, San Francisco, CA.

Wood, J. (2009). *Gendered lives: Communication, gender, and culture* (9th ed.). Belmont, CA: Wadsworth.

Wood, J. T., & Lenze, L. F. (1991). Gender and the development of self: Inclusive pedagogy in interpersonal communication. *Women's Studies in Communication, 14*(1), 1–23.

Woolfolk, A. E., & Brooks, D. M. (1983). Nonverbal communication in teaching. In E. Gordon (Ed.), *Review or research in education*. Washington, DC: American Educational Research Association.

Wrench, J., & Punyanunt, N. (2004). Advisor-advisee communication: An exploratory study examining interpersonal communication in the graduate advisee-advisor relationship. *Communication Quarterly, 52*(3), 224–236.

Wrench, J., & Richmond, V. (2004). Understanding the psychometric properties of the humor assessment instrument through an analysis of the relationships between teacher humor assessment and instructional communication variables in the college classroom. *Communication Research Reports, 21*, 92–103.

Wycoff, V. L. (1973). The effects of stimulus variation on learning from lecture. *Journal of Experimental Education, 41*, 85–90.

Young, K. (1931). Language, thought and social reality. In K. Young (ed.) *Social Attitudes*. New York: Henry Holt.

Young, R. L. (1993). Cross-cultural experiential learning for teacher trainees. *Teacher Education Quarterly, 20*(3), 67–76.

Zeichner, K. M. (1980). Myths and realities: Field-based experience in pre-service teacher education. *Journal of Teacher Education, 31*, 45–55.

Zorn, T. E. (1993). Motivation to communicate: A critical review with suggested alternatives. *Communication Yearbook, 16*, 515–549.

Index

('f' indicates a figure; 't' indicates a table)